CONTENTS

Opposite: Gleneagles.

SCOTLAND
WHERE GOLF IS GREAT

SCOTLAND
WHERE GOLF IS GREAT

JAMES W. FINEGAN

Photography by LAURENCE C. LAMBRECHT *and* TIM THOMPSON

ARTISAN | NEW YORK

Overleaf: Kingsbarns.

Copyright © 2006, 2010 by James W. Finegan

Golf-course photographs copyright © 2006 by Laurence C. Lambrecht
Other photographs copyright © 2006 by Tim Thompson
For other photography credits, see page 271

The material in this book originally appeared as part of a larger volume, *Where Golf Is Great: The Finest Courses of Scotland and Ireland*, which was published in hardcover by Artisan in 2006. This is its first time in a paperback format.

Published by Artisan
A Division of Workman Publishing Company, Inc.
225 Varick Street
New York, New York 10014-4381
www.artisanbooks.com

Library of Congress Control Number: 2009942066

ISBN-13: 978-1-57965-428-3

10 9 8 7 6 5 4 3 2 1

Printed in China

Book design by Susi Oberhelman

Map by Rodica Prato

North Sea

Skibo Castle
Brora
Royal Dornoch

Moray
Cruden Bay
Nairn
Grantown-on-Spey
Boat of Garten
Royal Aberdeen

SCOTLAND

Montrose

Blairgowrie

North
Atlantic
Ocean

Carnoustie
St. Andrews/St. Andrews Bay
Kingsbarns
Gleneagles
Crail
Lundin
Elie
Leven
Gullane
North Berwick
Loch
Lomond
Dunbar
Musselburgh
Muirfield
EDINBURGH

Lanark

The Machrie

Western Gailes
Royal Troon

Machrihanish

Prestwick
Shiskine

Turnberry

NORTHERN
IRELAND

ENGLAND

N

0   50 miles

INTRODUCTION

I t was in Scotland, about 600 years ago, that golf was born. This may have happened in Musselburgh, Leith (now part of Edinburgh), St. Andrews, Montrose, Aberdeen, or Carnoustie—no one knows for certain. Generally agreed is that the specific birthplaces was somewhere in the east of the country. Even so, golf could scarcely be said to have thrived from the outset: by 1850, there were fewer than 20 courses. Still, by 1910 there were 280 (admittedly, a number of them were nine-holers), and today, in a land that is actually a bit smaller than the state of Maine, there are more than 560 golf courses.

Among the bona fide Scottish shrines are the Old Course at St. Andrews, Carnoustie's Championship Course, Muirfield, Royal Troon, and Turnberry's Ailsa. These five British Open Championship venues provide unlimited opportunities to play in the very footsteps of the game's towering figures: such legends as Vardon, Braid, Hagen, Sarazen, Jones, Armour, Hogan, Palmer, Nicklaus, Player, Watson, and Woods, all of whom triumphed in Scotland.

And even if you are familiar with the legendary Scottish courses as well as the players who can point to victories on them, there could still be venues you might be less likely to call up. These include unheralded seaside gems like Brora, The Machrie, Murcar, the Burnside course at Carnoustie, and Shiskine (a knockout 12-holer on the Isle of Arran), not to mention such worthy inland layouts as Edzell, Boat of Garten, the Rosemount eighteen at Blairgowrie, and Belleisle.

Ninety-nine courses are covered in the thirty-one chapters of this book, which originally formed the first half of my *Where Golf Is Great* (that book also covered Irish courses). In addition, six notable courses have opened since *Where Golf Is Great* was published in 2006, and each of them is no less than good. The Carrick Course on Loch Lomond has solid shot values and scenic splendor aplenty. Spey Valley, about a half hour south of Nairn, has attractive but not extreme elevation changes and a testing set of greens. Tom Doak's first course in Scotland, the Renaissance Club, which is adjacent to Muirfield, features rolling sand-based turf that plays to his liking, firm and fast. David McLay Kidd's Castle Course provides an incandescent routing plus captivating views of the medieval quarter of St. Andrews. Smack up against Machrihanish Golf Club is another Kidd links course, Machrihanish Dunes, even finer than the original eighteen here. And Castle Stuart, a contemporary links designed by Mark Parsinen and Gil Hanse on the Moray Firth, is widely viewed as the single best course to open in 2009–2010.

Of the 99 courses here, 62 are links, the earliest and most natural form of the game. By most experts' count, the entire world has no more than 180 authentic links courses, and the great majority of them are in the British Isles. The game played on linksland—along the rumpled ground almost as much as through the air—is exhilarating. Generally speaking, a links course is one that is seaside, sea level, and routed over quick-draining, sand-based terrain. This land serves as the buffer—the link, if you will—between the sea and the fertile stretches at some remove from the salt water. Dunes—whether modest (as in the case of the Old Course at St. Andrews) or magnificent (as at Royal Aberdeen)—are almost always present. Over tens of thousands of years, this linksland evolved as the sea receded, leaving behind sandy wastes that the winds fashioned into ripples and knobs and knolls, into gullies and swales and hollows and hummocks. Then grass began to grow, and other vegetation, such as broom and gorse and heather, took root. The seaside terrain of these links is essentially treeless, with a sense of openness and freedom about it; the beauty is severe, sometimes even stark.

The diversity of shots executed over this land sets links golf apart. In the ever-present seaside breezes, we must hit low and piercing drives, take two or three clubs more than we first thought was necessary on our irons to the green, and manufacture shut-face little 6-iron run-ups that skip or skate, not to mention putts from fifty yards off the putting surface. The irresistible challenge calls for imagination and ingenuity, for finesse and feel. On any of Scotland's famed links courses, you get to play the game as it was in the beginning, and as it still can be.

Opposite: St. Andrews Bay
Torrance Course, 17th.

Also, the game remains open to visitors—as it so rarely does in the United States. Of all the clubs and courses dealt with in this book, only three do not welcome the stranger. This differs from what Americans are accustomed to at home, where private clubs are by definition private. But in Scotland, with the exception of Loch Lomond, the Carnegie Club, and the Renaissance Club, even the most prestigious clubs accept the unaccompanied visitor. And it's worth keeping in mind that golf carts are widely available today.

Some courses (for instance, the Old Course, Muirfield, and Royal Dornoch) have a policy requiring visitors to present a current handicap card or a letter of introduction with handicap confirmation. Also, in all likelihood you will be playing from the daily or regular markers. Only very rarely will you use the back tees; these are almost always reserved for competitions. I've acknowledged this policy by consistently providing the yardages from the regular markers in the pages that follow.

Tee times in season can be more difficult to pin down than hotel reservations. You may have to contact the club or course far in advance—say, eight months or even a year. In some cases, nearby hotels may have special relationships that facilitate getting tee times.

Speaking of hotels, the seventy-two accommodations in this book range from sturdy B&Bs, such as Ardell House, which overlooks the original Machrihanish eighteen, to the splendor of Culloden House, near Nairn, with its strikingly symmetrical brick Georgian exterior. I also include such charming spots as Shore Cottage, outside Campbeltown on Saddell Bay, whose "old shoe" comfort is something to relish.

For years, the leading hotel in East Lothian was Greywalls, next door to Muirfield. Regrettably, Greywalls no longer functions as a hotel in the classic sense. To stay there now you have to rent the entire mansion, which can sleep as many as forty-three. Smaller parties are accepted from time to time.

For the first dozen years of its existence, the Carnegie Club at Skibo Castle, near Dornoch, welcomed nonmembers to spend twenty-four hours at its luxurious 7000-acre enclave, where they could give serious consideration to joining the club. The tariff for the accommodation, the cuisine, the golf, tennis, swimming, fishing, canoeing, clay target shooting, and rather more came to something over $2,000 per diem for a couple. Relatively recently, this "testing of the waters," as it were, was canceled, and now you can experience this exceptional lifestyle only *after* you have joined the Carnegie Club or if you visit as a guest of an already existing member.

As for dining, Scotland's standards today are often high. A handful of examples from all over the map suggests the quality of the cooking: the French-influenced Peat Inn, ten minutes outside of St. Andrews and our favorite place to eat in Scotland; the Waterside Bistro, fifteen minutes from Gullane and perched on the bank of the River Tyne, serving delicious bar snacks as well as complete meals; MacCallums Oyster Bar, on the harbor in Troon, specializing in fresh oysters, steamed mussels, and fried calamari; and the Library Restaurant, inside the Open Arms Hotel in tiny Dirleton, which provides a saddle of wild venison wrapped in pancetta and presented on a bed of chive mash with roast parsnips.

As for sightseeing opportunities, they are enormously rewarding. There are amazing man-made monuments, such as Edinburgh Castle and St. Giles' Cathedral. The catalog of natural beauty spots is endless; to spotlight just one here, the scenic road between Kylesku and Durness (Route 56), in the north, winds through a forbidding mountain wilderness of rock-ribbed glens, glacial boulders, and somber lochs, here and there touching an unruly and broken coast studded by small islands. Scotland is crowded with things to see and do. Golf here is far from being the only diversion that will find a permanent place in your memory bank. The appeal of this land is well-nigh inexhaustible.

Opposite: Crail Balcomie, 17th and 18th.

ANCIENT ST. ANDREWS
AND THE KINGDOM OF FIFE

ST. ANDREWS

The first of my more than thirty visits to Scotland took place in mid-September 1952. I was twenty-one, a lowly ensign on the aircraft carrier USS *Wasp*, which had anchored in the Firth of Clyde, several miles below Glasgow. At liberty for a day, a shipmate and I took the train to St. Andrews, lightweight golf bags over our shoulders. We walked directly from the terminal to the Royal and Ancient clubhouse, blithely assuming that this was where we would change our clothes. The porter politely informed us that unless we were guests of a member, we could not be admitted. Suggesting we try the St. Andrews Golf Club, he pointed to a building just beyond the 18th green. Here, in a plain room at the top of the clubhouse, we hung our uniforms on pegs—there were no lockers—donned golf clothes, then clattered down the uncarpeted stairs in our spikes, crossed Links Road and the 18th fairway, and paid our green fee, 25 pence, at the kiosk. There were no other players about on this pretty afternoon, a brisk breeze driving high clouds out over St. Andrews Bay.

From the outset I loved this ancient links, but it baffled me. I had grown up caddieing and playing in suburban Philadelphia, so the Old Course did not resemble any golf course I had seen before: treeless, only two fairways wide, unimaginably vast greens serving two holes, corresponding "double fairways," sand bunkers with steep, stacked-sod faces that looked as though a bricklayer must have fashioned them. Not to mention gorse and heather and, above all, the rippling, heaving, hummocky terrain. After the round we took high tea in the town. From our window table we watched the university students in their traditional red robes going back to their lodgings, and the townspeople, putters in hand, trooping down to the wildly undulating putting green (it is not called the "Himalayas" for nothing) between the 2nd hole and the beach.

For a dozen years my wife, Harriet, and I spent most of the summer in St. Andrews, in a rented flat overlooking the 1st and 18th holes of the Old Course and providing a view of the R&A clubhouse, the beach, the bay, and the coastline. I would write in the morning and play in the afternoon or evening, on the New Course or the Jubilee or the Eden or on what seems to me the most complex great course in the world, the Old.

By now I have played the Old Course more than a hundred times and can report that it is shamelessly deceitful (just where *are* those hidden bunkers in the center of the 12th fairway?) and capricious (George Duncan, 1920 British Open champion, once said, "You can play a damned good shot there and find the ball in a damned bad place") and frustrating, from the gathering Swilcan Burn that fronts the 1st green to the gathering Valley of Sin in the forepart of the 18th green.

Some form of golf, however primitive in the beginning, has been played over this ground for close to six hundred years. Virtually every great champion—Ben Hogan is the glaring exception—has competed on this links. The British Open (properly called the Open Championship) has been contested here twenty-seven times, the Amateur Championship fifteen times, the Walker Cup eight times, and the British Ladies' Amateur four times. The R&A does not own the Old Course. Ownership of it, as well as of the other five St. Andrews links, is vested in the Northeast Fife District Council. The game upon these courses belongs to the world.

The design of the Old Course cannot be attributed to any single golf architect; the layout simply evolved over time. However, certain features were introduced and certain revisions were effected by Allan Robertson, Old Tom Morris, Alister MacKenzie, James Braid, and Donald Steel.

ON THE OLD COURSE

The most useful tip I can provide about playing the Old Course is one you won't get from a caddie (for obvious reasons): roughly 80 percent of the putts are straight, whether from 40 feet or 4 feet. So unless you are faced with a putt that unequivocally proclaims a break, don't borrow anything. Just stroke the ball directly at the cup. Few people believe this, but those who do—and possess a sound stroke—will run the table.

All right, now we are—you and I—on the 1st tee, gazing out over a monotonous stretch of flattish fairway, a good hundred yards wide in the tee-shot landing area because it encompasses both the 1st and 18th holes. There is little to arrest the eye, even less to please it. The scorecard shows 6,566 yards, par 72; but what I call the "tourist tees" make it some

Opposite: St. Andrews Old Course, 18th. Previous spread: 4th.

250 yards less, as a rule. This opener, all of 350 yards, can be very diffi- cult, because the Swilcan Burn actually defines the front of the green. With the wind at our back and the cup down front, our 9-iron will finish so far past the hole that three-putting becomes a clear danger. If, how- ever, the wind is in our face, the playing value of the hole is rather like 400 yards, and it is the stream that becomes a clear danger.

With the 2nd hole, we find ourselves abroad in a sea of heaving turf and playing to the first of the seven double greens, this one also con- taining the cup for the 16th. The ground from here on will be undulating, everlastingly in motion, triggering awkward lies and stances. And though the flag will generally be in sight, there is nothing to serve as a back- ground for it. Often there is a shimmering, miragelike quality to what our eye takes in, with the green itself maddeningly ill-defined.

There is a similarity to most of the par 4s going out—2, 3, 4, 6, 7— that makes it difficult to tell one from another. All head in much the same direction, and all present blind or semiblind forced-carry drives over rough or broken ground. The inbound half, on the other hand, is remarkably diverse. It is also one of the very best nines in the world. At least five holes are great.

From an elevated tee, the 170-yard 11th—the shortest hole on the course—plays squarely across the 7th fairway to a mildly elevated green backdropped by the Eden estuary. In the landmark book *The 500 World's Greatest Golf Holes*, by George Peper and the editors of *Golf Magazine*, the 11th is singled out as one of the world's hundred greatest holes. Hill Bunker, nearly 10 feet deep, patrols the left side of the green. (All 112 Old Course bunkers have names, some with an ominous ring: Coffin, Grave, Hell.) Strath Bunker, a mere seven feet deep but decidedly less roomy, eats into the right front of the green. There is considerable space between the two, and we ought to be able to steer clear of both. Aye, there's the rub: *steering*, instead of swinging full out with confidence. Moreover, because the green tilts steeply down from back to front, putting from well above the hole is a test. Wrote Alister MacKenzie in *The Spirit of St. Andrews:* "The eleventh hole at St. Andrews requires a greater variety of shots under different conditions of wind and changes in position of the flag than any other short hole. It also produces more interest, excitement, and thrills than any other hole, and for these reasons I consider it the greatest of all short holes." High praise indeed from the man who had already created the imperishable "trans-Pacific" 16th at Cypress Point.

Step off the back of the 11th green now onto the 12th tee. Is this, in the world of golf, the one place to be above all others? Gaze out over the broad Eden estuary as it stretches away to the North Sea. Face left and, beyond the flags for 11 and 7, lie the New Course and the Jubilee, both covered with golfers, and beyond these two eighteens are the white-capped waters of St. Andrews Bay, tumbling onto the West Sands. Immediately to your right is the Eden Course, and next to it, the Strathtyrum. More golfers. What an immense playing field it all is—links, links, links, gray green and undulating, studded with low dunes and gorse and heather and fearsome sandpits, not beautiful in the conventional sense, perhaps, its ineluctable charm the product of its naturalness. And now look dead ahead, down the 12th fairway and beyond the red flag. In the far distance lies the beloved old town itself, above the rocks and the sea on a gentle bluff, its low, gray silhouette punctuated by a handful of church spires. As we play our way home, each stroke draws us closer to it.

As for the 12th hole itself, 316 yards long, it was here in the 2000 Open that Tiger Woods unveiled a new concept in course management. Leading by 4 or 5 strokes as he came to this hole in the final round, he elected to take the trouble—the gorse and sand short of the green—out of play by the simple expedient of firing his tee shot *over* the green. The little pitch back could hardly produce more than a 4.

At the great 400-yard 13th, the drive must be kept right of the three Coffins bunkers; the blind second shot, anything from an 8-iron to a 3-metal, depending on the wind, must clear a low ridge first and then a nightmarish tangle of broken ground, bunkers, and deep rough.

This is followed by the even greater 14th, for me the finest par 5 on the planet. Littered with 15 bunkers and bordered tight on the right by a low stone boundary wall separating the Old Course from the Eden, this 523-yarder strikes us at first as classically penal. In fact, it is classically strategic. There are three routes to the green: the conservative path, left down the 5th fairway; straightaway, for a chance of getting nearly home in two if we can carry Hell Bunker; and right, taking the sand out of play but flirting with the boundary. In the 1995 Open, Jack Nicklaus found cavernous Hell Bunker with his second shot and struggled ingloriously to

Opposite, top: St. Andrews Old Course, 11th; bottom: 12th. Below, the 4th and 14th greens.

18 in the 500 *World's Greatest*. The blind drive must wing its way over the addition to the Old Course Hotel, which simulates the train shed that for decades stood there in the crook of the right-hand dogleg, squarely on the line of flight. The rectangular green, situated diagonally across the second shot and built on a plateau three or four feet above the fairway, is backed at the right and the rear first by a gravel pathway, then by a paved road, and finally by a stone wall, all of them in play. There is no free drop here. A devouring and claustrophobic sandpit, the merciless Road Bunker invades the left side of the putting surface. In short, this hole is an instrument of torture. In 1984 Tom Watson finished second in the Open, 2 strokes behind Seve Ballesteros, having played the hole 5-6-4-5.

The 18th, by contrast, is altogether congenial—354 yards, the broadest of fairways, an immense single green, not a bunker to be found. We drive well left of center, aiming for the red-and-gold clock on the Royal & Ancient clubhouse and giving a wide berth to the out-of-bounds on the right. Determined not to come up short in the Valley of Sin, we now play the approach too boldly and finish 35 feet past the cup. Leaning over the railing behind the green are spectators—3, 7, 10, 20—regardless of the time of day (I once completed a round in late June in the dark, at eleven o'clock, and was warmly applauded for my intrepid two-putting). Minimally downhill, this 35-foot lag is somehow not disturbing. Surely if we lay our hands softly on the grip and put an unhurried stroke on the ball, it must feed its way down and expire somewhere within the haven of a two-foot circle. And so it does. We tap in for a 4, retrieve the ball—and slowly exhale.

On a hole that has witnessed more than its share of Open history, the dramatic victory of Jack Nicklaus in 1970 remains vivid in memory. Doug Sanders, he of the peacock wardrobe and the truncated backswing, missed a three-footer for the title on the 72nd hole to give Nicklaus new life. In the 18-hole playoff the next day, Nicklaus clung to a 1-stroke lead as they came to the home hole. Hitting first, Sanders drove to within 25 yards of the green. Now the thirty-year-old Ohioan, after shedding his sweater in an unconscious gesture that suggested it was high time he took off the wraps, launched a colossal drive (Have we forgotten how truly long he was, pregraphite, pretitanium, and pre-rocket-balls?) that skimmed through the Valley of Sin, just missed the flagstick as it raced across the green, and finally stopped on the overgrown bank behind the putting surface, some 375 yards from where it had begun its journey. Sanders ran his chip to within four feet of the cup for a likely birdie. Nicklaus's pitch from the heavy grass pulled up seven feet short of the hole

a 10. Over the months that followed, visitor after visitor came to the 14th bent on "beating Jack Nicklaus." I played with a few of these giant-killers. I recall one fellow who, after finally managing to extricate himself from Hell, reached the green in 8 and holed a 14-footer for 9. His joy knew no bounds. This hole was named one of the 500 *World's Greatest*.

The 16th, 351 yards, is also great and also hostile. A tight cluster of three bunkers called the Principal's Nose awaits in the left center of the fairway, 200 yards out. The right side of the hole is bordered by an out-of-bounds fence 29 yards from the triune hazard of the Nose. The timorous tee shot will be kept left of it, but the approach shot will then be imperiled by Wig Bunker, which knifes into the left front of the low-plateau green. Aiming right of Wig brings into play the boundary fence, which lurks only a few feet from the right edge of the putting surface. Of course, a strong and straight drive over the Principal's Nose sets up an easy short iron to an open green. The 16th is a model of risk/reward golf.

The 17th is the hardest par 4 in major championship golf. Called the Road Hole and measuring 461 yards, it was chosen as one of the top

Ten years later I would ask Jack whether, when the ball left his putter blade, he thought he had holed the seven-footer.

"Yes," he replied. "Of course, that putt breaks a little left to right and the ball did go into the right center of the hole. But I knew I'd stroked it well." He paused, then added with a smile, "As a matter of fact, it came closer to missing than I thought it was going to."

From time to time I am asked how a visitor gets to play the Old Course. There are five ways. First, you can reserve a tee time by contacting the Links Trust long in advance. Second, you can book a package with any of several St. Andrews hotels or international tour operators that are regularly allocated Old Course tee times. Third, sign up for the Old Course Experience, a costly investment that covers a round on the Old, a round on one of the other courses, a caddie, a five-star hotel, and fine meals. Fourth, enter the ballot, no later than 2:00 P.M. the day before you wish to play, and hope your name is drawn. And finally, speaking of luck, you can try yours the same way I do, as a standby. Simply give the starter your name—first come, first served. Though all tee times are taken, some will be the property of twosomes or threesomes, thus creating an opportunity for a standby or two. An average of twenty to twenty-five are put out daily. The starter can be counted on to be courteous and helpful.

Over the years I've played the Old Course with more than two hundred and fifty people. All kinds of people: Flora, a ninety-six-pound middle-aged Filipino opera singer, who was unable to break 150 but relished every stroke she played. . . . Brian, in his early fifties and one of the two or three best one-armed golfers in the British Isles (left arm off at the shoulder), who drives the ball 230 yards and who finished that day with 81 (38–43: fierce headwind on the second nine). . . . Lars, a twenty-year-old Swede who fired a 2-under-par 70 and was working as a dishwasher in one of the St. Andrews University dorms while he went on honing his game "for as long as it takes." . . . Gary, a thirty-four-year-old who owned two stalls (games of chance, two pounds to play) on the seaside promenade down in Blackpool, England, minutes from Royal Lytham & St. Annes. . . . Bill, a husky retired U.S. Navy pilot who flew six hundred missions in Vietnam, who plays golf daily, and who said, "If I ever find that I can't drive the ball two hundred eighty yards anymore, I'll give up the game" . . . Steve and Michael, a life insurance salesman and his fifteen-year-old son, from San Luis Obispo, California, who insisted that I accompany them to the Quarto bookshop, just around the corner from the 18th green, so they could buy a copy of my Scotland book and have me inscribe it.

I don't think you could meet such a diversity of golfers on any other course in the world. But then, the Old Course is unlike any other course in the world. It is sui generis, a law unto itself. It stands alone, the shrine of shrines. Several years ago in a game at Pine Valley, I said to Alan MacGregor, manager of the St. Andrews Links Trust, as we stood on the hilltop 18th tee, "I hope you agree that Pine Valley is the greatest course in the world."

He hesitated, then replied, "I agree that Pine Valley is the *best* course in the world, but the Old Course is the *greatest*."

OTHER ST. ANDREWS LINKS TRUST COURSES

There are five more links courses at St. Andrews. Old Tom Morris designed and built the **New Course** in 1895. Enjoying much the same undulating linksland as the Old, which is right beside it, it measures 6,362 yards from the regular markers; par is 71. Three holes show the New at its best: the par-5 8th, where a narrow gap between two high sand hills defines the approach to a hidden green; the 225-yard 9th, a rising shot along the Eden estuary to a punch bowl green; and the great par-4 10th, 464 yards, played from an elevated tee to a blind and sloping fairway, the exacting second shot

Opposite: St. Andrews Old Course, 18th.

along a dune-framed valley to a green backed by low sand hills. The New appears regularly on lists of the top hundred courses in the British Isles.

On the seaward side of the New—and even more testing—is the **Jubilee**, which opened in 1897. The holes today are largely the work of Donald Steel, who has imbued this eighteen with character and variety by skillfully employing two parallel spines of sand hills. Par is 72 on this 6,424-yard layout.

The **Eden** was a collaboration in 1913 by two of the very greatest figures in golf course architecture, Harry Colt and Alister MacKenzie. Despite many changes over the years, some top-notch Colt-MacKenzie holes remain, including two short par 4s that play right beside the estuary to plateau greens perched teasingly above it. The Eden measures 6,200 yards against a par of 70.

The **Strathtyrum Course**, which opened in 1993 (5,100 yards, par 69), was designed by Steel expressly for high handicappers. Fairways are wide, bunkering is light. Adjacent to the Strathtyrum is a little nine-hole layout called **Balgove** (1,530 yards, par 30), an ideal spot for youngsters to get their first taste of the game.

An important addition to the St. Andrews Links lineup has just opened. The **Castle Course** (6,376 yards, par 71) was built on high ground along the coast between Kinkell Braes and St. Andrews Bay Golf Resort & Spa. Scottish-born David McLay Kidd, architect of Bandon Dunes and suburban London's Queenwood course, designed the new eighteen, which opened in July 2008. Favorable reviews and several international awards strongly suggest that this course can take its place among the very best in Scotland.

THE DUKE'S COURSE

Herb Kohler (bathroom fixtures, Whistling Straits, and much more) rather recently acquired the Old Course Hotel and with it the Duke's Course, which was laid out by Peter Thomson in 1994. Mr. Kohler promptly ordered a revamping of the Australian's layout. The net of it is seven extensively redesigned holes, a number of remodeled tees, and a new drainage system. The "new" Duke's is excellent. Time will tell whether it is better than the "old" Duke's.

In 1910 Bernard Darwin, grandson of the great naturalist Charles Darwin, wrote, "I once met, staying in a hotel at St. Andrews, a gentleman who did not play golf. That is in itself remarkable, but more remarkable still, he joined so unobtrusively in the perpetual golfing conversation that his black secret was never discovered."

Yes, there is in St. Andrews life apart from golf. The compact and level "ault grey toon," a place of exceptional richness and antiquity, is ideal for walking. Of the three principal streets—North, Market, South—it is South Street that most fully embodies the ancient heritage of St. Andrews. Let's enter it through the West Port, carved out of a still-intact section of the fourteenth-century wall. We now stroll up the spacious cobbled thoroughfare. Landmarks dot the way: the roofless remains of Blackfriars' Chapel (1525); Madras College, a coed preparatory school founded in 1832; the Town Hall; Holy Trinity Church, dating from 1410.

A bit of a detour now for the Lade Braes Walk, roughly a mile and a half long. Much of it follows the embowered Kinness Burn, where several sylvan scenes (Law Hill provides one of them) are straight out of Constable.

The final leg leads down a narrow lane of gardens belonging to houses of all shapes and sizes and ages that may be short on grace but are long on personality. Where must the Lade Braes walk end? Why, back at South Street, practically next door to Blackfriars' Chapel.

A block or two farther along, we enter the lovely old quadrangle of St. Mary's College, dominated by a mighty oak tree. The first student matriculated in 1522; upstairs, a room from that period is preserved as it was.

In the last block of South Street is a house where Mary Queen of Scots is believed to have resided for a time in 1564 and where Charles II certainly did in 1650. Quite nearby is the Pends, a harmonious arched stone gateway leading to the cathedral precincts. Legend has it that the Pends will collapse when the wisest man in Christendom walks through the archway. The Pends still stands.

Regrettably, the same cannot be said of the cathedral, which is largely in ruins. But what evocative ruins they are, here on a splendid promontory above the sea. What brought the once-exalted house of God so low was the Protestant Reformation, with mobs sweeping down South Street to this seat of popery, there to sack and smash and loot. For years, local stonemasons found the cathedral to be a convenient quarry; many of the best houses in St. Andrews incorporate fragments of the noble church.

An unusual assortment of monuments and tombstones lures us to the graveyard. Old Tom Morris is buried here. Next to him is Young Tom, also a four-time Open champion, who died heartbroken, at the age of twenty-four, three months after his wife succumbed in childbirth, as did the son, their first offspring.

Just east of the cathedral, on The Scores, is the castle, begun in 1200 and long the seat of the Archbishop of St. Andrews. Guarded by cliffs and the sea, this haunting ruin was the setting for bloody drama on more than one occasion as the Reformation engulfed Scotland.

Over on North Street, a block away, are the Crawford Centre for the Arts, St. Salvator's Church, and Younger Graduation Hall, site of one of the most poignant moments in the history of St. Andrews. When Bob Jones came back in 1958 as nonplaying captain of the United

From left: the practice tee;
Market Street; Union Street
sign (top) and Old Cathedral
(bottom); Old Cathedral.
Opposite: the Old Cathedral.

24

SCOTLAND

In 1910 Bernard Darwin, grandson of the great naturalist Charles Darwin, wrote, "I once met, staying in a hotel at St. Andrews, a gentleman who did not play golf. That is in itself remarkable, but more remarkable still, he joined so unobtrusively in the perpetual golfing conversation that his black secret was never discovered."

Yes, there is in St. Andrews life apart from golf. The compact and level "ault grey toon," a place of exceptional richness and antiquity, is ideal for walking. Of the three principal streets—North, Market, South—it is South Street that most fully embodies the ancient heritage of St. Andrews. Let's enter it through the West Port, carved out of a still-intact section of the fourteenth-century wall. We now stroll up the spacious cobbled thoroughfare. Landmarks dot the way: the roofless remains of Blackfriars' Chapel (1525); Madras College, a coed preparatory school founded in 1832; the Town Hall; Holy Trinity Church, dating from 1410.

A bit of a detour now for the Lade Braes Walk, roughly a mile and a half long. Much of it follows the embowered Kinness Burn, where several sylvan scenes (Law Mill provides one of them) are straight out of Constable.

The final leg leads down a narrow lane of gardens belonging to houses of all shapes and sizes and ages that may be short on grace but are long on personality. Where must the Lade Braes walk end? Why, back at South Street, practically next door to Blackfriars' Chapel.

A block or two farther along, we enter the lovely old quadrangle of St. Mary's College, dominated by a mighty oak tree. The first student matriculated in 1522; upstairs, a room from that period is preserved as it was.

In the last block of South Street is a house where Mary Queen of Scots is believed to have resided for a time in 1564 and where Charles II certainly did in 1650. Quite nearby is the Pends, a harmonious arched stone gateway leading to the cathedral precincts. Legend has it that the Pends will collapse when the wisest man in Christendom walks through the archway. The Pends still stands.

Regrettably, the same cannot be said of the cathedral, which is largely in ruins. But what evocative ruins they are, here on a splendid promontory above the sea. What brought the once-exalted house of God so low was the Protestant Reformation, with mobs sweeping

down South Street to this seat of popery, there to sack and smash and loot. For years, local stonemasons found the cathedral to be a convenient quarry; many of the best houses in St. Andrews incorporate fragments of the noble church.

An unusual assortment of monuments and tombstones lures us to the graveyard. Old Tom Morris is buried here. Next to him is Young Tom, also a four-time Open champion, who died heartbroken, at the age of twenty-four, three months after his wife succumbed in childbirth, as did the son, their first offspring.

Just east of the cathedral, on The Scores, is the castle, begun in 1200 and long the seat of the Archbishop of St. Andrews. Guarded by cliffs and the sea, this haunting ruin was the setting for bloody drama on more than one occasion as the Reformation engulfed Scotland.

Over on North Street, a block away, are the Crawford Centre for the Arts, St. Salvator's Church, and Younger Graduation Hall, site of one of the most poignant moments in the history of St. Andrews. When Bob Jones came back in 1958 as nonplaying captain of the United

From left: the practice tee; Market Street; Union Street sign (top) and Old Cathedral (bottom); Old Cathedral sign. Opposite: the Old Cathedral.

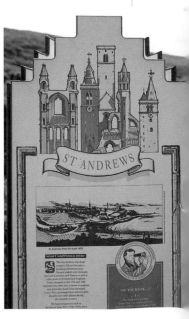

States squad in the inaugural World Amateur Team Championship, the town fathers took the opportunity to make him a freeman of the Burgh of St. Andrews. Only Jones had won both the Open (1927) and the Amateur (1930) on the Old Course, an achievement unlikely to be equaled. And his fineness of character and gentlemanly demeanor had registered as powerfully upon St. Andrews as his flair for playing links golf. Now crippled by a rare spinal disease, he needed a golf cart to get around.

More than two thousand people crammed Younger Hall that evening. After the provost spoke of the abiding friendship between Jones and the townspeople, Bob edged his way painstakingly along a supporting table to the lectern. Without benefit of script or notes, he recounted the high and low points of the championships in which he had competed on the Old Course. "I could take out of my life everything except my experiences at St. Andrews," he said, "and I would still have had a rich and full life." He concluded by speaking of friendship: "When you have made me aware on many occasions that you have a kindly feeling toward me, and when you have honored me by every means at your command, then when I call you my friends I am at once affirming my high regard and affection for you and my trust in the sincerity of your expression. And so, my fellow citizens of St. Andrews, it is with this appreciation of the full measure of the word that I salute you as my friends."

As he guided his "electric buggy" down the center aisle, the entire gathering rose and broke into an unutterably moving rendition of the old Scottish song "Will Ye No' Come Back Again?" As it happened, he never would.

My wife and I customarily stroll The Scores (the hotel takes its name from the street) after dinner, as you might a boardwalk. The sea is close at hand. We pass the bandstand and Martyrs' Monument, then a number of appealing hundred-year-old residences, several small hotels, and university buildings, including St. Salvator's. Sometimes we sit on a bench beneath the trees, gazing at the ruins of the castle. Other times we walk a block farther, to a spot that commands not only the sea but the cathedral and its graveyard, with the monument to Young Tom Morris in full view. And then it is time to retrace our steps, back along The Scores.

I remember the November evening many years ago when, on the return leg of our walk, we discovered a way into the grounds of St. Salvator's from The Scores. Turn down Butts Wynd, a narrow lane linking The Scores with North Street, and your venturesomeness will be rewarded by finding a gateway in the wall surrounding the college. That night, for the first time, we passed through it into the beautiful quadrangle. Shadows and silence, the great collegiate church mantled in darkness, its cloistering scarcely discernible, and, on the far side of that perfect lawn now dampened with dew, a light or two in the Jacobean facade of Lower College Hall. Ancient universities (this one founded in 1412), beguiling by day, can be even more bewitching by night. No student stirred as we stood peering up at the church spire, its pinnacle soaring above North Street and lost in the night, before we retreated through the gateway in the wall and down Butts Wynd to The Scores.

Along the seaward side of The Scores now, if it is a clear night, with stars thickly sewn in the heavens and perhaps the moon glinting off the gentle swells of the North Sea, the lights on the Angus coast—Carnoustie, even Arbroath—will glow softly golden far across the water. But if there should be a mist, why then, we are content with the shushing of the surf on the rocks at the base of the bluff. It is sweet indeed.

Fife has a number of nongolf attractions a short drive from St. Andrews. The royal burgh of Falkland revolves around Falkland Palace, begun in the fifteenth century as a hunting lodge for the Stuarts. Flemish tapestries, carved oak ceilings, and stained-glass windows all lend a regal look to the great house. And in the exquisite garden is a royal tennis court that dates from 1539. Court tennis is an eye-opening combination of squash and tennis. In the village are two good eating spots, The Covenanter Hotel, on the square, and, just off the square, the Stag Inn—dim, snug, and with old wooden booths.

Some twenty minutes northeast of Falkland, in pretty Ceres, is the Fife Folk Museum: costumes, tools, and utensils from the farms, homes, and workshops of bygone days. Also in Ceres is an unusual shop that specializes in linens and antique children's clothes, and no dis-

Opposite: the Old Cathedral. This page: views of Falkland Palace and its gardens, except the monument to Young Tom Morris (top left) and the inside walls of Old Cathedral (top right).

27

tance outside the village is Hill of Tarvit Mansionhouse, an imposing Edwardian manor that showcases the late Frederick Sharp's collection of Flemish tapestries, Chinese porcelains and bronzes, French and Regency furniture, and European paintings. The gardens are still carefully maintained, but gone is the nine-hole golf course that Sharp built for himself and his friends and made available, free of charge, to the residents of Ceres.

DINING

Eating in St. Andrews can be a town or country pleasure.

- Leading the town restaurants is the **Road Hole Grill**, on the top floor of the Old Course Hotel. The dishes, beautifully prepared and presented, incline to be sophisticated, and the wine list and service in this stylish milieu are equally outstanding.

- Not to be overlooked is the dining room in the **Links Clubhouse**, where the setting sparkles, the menu is imaginative, and the view over the links is irresistible.

- In the heart of town is the **Vine Leaf**, with eclectic decor and an equally eclectic menu.

- The **Balaka Bangladeshi** is consistently ranked among the best of the United Kingdom's eighty-five hundred Bangladeshi, Indian, and Pakastani restaurants by the *Good Curry Restaurant Guide*.

- Another good ethnic restaurant, this one Thai, is **Nahm-Jim**, on Crails Lane.

- Just beyond the bandstand on The Scores and hanging over the sea is the smartly contemporary **Seafood Restaurant**.

- For a pub lunch or a nightcap, duck into the old and atmospheric **Jigger Inn**, beside the Road Hole; or the lively **Dunvegan Hotel**, on Pilmour Place, with its American proprietors and its first-rate cheeseburgers; or the **St. Andrews Golf Hotel**, on The Scores, where, if the university is in session, college kids throng the rathskeller nightly.

In the countryside ringing St. Andrews is a quartet of superior restaurants:

- The **Grange Inn** (beam ceilings, log fires), on a hillside immediately south of town and with enchanting views of it, used to be renowned for its soups. Now, just about everything on the menu turns out to be delicious.

Clockwise from top: Myres Castle; Hill of Tarvit interior; a view of St. Andrews; exterior of Hill of Tarvit.

- Perhaps 15 minutes northwest of town is **Craigsanquhar House**, whose dining room provides a long, captivating view over the fertile fields of Fife.
- About ten minutes southwest of town is the **Inn at Lathones**, where the cooking bows toward France and the dining room has a warm informality that inclines us to linger over the wine.
- Not five minutes from Lathones is the **Peat Inn**, our favorite place to eat in Scotland. The principal dining room in this old whitewashed stone farmhouse looks over a simple garden to uncultivated fields. The French-influenced menu is chock-full of exceptional choices: julienne of pigeon breast on a confit of spiced pork, saddle of venison with a wild mushroom and truffle crust in a red wine sauce, *feuilleté* of white chocolate ice cream with a dark chocolate sauce. The impressive wine list even contains some attractive vintages for less than fifty dollars. The Peat Inn, it might be noted, is *in* Peat Inn.

LODGING

Since St. Andrews is, as much as anything, a seaside resort, it offers a variety of places to stay. You can find a room in a university dorm (often with bath) or in one of the countless B&Bs, a number of them on Murray Place.

- **Waldon House**, smack on the 18th hole of the Old Course, is a B&B owned and operated by the R&A. When any of the eight rooms is not occupied by a club member or his guest, that room is generally made available to the public.
- In the countryside outside the village of Auchtermuchty (thirty minutes from St. Andrews) is **Myres Castle**, which dates from the sixteenth century. A private and luxurious house, it is rented exclusively to parties ranging from six to eighteen; minimum stay, two nights. The nine bedrooms in this period paradise, each with its own bath, are individually appointed. The cooking is superb.
- The five-star **Old Course Hotel & Spa** is all that a great hotel should be: stylish, luxurious, supremely comfortable; world-class amenities, cuisine, and views; an up-to-date spa with a small but pleasant pool; faultless service. Very recently refurbished by

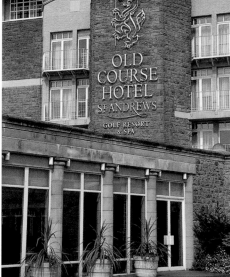

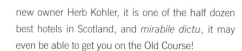

new owner Herb Kohler, it is one of the half dozen best hotels in Scotland, and *mirabile dictu*, it may even be able to get you on the Old Course!
- A couple of miles out of town on the Strathkinness Low Road is **Rufflets**, an inviting country-house hotel. Accommodations are bright and cheerful, cooking is creative, and the topiary garden, beside a stream, is idyllic. Rufflets was for years the choice of Jack and Barbara Nicklaus.
- Another legendary golfer's favorite is **Rusacks Hotel**, where Bob Jones stayed. Overlooking the first and

last holes of the Old Course, it is casual and hospitable, with good food and unforgettable views.
- The **Scores Hotel**, where we first stayed in 1971, is a traditional haven for golfers, sitting on a rise above the R&A clubhouse. Comfortable accommodations, worthy cooking, and a kindly welcome are the chief reasons why travelers return to it regularly, not to mention the stunning views of the sea and the West Sands from the front rooms and the thirty-eight-second walk to the 1st tee of the Old Course from the front door.

Clockwise from top left: Jigger Inn; Grange Inn; Rusacks Hotel; Royal & Ancient Golf Club; Old Course Hotel.

ST. ANDREWS BAY

I n 1998 American pharmaceutical magnate Donald Panoz (his Elan Corporation devised the nicotine patch) flew in from Atlanta. For all of five minutes, he surveyed the potential site for a golf resort on the outskirts of St. Andrews. Then he said simply, with a smile, "This'll do me."

It's no wonder the decision on the 520-acre tract was so easy. In addition to sea frontage of more than a mile, this property, which varies between twenty and eighty feet above the rocky strand, offers mesmerizing views across the bay to the medieval quarter of St. Andrews.

At the heart of the St. Andrews Bay Golf Resort & Spa are a 209-room hotel and two outstanding eighteens, the Torrance Course and the Devlin Course. Sam Torrance, captain of the 2002 European Ryder Cup team and himself an eight-time Ryder Cupper, was assisted on his design by Atlantan Denis Griffiths and by the late Gene Sarazen, who, at age ninety-six, visited the site and drafted some key recommendations.

ON THE TORRANCE COURSE

The Torrance is an aesthetic delight—sea views from every hole, St. Andrews views from many holes—and a challenge. It can play as long as 7,020 yards, as short as 5,380; par is 72. The overall elevation change is about 40 feet. There are numerous opportunities to play links-style running shots. Stone walls, golden fescues dotted with wildflowers, and winding burns are all part of the game here. Trees are not.

The course is studded with holes that combine charm with test. At the 167-yard 11th, our eyes first spot the flagstick and then, on the same line but on the far side of the bay, take in ancient St. Andrews—the town wall, St. Rule's Tower, the spire of St. Salvator's, the cathedral and its graveyard—all of it perfectly framed in the distance. Golfers have never before been blessed with this vista. It is incomparable and it is unforgettable.

The penultimate hole, one of the cliff-toppers skirting the sea, is also marvelous. On this 427-yarder the prevailing wind is into us and left to right, blithely tossing the frail drive over the cliff and down into the sea, where basking seals bark mockingly.

ON THE DEVLIN COURSE

Bruce Devlin, who has played a principal role in the design or remodeling of more than one hundred fifty courses worldwide, was given more land and more sea frontage than Torrance, to say nothing of ground with greater elevation change. This acreage is also richer topographically, with more features, including Kittock's Den, a vast and deep hollow with trees and scrub and the promise of several adventuresome golf holes. Two sizable ponds have been introduced in this par-72 layout. Championship markers are set at 7,100 yards, daily tees at 6,200.

Opposite: St. Andrews Bay, 17th. Above: 10th.

Above, left: St. Andrews Bay, Torrance Course, 14th; right: 11th. Opposite: 17th.

Following a pleasant 512-yard opener, we face a short par 4 and a short par 5, both long on peril thanks to those two ponds. But having sufficiently unnerved us, Devlin and his associate, Denis Griffiths, now back off, all the way: no more artificial water hazards.

The 6th is nothing less than a great two-shotter. From the back tees, it measures 467 yards; for mere mortals, 410. Kittock's Den rears its intimidating head here for the first time. A proper drive leaves us on a fairway plateau short of a steep descent into the wicked scrubby hollow. There is no mystery to the second shot, a forced carry of 180–190 yards over this hazard to the safety of the green on the opposite hill. Thin the shot or pull it or push it or pop it up, and the result will be calamitous.

It is at the 361-yard 9th that we reach the sea for the first time, playing along it and high above it, much of the hole downhill. The 330-yard 10th and the 13th, 510 yards, head inland to climb the same steep hill, but the 11th and 12th find us back at the sea, their greens at the cliff's edge. This routing plan is a jewel, not simply unpredictable but also taking full advantage of every natural feature here.

Kittock's Den is much in play at the 14th, 16th, and 17th. The 403-yard 17th is the single best—and most thrilling—hole at St. Andrews Bay. The green cannot be seen from the tee. A drive clearing the bunkers on the right brings us to the crest of the hill. Far below, sitting defiantly on an old Roman fort with nothing but the slate-blue North Sea behind it and

Time now to head to the thoughtfully appointed clubhouse. The enthralling views take in St. Andrews to the west; the Angus coast to the north; the Torrance Course to the south; and the Devlin to the east. The **Fairmont Andrews** has an exterior design that leans vaguely toward France and an overall feeling that may be more Scottsdale than Scotland. All 209 guest rooms overlook golf holes; most have sea views and/or views of St. Andrews. The spa has a gym, a heated indoor swimming pool, Jacuzzi, whirlpool, sauna and steam room, plus a wide range of body and beauty therapies. The resort offers five places to eat, the dining room in the clubhouse and four restaurants in the hotel:

- The informal **Atrium** is the centerpiece of an immense four-story-high enclosure of space guaranteed to stop you dead in your tracks at the top of a sweeping divided staircase. The cooking, bistro style, is good.
- Overlooking the atrium, and boasting a large fireplace, is **Kittocks Den**, which serves drinks and snacks throughout the day.
- **Esperante**, the fine-dining restaurant, is a stylish and intimate room, with the emphasis on Mediterranean-type dishes.
- **The Squire**, Scottish dining with a contemporary flair.

little but sand in front of it, is the green. Threatening on the right the length of this heroic second shot is the Den. All that is required of us here is a lifetime swing. If we should somehow manage to unfurl just that, gain the green, and get down in two putts, the result will be euphoria.

The 18th is a rare occurrence on a championship-level course, a par 3 to conclude the round. This one tiptoes along on the brink—187 yards from all the way back, 147 from the daily tees—scarily close to the cliff edge from tee to green, some 75 feet above the shore. The shot hit even minimally out to the right is out to sea. To the very end, Devlin and Griffiths have provided shot values of a very high order and just about the right degree of pressure on the swing.

KINGSBARNS

Just down the coast road from St. Andrews and about ten minutes beyond St. Andrews Bay lies the Kingsbarns Golf Links. It was designed and built by two Californians, Kyle Phillips and Mark Parsinen. What they accomplished here is pure magic. They took 190 acres of what had been pasture and crop lands (wheat, beets, corn) along the sea and created, out of whole cloth, a magnificent and sublimely natural-looking links course. This was legerdemain on the grandest scale, with dunes of various shapes and sizes, crumpled fairways, a plethora of humps, hillocks, and hollows, cunning little rough-cloaked mesas and promontories, and spirited greens that are a clear by-product of the immediately surrounding terrain. But this links is entirely manufactured. Nature had essentially no hand in it, except to provide the entrancing seaside setting with the surf surging against the rocky foreshore. Yet even the most experienced observer would swear that it is authentic, its contours surely the result of the receding seas and the persistent winds over tens of thousands of years.

Not so. It was excavators, dumpers, bulldozers, and backhoes.

In late July 1998, two years before the course was completed, I visited the site, touring it with Mark Parsinen in his mud-caked black Range Rover. Solidly built and then in his early fifties, he struck me as the kind of man who would not hesitate to dig in—*literally*—to get the job done.

"I was studying at the London School of Economics in 1969," he said, "and every chance I got I'd head up to St. Andrews and Carnoustie or to Muirfield or Troon or Dornoch. During the eighties and nineties I made some money in the computer business, but I knew this would never be as satisfying as building golf courses. So I teamed up with Kyle Phillips—he'd been designing courses all over the world with Robert Trent Jones Junior—and along came the chance for us to do Kingsbarns: not only in Scotland and smack beside the sea, but practically on the doorstep of St. Andrews.

"We jumped at it. I realized that if we were going to create a links at Kingsbarns—you know, there was a nine-hole course here for over a hundred years, but they had to give it up when the war broke out in 1939—anyway, I figured I better learn a lot more about links courses than I knew from just playing them.

"I read Robert Price's book *Scotland's Golf Courses*, which concentrates on how the natural landforms themselves have played such a critical role in the development of the courses, and then I hired Dr. Price to consult on Kingsbarns. He and I walked the Old Course, looking closely at the little ridges there, then over to the Jubilee, where you have much bigger dunes. The two of us would get down on the ground to examine just why it is that things look the way they look."

Mark Parsinen and I bumped along over the embryonic layout that day, often high above the strand, from one end of the mile-and-a-half-long sea frontage to the other. He talked animatedly while he drove (also animatedly). Again and again he stopped so we could jump out and he could explain the particular hole. He made the point that every hole views the sea and that six holes play along it. His enthusiasm was contagious.

"After I got Dr. Price on board," he continued, "I went back to a number of those wonderful links I'd been playing, in Ireland as well as Scotland. I was examining their dune systems—they're not all the same, by any means—and their green sites and green complexes. I even sent our two shapers over to Troon and Turnberry and up to Cruden Bay to see firsthand what I was talking about.

"And then, to make sure we would end up with real links turf—the right grasses, the fescues, the bents, in the right combinations, growing in the right soil—I retained Walter Wood, who had just retired as greens superintendent at St. Andrews, to consult with me on an ongoing basis. We spent fifty thousand pounds on soil analyses to make certain we could produce consistent soil conditions for sand-based fairways throughout the links."

ON THE COURSE

Kingsbarns, which opened in 2000, can be played as long as 7,120 yards, as short as 5,140. Because it is quick-draining, in season the fairways are firm and fast. The game on the ground is at least as important as the game in the air. Run of ball was a major consideration in the design; angles of play would be strong elements in the course's defense against the attack of an accomplished golfer.

Opposite: Kingsbarns, 15th.

game here enormously—they are marvelous fun—and distinguish it markedly from dart-throwing parkland golf.

Strategy is at the core of the design, strategy clearly based on the risk/reward principle. So, if we adopt the more courageous line off the tee, a well-struck drive will earn the easier approach to the green. Timid tee shots often leave second shots over bunkers or rough or dunes or swales.

On a course where no hole is less than very good, there may be eight that are great, four on each side. Going out, the four are consecutive—4, 5, 6, and 7—and all two-shotters, yet they could scarcely be less alike.

At the 390-yard 4th, a drive carrying some 210 yards over a deep bunker is the only way to get into position for a straightforward iron to an exposed, windswept green open across the front. On the next hole, 20 yards shorter, with the green hidden away to the right in a dell of dunes, a clear shot into it will be merited only by a drive that is lined farther left than we can comfortably envision.

The 6th is spellbinding. The tee on this 318-yarder, well up the side of an imposing sand hill, discloses a majestic panorama of golf holes rippling along far below, waves cascading onto the foreshore, and, miles away down the coast, the clubhouse at Crail perched on its promontory. Drive straight at the flag and you are left with a blind short pitch to a green ringed by low dunes and rough and abrupt little falloffs. But there is another route. Drive well out to the right, up onto a raised and generous plateau of fairway. Gazing down from here, you enjoy not only a good view of the putting surface but also an approach angle for this very short falling pitch that enables greenside contours to feed the ball neatly toward the flagstick.

The 7th, on the other hand, is a model of decorum. It is muscular, 436 yards long, uphill, with emphatic right-to-left contours all the way. Two aggressive hits, both held determinedly to starboard, will be the ticket.

On the second nine the great holes are 12, 15, 17, and 18. Measuring 566 yards from the white markers, the 12th sails along spectacularly beside the sea all the way, high above it from the hilltop tee, then plunges to a broad and tumbling fairway, now curves left to begin a moderate ascent to the astounding green set on the diagonal and itself continues the ascent, all 72 yards of it! The difference in extreme cup positions, right front as opposed to left rear, will be at least five clubs. The word *exhilaration* does not do this hole justice.

The 185-yard 15th is more of this tremendous stuff. The target is sited on a spit of land jutting into the sea to our right. If the wind is into us, the playing value from the elevated tee of this forced carry over surf-

Above: Kingsbarns, 6th.
Opposite: 8th.

In addition to the pleasure of runups from as far out as 100 yards off the green, here at Kingsbarns we relish the thrill of a 3-metal shot skimming up a slope to reach a putting surface that may be as much as 235 yards away. The course plays shorter than the card suggests, but the ball is inclined to be less obedient than we might wish.

Bunkering is not heavy—some eighty sand hazards all told. But these pits, most with steep revetted faces, are frequently deep, and because of crafty fairway contouring, they tend to gather a ball that had seemed to be skating safely clear of their clutches. The greens, large enough to be hittable targets in a robust wind, are splendid, though perhaps, on occasion, a little too festive. Even a player with a solid short game may find himself three-putting four or five times and failing two or three more times to get up and down from just off the green. That's a lot of strokes to surrender. Still, these slopes and curls and angles enrich the

spattered rocks can easily be 200 yards. Is there any hole at Kingsbarns where the embrace of the sea is more powerfully felt?

Like the 7th, the 17th is brawny, 432 yards. The green sits far above the fairway. Only the sloping false front is visible, to remind us that a ball landing here will retreat well down the hill. There may be no more rewarding full-blooded shot on the course than the one that gains this green.

The home hole offers little in the way of refuge. It is 414 yards long, with concealed bunkers down the left on this blind drive. Then, for the last swing of the round, comes a win-or-woe second shot that must traverse a deep valley with a trickle of burn at the bottom to devour the ball that fails by feet to reach the elevated bilevel green. It is a rousing finish.

Kingsbarns is inordinately rich, complex, full of feature and of shot-making options. This is one of the two best courses (Loch Lomond is the other one) to open in Scotland since Turnberry was rebuilt after the Second World War. From start to finish, it is a triumph of study and creativity, of artistry and daring and challenge and beauty, and, yes, of money over nature. It is links golf of the highest order, deserved to be ranked among the top fifteen courses in the British Isles and among the top fifty in the world. Could this breathtaking faux links be the single most extraordinary achievement in the history of golf-course construction? Or should it be viewed as one of a triumvirate, the other two in this rarefied air being Pete Dye's Whistling Straits and Tom Fazio's Shadow Creek?

Opposite: Kingsbarns, 12th.
Above: 17th.

CRAIL

N ot ten minutes farther along the coast road from Kingsbarns is the seventh-oldest golf club in the world, the Crail Golfing Society, founded in 1786. Initially, the society played on the narrow strip of linksland at Sauchope, at the northeast end of town. Sandy Herd, who won the 1902 Open Championship and had worked for several years as a plasterer in Crail, attributed his straight driving to the tightness of the eight holes at Sauchope.

In the late 1850s the society began to play much of its golf on the Balcomie Links, generally regarded as the windiest spot in the East Neuk of Scotland. Crail golfers made a lasting contribution to the art of greenkeeping in 1874, when its committee agreed that "iron cases be got for the eight holes on the links to prevent the holes from being destroyed." There exists no earlier record at any course of the insertion of metal cups into the holes.

It was Old Tom Morris who laid out a proper nine-hole course at Balcomie, in 1895. Four years later he added a second nine. Though there have been some changes over time, the Balcomie eighteen today is largely the one laid out more than a century ago. Golfers come from all over the world to play Balcomie—it is almost a point of pilgrimage—for several reasons: its age, its quirky charms, and its attribution to Old Tom alone.

Over the years, I have come to prize a friendship with Crail's head professional, Graeme Lennie. With his many duties—giving lessons, selling equipment, collecting green fees, and administering the game on two eighteens—he plays very little golf. So whenever I've been in St. Andrews for an extended stay, I have insisted that he accompany me to Carnoustie or Royal Aberdeen, to Murcar or Cruden Bay or Peterhead. And at one or another of our stops, I can count on him to say, with wry resignation, "If you didn't come to Scotland, I'd never get to play."

Graeme is a member of the James Braid Society and the British Golf Collectors' Society. The Scottish PGA honored him by naming him its captain for 2003 and 2004. The post is largely ceremonial, but a professional is not elected to it unless he has earned the respect and regard of his peers. I recall how pleased he was when, scheduled to preside for the first time over an assembly of the membership, in

Glasgow, he called British PGA headquarters, at the Belfry, to ask whether it might be possible to display the Ryder Cup at this meeting. The small gold trophy was delivered to him by courier.

ON THE BALCOMIE COURSE

Total yardage on the Balcomie Links is 5,922, against a par of 69. Two of the six par 4s on the outbound nine measure 459 and 442 yards; the other four range from 306 to 349. The second nine is a crazy quilt of golf holes—two par 5s (back to back and side by side), three par 4s, and four par 3s (two of them over 200 yards). You never know what to expect next.

On the 1st tee, where the drop to the fairway may well measure 100 feet, we get a feel for the entire course because so much of it is spread out below us. What we observe from our hilltop is a vast and well-nigh treeless meadow sweeping down, in vaguely terraced formation, to the sea. There seems to be minimal separation between holes and little definition to them. It all appears to run together.

Balcomie's appeal lies principally in the surprising diversity of shots called for, many of them requiring skill at the ground game and virtually every one of them executed within sight of the sea. The very walk over the rolling, sometimes hilly, terrain is a treat, so enthralling are the views. Simply to be out on Balcomie is cause for rejoicing. As a long-ago member, Professor Dow, never tired of saying, "One half hour of the air at Balcomie is worth more than all the medicines in Jimmy Smith's [apothecary] shop."

But, you insist, that is hardly enough. Wherein lies the test, the challenge? Largely in a single circumstance: the wind. No hole is sheltered from it. On a course where conventional hazards—bunkers, burns, boundaries—rarely vex us, the wind harasses us relentlessly.

The 2nd hole (a grand uphill par 5, its small green full of slippery slopes), the 3rd (a blind 184-yarder with a long, narrow green), the 4th and the 5th—all play along and above the sea, with the tee shots on 4 and 5 daring us to bite off large chunks of these perilous right-turn doglegs, disaster waiting on the wave-washed rocks below. At 459 yards, the par-4 5th, with the sea menacing both of our all-out swings, is a genuinely heroic hole and,

Opposite: Crail Balcomie, 1st.

in fact, the strongest test on the course. Now little more than a dozen years old, it was impudently saluted by a member the day it opened for play: He holed his second shot!

The next eight holes, though not seaside, are nonetheless peppery, and the final hole in this inside stretch is a particular favorite of mine. A 219-yarder, the 13th plays forcefully uphill over a rocky escarpment smothered in long rough grasses. The climb itself looks daunting, and into the wind, as seems often the case, the shot to the blind green is fearsome.

And now that we have played straight up, we turn our back on the nearby clubhouse and, from the 14th tee, play straight down, 150 yards, to a green far below ringed by six bunkers. The world of Balcomie lies all around us, links and sand and sea importuning us to pause and drink it all in.

The par-4 15th, 265 basically level yards, is a bona fide birdie hole, if only we can time our driver swing between the waves crashing on the shore, perhaps a dozen paces away. Sixteen, up a steep hill, calls for a very soundly struck iron—the measured 163 yards plays at least 175. The 462-yard 17th, often downwind from its hilltop tee, is the number-two

Left: Crail Balcomie, 15th.
Above: 16th.

stroke hole and a stiff par 4 (or certainly *used* to be). And the 18th, though hospitably open across the green's broad front, is, at 203 yards, tough to par when par is what we must have to rescue the match.

So much for the morning round. It was nonstop fun, where the sea was always in sight, the target was generally within reach, and the penalty for failure was rarely stringent. We may even have played to our handicap.

Time for a sandwich and a beverage now in this brilliantly sited clubhouse atop an old quarry on the property's highest point. The rambling stone structure, with its abundance of glass, was obviously built with the view in mind. And what a view it is! On a day that is truly crystalline, we can take in from this pinnacle (we may have to step outside to appreciate some of the noble panorama) more than a hundred miles of coastline, from Montrose in the north, then south across the Firth of Forth and down the East Lothian coast past Dunbar to St. Abb's Head, near Berwick-upon-Tweed (and just a few miles from the English border). You may want to pull out a map and see what it is I'm trying to convey here—I know that my words are inadequate.

ON THE CRAIGHEAD COURSE

If the Balcomie Links is true holiday golf, its sister course, Craighead, next door, is true championship golf. It came along a hundred years later (the Crail Golfing Society does not incline to rush into these things) and it is the work of America's Gilbert Hanse. Among his most highly regarded courses are Applebrook and French Creek, outside Philadelphia; Rustic Canyon, Los Angeles; and the Boston Golf Club.

In order to produce a genuinely natural course, Hanse moved little earth, accepting the gently sloping terrain much as he found it. The eighteen is laid out high above the sea and, for the most part, at a bit of a remove from it, as is the case with Muirfield. Indeed, the similarity in appearance to the great East Lothian course is unmistakable, with the fairways here also framed by thigh-high golden-beige native fescues, which look like wheat waving in the wind. Craighead's fairways, however, are very broad, averaging a good 60 yards across. Still, in a 30 to 40 (to 50) mile-per-hour wind, a ball with even a scintilla of sidespin can sail alarmingly wide of the mark.

If the wind and rough are deterrents to low scoring here, so are the green complexes. Admittedly, most putting surfaces are open across the front, so there is plenty of room to play the ball along the ground. But a number of greens incline to shed the approach shot, to shrug it off. In fact,

half a dozen of them—the 2nd, 7th, 9th, 12th, 15th, and 17th—are among the least receptive greens you will ever play to. And when you miss these targets, be prepared to recover from the base of a steep little falloff or from the bottom of a deep revetted bunker with a sheer front wall.

This layout—it has a par of 71 and can be tackled at 5,400, 6,250, or 6,725 yards—is studded with outstanding holes, particularly the final five. The 414-yard 14th walks a tightrope along the clifftop from tee to green, with the sea far below on our left. It may be the most dramatic hole on the course.

Gil Hanse said to me, "This green, which is tilted from right to left, is a reflection of the slope that was here. The hole is a natural, and I left it as I found it."

At 516 yards from the regular markers (554 from the back) and dog-legging smartly right, the 15th plays from a tee quite near the cliff edge to a landing area corseted by sand and with a tiny pot bunker in the center of the fairway. The uphill second shot calls for a decision: Either lay up short of Danes Dyke, leaving a semiblind third shot to the world's knobbiest green, or clear the ancient stone wall (shades of North Berwick) with a

Opposite: Crail Craighead, 9th. Above: 17th.

Crail Craighead, 18th.

fairway metal and now enjoy the luxury of a 70-yard pitch. Terrific stuff, whatever you elect to do.

From a platform tee the 16th, 373 yards and bending left, recrosses Danes Dyke to a fairway with a massive bunker complex in the crook of the dogleg. The smallish green is crowned; it is also guarded at the left by four deep pits.

On the last par 3 (17, 175 yards), a pair of large and deep and fanciful bunkers pinch the entrance to the green. The only way on is up and on. And when we get there, the rollercoaster green makes putting perilous. This is a great—and memorable—one-shotter.

At 425 yards, the home hole calls for solid hitting, not to mention real control if we are to avoid the cluster of bunkers on the right eating into the tee-shot landing area and then, on the long second shot, skate through the Valley of Sin (a bow to the Old Course) immediately short of the green.

After taking a good look at Craighead, Peter Thomson volunteered that it could serve well for final qualifying in the Open Championship.

Crail Golfing Society annually hosts a tournament that is a test not only of skill but of endurance. The competition, which dates to 1895, is called the Ranken-Todd Bowl, the bowl itself a huge ribbed silver vessel that looks to be worth the crown jewels. Eight or nine local golf clubs, including St. Andrews, Leven, Lundin, and Elie, are invited to send a four-man team. Each team plays only two balls, both balls counting in this alternate-stroke arrangement. A qualifying round is held in the morning to eliminate all but four clubs. The semifinals are held in the afternoon, and in the evening the 18-hole final is contested. Though the world is full of 54-hole invitational tournaments, this may be the only one that is settled in a single day.

The East Neuk fishing villages of Crail, Anstruther, Pittenweem, St. Monance, Elie, and Lower Largo are picturesque without being precious, some more workaday than others. All reward even the most casual sightseeing. But if you had to settle on just one as the most appealing example of the genre, it would probably be Crail. Here we find a spacious and well-proportioned town square, called Marketgate (poke your head into the Jerdan Gallery and enjoy the paintings in the house and the sculpture in the garden); the Collegiate Church of St. Mary, parts reaching back to the twelfth century; the Tolbooth, dating to the 16th century and formerly containing the council chamber, courtroom, and prison cells; the seventeenth- and eighteenth-century stone cottages, with their crow-stepped gables and red tile roofs; and the narrow, cobbled lanes spilling down to the protected harbor.

Crail has a couple of small hotels that might catch your fancy. Closest to the golf courses is the **Balcomie Links Hotel**: several rooms with distant sea views; nonsmoking dining room; live music in the lounge bar at weekends. On a bluff above the sea is the **Marine Hotel**, within a five-minute walk of the harbor: smallish but spiffy rooms, most of them with beautiful views over the Firth of Forth; al fresco dining in the garden.

Views of Crail.

ELIE

Less than twenty minutes driving west on the coast road from Crail brings us to the seaside town of Elie and to The Golf House Club, Elie. You may wonder about the origin of this unusual name.

The original golf club in these parts, and the one that first used this linksland, was the Earlesferry & Elie Golf Club, founded in 1858 (Elie and Earlesferry were adjacent villages). The club did not own the links; it just had the right to play there. Nor did the club have a clubhouse. It used the Golfers' Tavern for most meetings. In 1875 a second and a third club were formed, also with the right to use this same links. The membership of the second club may have been a shade tonier than that of the Earlesferry & Elie club and of the other new club, the Thistle. In any event, this second club, at its inaugural meeting, vowed to erect a clubhouse. It was this decision that gave the club its peculiar name: The Golf House Club, Elie. Which is to say, the club that had a golf house, as distinguished from the two clubs that did not. The Earlesferry & Elie Golf Club disbanded in 1912.

Elie's women golfers have their own organization, the Elie & Earlesferry Ladies Golf Club, founded in 1884. Over the next forty years the ladies applied again and again for permission to occupy some modest space in what was viewed as the men's clubhouse. Again and again they were rejected. Then, in 1927, an outrageous incident occurred. A deputation of three ladies, including the club secretary, was invited to The Golf House Club to discuss the possibility of using a room in the clubhouse. However, on arriving they were advised that ladies were forbidden to enter by the front door and that, unfortunately, the steward had gone out, locking the back door. The only way to get in, it was suggested, was to climb through a window. This proved relatively easy for two of the ladies but intimidating for the secretary, who was elderly and of ample girth. Finally, that good woman also made her way in, amid a flurry of petticoats. The personal indignity she suffered so shocked both organizations that the Ladies Club was granted space in the clubhouse at last.

Ironically, the clubhouse today has something of a feminine aspect, at least on the exterior. There is a lightness about it, and a fanci-

ful nature, a sunny holiday spirit. My good friend Alec Beveridge, a longtime member of The Golf House Club, calls the clubhouse "couthie," a Scottish word that suggests niceness, in this case a hospitable niceness that inspires affection and hymns the joy of the game.

The clubhouse is one thing, the starter's hut quite another. This shack is one of golf's great curios. Mounted within it and jutting boldly up out of it through the roof is a submarine periscope. Dubbed Excalibur, it was presented to the club forty years ago. It enables the starter to see over the hill that rises precipitously in front of the first tee, in this way making certain that the players who have disappeared beyond the crest are now out of range.

From time to time over the years, the starter has had considerable authority with respect to the order of play. So if one wished to tee off at 9:00 A.M., it was well to be in the starter's good graces. According to a

Opposite: Elie, 13th.
Above: The clubhouse and starter's hut, with periscope.

favorite club story, a visitor arriving for a week's holiday slipped the starter a banknote to assure a favorable tee time throughout his stay. For several days he got just what he wanted. Then, abruptly, he found himself with an eleven o'clock starting time. When he asked the starter for an explanation, what he got was a laconic, "Yer money's run oot!"

ON THE COURSE

The course we play today was laid out by Old Tom Morris in 1895 (the same year he laid out the first nine at Crail), with revisions by James Braid in the 1920s. Braid, who would win the Open Championship five times, was born and raised in Elie and learned to play the game here.

The course measures 6,273 yards against a par of 70. There are no par 5s and only two par 3s. On the face of it, Elie ought to be a bore. It emphatically is not. Its 16 two-shotters range from 252 to 466 yards, they run to every point of the compass, the wind is frustratingly fickle, and blind shots pop up with bewildering frequency. What's more, the greens are full of fun, the bunkers are full of woe, and the topography overall is remarkably varied.

Elie's opener is a bear: 420 yards long, a blind drive, a low stone boundary wall along the right, and bunkers on both sides of the green. And if the 1st is a likely bogey, the uphill 2nd, only 284 yards, is a possible birdie. The green here affords one of golf's memorably lovely moments. It is the highest point on the links, and from it we look down on the rooftops of the town in the foreground and, beyond them, to the Firth of Forth itself: The Isle of May, Berwick Law, and Bass Rock all vie for our attention in the distance. The East Lothian coast—Muirfield, Gullane, North Berwick—stands out in bold relief across the water, and backdropping it is the shadowy outline of the Lammermuir Hills. The distance across the sea to Muirfield is only ten miles, but it's the best part of two hours by car.

Below: Elie, 10th. Opposite, left: 2nd; right: 3rd.

Only on the 1st and 18th is the sea out of sight. On holes such as the 4th and 5th, we catch glimpses of it down lanes or between houses, a patch of frothy blue bobbing up here and there if we look left as we walk down the fairway. At the 5th, 365 yards, our drive comes to rest in a patch of tumbling fairway that reminds us not of the seas receding to those thousands of years ago but rather of coal miners retreating to those hundred and fifty years ago. And at the 316-yard 6th, with its downhill pitch to a green running away, we command the full sweep of West Bay 'round to Kincraig Point and its extraordinary rock formation called "Daniel Preaching to the Lion."

Out at the far end of the links there is a cluster of four holes that is characteristically Elie, the first two cunning and old-fashioned, the other two classic and rigorous. At the very short par-4 10th, our tee shot sometimes scales a steep hill and races down an even steeper one, perhaps to finish on the sloping green above the beach. Here the seabirds strut on the rocks, and holiday makers build castles on the sand.

Only the flag is visible on Sea Hole, the level 125-yard 11th, where the sea wall is scant steps from the green's left edge. In days long gone

caddies who were stationed in the rocks beside the green would fabricate a hole-in-one here in the hope of pocketing a bigger tip. When a shot would finish quite close to the cup but out of the player's sight, three of the four boys would leap up, cheering and gesticulating, while the smallest one would steal onto the green and pop the ball into the hole.

The 466-yard 12th clings to the curving shoreline, with MacDuff's Cave barely discernible in a distant cliff. From the scrap of tee just above the strand, only the strong and brave will cut off enough of the beach to get home in two. This is a risk/reward hole, and a great one.

The 13th is also great. Braid once called it "the finest hole in all the country." Its measured length, 386 yards, is not disheartening, but the second shot, often into a left-to-right wind off the bay, tends uphill to an angled shelflike green that is 190 feet wide! A deep swale captures even the slightly underhit approach. Immediately behind the putting surface is a steep bank, which used to be counted on for a kindly roll if we had overclubbed. (In the 1973 British Senior Professional Championship, Roberto de Vicenzo deliberately overclubbed here in the final round and

and a mutual friend were awaiting our turn to begin the round. Immediately ahead of us was a couple in their early fifties who sounded Swedish to me. He sent his drive over the blockading hill. She did not follow suit. Demonstrating one of the most unconventional swings I've ever seen, she lurched back on the takeaway so far off the ball that for an instant I thought I was in danger of being brained, then lunged violently forward to stab the turf with the driver head and bounce it neatly over the ball, which stayed steadfast on the wooden peg. Assuming her stance again, she proceeded to repeat the swing, this time, however, cleanly fanning the ball without touching the ground. On her third attempt she fanned once more. Her fourth swing propelled the ball vigorously along the ground and markedly to the right, skipping between the starter's hut and the clubhouse. Trolley now in tow, she briskly set out after her version of a successful drive. Seconds later the starter emerged from his headquarters and approached us, displaying a trace of a smile. He summarized her performance as "one divot, two fresh airs, and a lucky hit," adding, "That woman will bear keeping an eye on." He promptly retreated to his hut and glued his eye to the periscope.

NEARBY COURSES

Midway between Crail and Elie lies Anstruther, an old fishing port. The **Anstruther Golf Club**'s course—nine holes, 2,000 yards long, par 31—contains one of the most thrilling, challenging, and eccentric par 3s on the globe. The 5th, called Rockies, is 236 yards long. Paralleling the shoreline (the sea is on our left), it plays downhill from a clifftop tee to a hidden green tucked around to the right, behind a small outcropping of rock. The shot is blind, and for most people the hole, generally played into or across the prevailing wind, is actually a dogleg. The net of it all is a blind dogleg par 3. A local who is not a member at Anstruther confided to me that in July 2000, when the Open was held at St. Andrews, a very great young golfer from America, not yet twenty-five, clattered in on a helicopter to examine this remarkable hole, did so, shook his head in disbelief, climbed back into the helicopter, and clattered away.

Just outside Colinsburgh and not ten minutes from Elie is a parkland eighteen called **Charleton**, now a dozen years old. It ranges from rolling to hilly, the pastoral views are gorgeous, and since there are no hazards, a stiff breeze is needed to make it testing. The lively green complexes lend character to a course whose green fees are appropriately low.

wound up with a tap-in birdie that led to victory.) Today, however, that bank in back is no longer shaved, and the ball that runs up it stays up it, presenting a vexing little pitch down the slope. The 13th was selected for the book *The 500 World's Greatest Golf Holes*.

To the surprise of absolutely no one, the final five holes are all par 4s, three of them well over 400 yards. Chances of making up strokes as we head for the "golf house" are not good unless we can birdie the 359-yard 18th, which in 1935 witnessed an astonishing double bogey: In it were 4 penalty strokes. A saddler named Ken Foster followed a good drive by firing his 135-yard second shot dead left through a clubhouse window. He dropped another ball and, now playing 4, flew it through the same window. He then dropped a third ball and holed it for 6.

Elie seems never to be short on anecdotes. Perhaps the goings-on that I witnessed in 2003 might be added to the stock. My elder son and I

Mellow and traditional Elie, with its charming seventeenth-century parish church, provides the best bathing in the East Neuk, not to mention windsurfing, sailing, and canoeing. All of five minutes away is Kilconquhar, a picture-postcard village on the shores of Kilconquhar Loch. Kellie Castle, three miles northwest of nearby Pittenweem (Lumsden Antiques, at the harbor, offers some choice pieces at reasonable prices) is a tower house—more fortress than mansion—dating to the fourteenth century and affording pretty views across farmland and woodland to the Firth of Forth. Also well worth visiting is the Scottish Fisheries Museum, in Anstruther, which illustrates with real boats as well as models many aspects of sea fishing and life in early fishing communities.

You might want to keep in mind two eating places in Anstruther:
- The **Dreel Tavern** is good for a pub-food lunch: beam ceilings, fireplaces, dark paneling, and, when the day is fine, dining in a simple garden above the Dreel Burn, a stream that runs through the heart of town.
- For dinner, the standout choice is **The Cellar**, hidden on a back street near the children's amusement pier and possessing an intimate, romantic ambience (log fire, beam ceiling, natural stone walls, candlelight). The cooking is superlative. After a hot quiche of smoked sea trout and lobster, try the roast monkfish and scallops flavored with herb and garlic butter and served with a sweet pepper risotto. The Cellar gets a pile of votes as Scotland's best seafood restaurant.

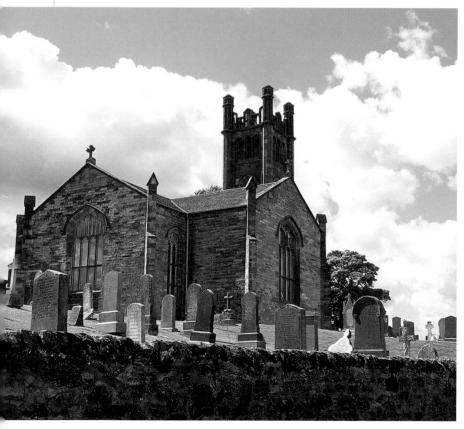

Clockwise from top: the gardens at Kellie Castle; the castle; the village of Anstruther; church in Kilconquhar.

LUNDIN AND LEVEN

The Lundin Golf Club and the Leven Golfing Society, two more of the old East Neuk clubs with authentic seaside links, were once coupled, bound together by their golf holes. But perhaps the explanation can wait a bit, till we arrive at the point on the courses where this is more easily understood.

It was about thirty years ago that I first visited the Lundin Golf Club, in Lundin Links, about fifteen minutes west of Elie. In the monastic changing room that day, I overheard a conversation between two quite elderly members. One was remembering a match in which "Jimmie whipped Sandy," on the 17th, by playing a miracle 4-iron from a bunker "to within six feet of the cup for his birdie, turning what had looked like a certain loss into a certain win."

Shortly afterward, in the lounge, as I was chatting with the secretary, the storyteller came up to us. His name was Fred Horne and, eighty-six years of age and a member since 1910, he was the club's oldest active member. I said I'd heard him talking about a match at Elie and couldn't help but wonder about the identity of the two players.

"Braid it was," he said, "Jimmie Braid. Braid and Sandy Herd. Over at Elie."

"You knew Braid?" I asked.

"Indeed I knew him," the old man answered. "There was a time when I would have a game with him once a year over at Elie. But of course he's been gone for some years now." Braid died in 1950.

ON THE LUNDIN COURSE

The start at Lundin is exhilarating: This 424-yarder is hard by the sea, the tee perched atop a ridge of sand hills, the beach itself some 40 feet below us on our left. We should swing freely, because the landing area, shared with the 18th fairway, is a very broad and inviting one and because a long drive will be useful when it comes to tackling the second shot, a rising one back up to the great dune ridge, where a large, lightly bunkered green awaits. This is one of the best opening holes in my experience, to be spoken of in the same breath as the 1st at Machrihanish, at Aronimink, and at Sand Hills.

The next three holes carry us farther west along the coast, the 2nd and 3rd a pair of beguiling short two-shotters played from high in the dunes down to fairways with sand on the right and greens with deep bunkers in front. A mighty 452-yard par 4, the 4th ripples determinedly straight along above the sea on a broad plateau for about 425 yards, at which point a sliver of burn crosses the fairway at the bottom of a steep and narrow dip. A crisp 5-metal may clear this implacable hazard. Or is a 3-metal called for? Or should we lay up and accept a bogey? This is a true death-or-glory hole, the only one on the course. A great second shot will produce an opportunity for a 3, and an almost great second shot will produce the likelihood of a 6.

Opposite: Lundin, 5th.
Above: 2nd.

Whatever the outcome of the altogether splendid 4th, we have come to a dead end on our trek down the coast from the clubhouse. We have reached Mile Dyke, a low stone wall. On the other side of it are golf holes like the four we've just played, stretching away beside the shore for what must surely be a mile. However, they don't belong to the Lundin Golf Club, though Lundin once co-owned them. Now they are the property of the Leven Golfing Society.

Here is how this happened. When the Lundin club was founded, in 1868, it shared an 18-hole layout with Leven. The course was two fair-

ways wide and nine holes long, fitting nicely between the sea and the railroad on ideal linksland, undulating and sand based.

Often in Scotland two (or three or four) golf clubs will play over the same course, especially if it's a municipal facility, as in the case of St. Andrews and Carnoustie. What was unusual—in fact, highly unusual—about this case was that Leven's clubhouse was at the west end of the links and Lundin's at the east end. Play began at *both* clubhouses, about two miles apart, with the golfers aiming to reach the halfway mark at the *other* clubhouse. Imagine the potential for confusion and crowding at the turns, not to mention the complexity of allotting starting times on an equitable basis, especially as the game became more and more popular. By 1907 Lundin had almost four hundred members and Leven almost a thousand.

In 1908 the two clubs agreed to cut the course in half. Each took the nine holes on its side of Mile Dyke, and never again would the twain meet. To come up with nine more holes, each club spilled over onto the inland side of the railway. Lundin seized the opportunity to call in Braid and have him lay out new holes and incorporate them into the eighteen we play today.

The same burn that gave us pause on Lundin's terrific 4th now bedevils us on its 140-yard 5th, corkscrewing across our path on a right-to-left diagonal and joining forces with bent-clad sand hills and clustering bunkers to demand a good short iron here. En route to the 6th tee, we cross the abandoned railway line—the trains and tracks are gone nearly fifty years—to play the nine "new holes," which were routed over what might be called a cross between links and parkland in both turf and topography. Following three solid par 4s, the nine ends with a gently rolling 555-yarder into the prevailing wind. It is a legitimate three-shotter.

Two difficult par 4s—the 10th finds a heavily bunkered green set in a natural dell shaped by sand hills, and the straightaway 466-yard 11th is simply very long—bring us to the sharply uphill par-3 12th. The green here, as well as the entire par-5 13th and the tee of the 175-yard 14th, is laid out on a broad plateau that provides panoramic views of the links far below and of the Firth of Forth to East Lothian. It is all of a heart-stopping grandeur.

Once we've returned to the less heady but more satisfying golfing country at sea level, with its tossing, tumbling terrain, we commence the march for the clubhouse, first with a long two-shotter for the 418-yard 15th to a blind green secluded in a hollow. Then it's two shortish par 4s that contain blind shots and a pitch over a burn—plenty of surprise and suspense on the double-trouble 16th. Finally, the uncompromising home hole: Its length alone—442 yards—is daunting. The landing area for the drive is generous (shared with the 1st fairway), but the long, narrow green is sited in a kind of saddle between the sea on the right and a boundary road on the left. To get home in two we must propel the ball more than 200 yards with little deviation from string straight.

Lundin is a thoroughgoing delight. It is full of character and charm, of variety and test, and of holes with strong shot values. What it is not full of is serenity. This is one of the most spirited courses in the land. There is a lot going on in these 6,377 yards (par 71). Six different factors—the breeze, bunkers (120 of them), burns, bents, boundaries (on 16

holes!), and the "blinds" (6 drives, 4 shots to the green)—contribute to the challenge. All of which helps to explain why this rather short course has hosted the Scottish Professional Championship, the British Seniors, the World Senior Professional Championship, the Scottish Amateur Stroke Play Championship, the East of Scotland Amateur, and final qualifying for the Open Championship. It is also the venue every summer for the Scottish Police Golf Association Championship.

My most recent visit to the club found me playing on an early evening when this competition was being held. My companion was Malcolm Campbell, longtime Lundin member and author of the informative and immensely readable *Scottish Golf Book,* to say nothing of nine or ten other works on the game. We could not ignore a temporary sign, black type on a yellow board, prominently displayed at the 1st tee: PLEASE REPORT ANY SUSPICION OF SLOW PLAY. OFFENDERS ARE LIABLE TO PENALTY OR DISQUALIFICATION.

ON THE LEVEN COURSE

Leven may well be next door, in a manner of speaking, but we do not simply walk over and hit off. In truth, reaching the 1st tee from Lundin requires a drive along the coast road for a couple of miles.

Dating back to 1820, Leven is the twelfth oldest golf club in the world. The clubhouse itself, a three-story redbrick building more than 110 years old, is stately, with high-ceilinged rooms that, though not luxuriously furnished, are attractive. Tom Anderson—small, animated, in his early sixties, an officer of the society—showed me around on my first visit. "Purpose built to be just what it is," Tom said, "a clubhouse for golfers. Only one or two others—the R&A, of course—are older than it and in continuous use as a clubhouse right down till today."

Leven has an impressive collection of trophies: silver cups, gold and silver medals, and the like. One of them, a handsome gold medal, was first competed for in 1870. Tom said, "That's the prize for the oldest open amateur tournament in the world. In the beginning it was restricted to players from local golf clubs. But today they come to Leven from all over the country to play for it. The tournament actually goes back fifteen years before the Amateur Championship itself."

Below: Leven, 7th.
Opposite: 10th.

In a wall of the billiards room, which is on the second floor, Tom raised a small panel that revealed a dumbwaiter. "No need to run up and down the stairs to get a pint," he said, with a smile. "A man can concentrate on the snooker." Downstairs, a sign on the bar caught my eye:

NOTICE

THE SUGGESTION BOOK WILL NOW BE KEPT
BEHIND THE BAR AND AVAILABLE THEREFORE
FROM THE STAFF, WHO HAVE BEEN INSTRUCTED
NOT TO RELEASE THE BOOK TO MEMBERS WHO
HAVE BEEN DRINKING EXCESSIVELY.

JOHN BENNETT, SECRETARY

Suggestions in the years that followed may not have been quite so stimulating as those that preceded Mr. Bennett's term.

The links we play today at Leven is to some degree the work of Old Tom Morris, but it is not easy to say precisely where his fine hand can be seen. In any event, as we stand on the 1st tee, the outlook is not appealing. Oh, the Firth of Forth is there, but blocking it from sight are several low, scruffy structures. Regrettably, nothing conceals the trailer park and a nearby jumble of nondescript buildings. A couple of low dune ridges signal the authentic linksland, but there is nothing akin to the restive topography on the adjacent links of the Lundin club. A well-nigh featureless tract awaits, gray green, austere, an occasional yellow or red flag contributing the only touch of color. But then, the Old Course itself is scarcely a visual feast at the outset. Perhaps, I thought, there is more here than meets the eye. From the medal tees, the course measures 6,435 yards against a par of 71. The visitors' tees add up to just over 6,000 yards.

The first four holes roll straight along, parallel to the sea, one after another like railroad cars. All are two-shotters, two of them, the 1st and 4th, long at 413 and 449 yards, respectively. The 381-yard 2nd may be the finest of the quartet. We can play safely right to an expansive fairway in a dune-framed valley, from which, however, there is no view of the green; or, with our drive, we can risk a long, forced carry over two bunkers in the face of a modest slope in order to gain a plateau of fairway on the left from which the entire green complex is visible. A classic risk/reward option.

Following the stoutly bunkered 158-yard 5th comes the longest hole on the course, 567 yards, with a boundary to unsettle the fader much of the way and plenty of sand at the green. Eight bunkers encase

Leven, 18th.

the relatively small green on the 184-yard 7th, and on the 8th, a 348-yarder, back comes that boundary on the right to beleaguer us.

I had a very odd experience on the 173-yard 9th, where the green, just over a rise, cannot be seen, though the flag can be. The hole was playing into the wind. I flared a 4-metal wildly right and out of sight over the rise. I hit a provisional—perfectly, in the literal sense of the word. My search for the first ball proved unsuccessful. The second ball, on the other hand, lay snugly at the bottom of the cup. This marked the only time I ever holed out from the tee but had to write 3 on the card.

The more I played Leven, the more admiration I had for its character and complexity. Gorse, heather, and the long bent grasses that cloak the ridges must be avoided. The rumpled fairways sometimes trigger awkward stances and lies; bunkers are often deep; blind shots surface with some frequency—on the 10th, for instance, both drive and second

shot. But there is nothing contrived about this. It's simply a reflection of the natural flow of this ancient linksland, untouched by a bulldozer.

Par on the second nine is 37, and the last four holes are hard. Well, at least three of them are: the 188-yard 15th, with its creatively contoured and inhospitable green; the 386-yard 16th, rising and into the prevailing breeze to finish within steps of the Leven Bowling Club's green; and the 414-yard 17th. The par-4 18th cannot be classified as hard: It is a killer, 457 yards long, more often than not into the wind. Those are the minor considerations. The major consideration is the broad Scoonie Burn, which crosses the hole just short of the green and then slinks beside its right edge. Even the powerful player is often confronted with a true go/no-go dilemma. In all of Scotland there may be no more lethal a finishing hole. When St. Andrews hosts the Open Championship, qualifying is sometimes conducted on the worthy links of Leven.

Five minutes from Lundin Golf Club and smack on the quay in Lower Largo is the **Crusoe Hotel**, so named because this village is the birthplace of Alexander Selkirk, the castaway sailor whose adventures were immortalized by Daniel Defoe in his novel *Robinson Crusoe*. All guest rooms, which are comfortable but not necessarily spacious, enjoy captivating harbor or sea views. The public rooms—fieldstone walls, fireplaces—are cozy.

Quite nearby, on the Leven Road, is the three-star **Lundin Links Hotel**, a mock-Tudor structure with attractive public spaces and guest rooms. Several accommodations afford striking views over the rooftops of the village and across the Firth of Forth to the East Lothian coast. The particularly spacious room with the canopied four-poster bed and the grand sea view—ah, we could gratefully settle into it for a week! The cooking at both hotels is generally reliable.

Views near Largo, and the Lundin Links Hotel.

CARNOUSTIE AND MORE ANGUS,
GLENEAGLES AND
MORE PERTHSHIRE

CARNOUSTIE

For very nearly thirty years, I had not been a fan of Carnoustie. "The terrain is flat, bleak, and uninviting," I wrote in *Golf Magazine*. "There are half a dozen mediocre to weak holes, and only two great ones." Another example: "If the finale [17 and 18] is mighty, it serves to point up the prosaic nature of too much that has gone before. This historic links simply sits there, flat, severe, dour."

Not everyone agreed. A number of years ago Jack Nicklaus said to me, "When I first went to Carnoustie in 1967 to play a television match with Arnold [Palmer] and Gary [Player], I thought Carnoustie was the worst golf course I'd ever seen. And by the time I'd finished the Open in 1968, I thought it was the hardest golf course I'd ever seen, but a darn good course, and I really had great respect for it. And the last time I went back, in 1975, I had even greater respect for it. Now Carnoustie is one of my favorites."

Did the great man's thoughtful reevaluation prompt me to back off? No. Carnoustie, with the brown silos of a malting plant looking sternly down on it, was for me ordinary and cheerless. I found it reassuring that the R&A had quietly dropped it from the Open Championship rota.

Serious efforts here to fashion golf holes as we know them began with Allan Robertson's laying out a ten-hole course in 1850. Over the next eighty years Old Tom Morris, Willie Park Jr., and James Braid all took a hand in either adding to or remodeling what is now known as the Championship Course.

A little over a hundred years ago, Carnoustie—the town, then, as now, a drab huddle of one-story gray stucco cottages—served in a very real sense as a fountainhead for American golf. Some three hundred of the young men of this Tayside town emigrated to the United States to earn their living as golf professionals, staffing the pro shops, making clubs, giving lessons, and competing in tournaments. Among them were the three Smith brothers (Willie and Alex both won the U.S. Open) and Bobby Jones's swing model, Stewart Maiden. Wrote Jones: "The biggest piece of golfing luck I ever had was when the Atlantic Athletic Club got Stewart Maiden for its professional. . . . Stewart never gave me any lessons. I just followed him around the course and watched him. I imitated his style, like a monkey, I suppose."

It was in 1931 that Tommy Armour, the Edinburgh expatriate who had won the 1927 U.S. Open and the 1930 PGA, captured the first Open Championship held at Carnoustie. Here, six years later, Henry Cotton carried off the second of his three Opens, turning back a powerhouse field that included the entire American Ryder Cup team (Nelson, Snead, Sarazen, Guldahl, et al.).

The British Open came back to Carnoustie in 1953. This marked the only time Ben Hogan competed in the most important of all championships. He won by 4 strokes, improving his score with each round: 73, 71, 70, 68. In a piece he wrote (with Gene Gregston) for the *Saturday Evening Post,* Hogan covered the championship in detail, including the qualifying round and his caddie:

> When I walked up to the first tee at Burnside for my first qualifying round and my first official shot in a British Open, I didn't see anyone in charge, no one announcing players as we do in America [Hogan had earlier that year won the Masters and the U.S. Open]. There was a little house off to the side and a woman sitting in it by herself. The twosome in front had teed off and hit their second shots; still no one . . . said anything to me about teeing off. So when I thought it was about time, I walked onto the tee and put my ball down. Some people shook their heads negatively.
>
> While I was waiting for some word, a train came up the tracks that run alongside the first fairway. The engineer gave me three short blasts on his whistle, stopped the train and waved. I didn't shoo him away, as the news stories reported. I merely waved back to him. Then I heard this horn go "beep-beep." The woman in the little house had blown the horn, and that was the signal to tee off. All the people lining the fairway on both sides nodded their heads, indicating it was now all right for me to drive. Valerie [Mrs. Hogan] said later that she could see I was about to burst with laughter, and I was. It was all new and funny to me, but, I guess, perfectly normal to them.

Opposite: Carnoustie, 17th.
Previous spread: Gleneagles
Queen's Course, 7th.

On that first qualifying round I also learned that my caddie, Timmy, is a very nervous fellow. He was a good caddie. He treated my clubs as if they were the crown jewels and . . . he took my shoes home with him every night to polish them. But when things got tight on the course . . . the more nervous he became the more he would talk. Each time, I'd stop and quiet him. Many times when I'd have a long putt he'd hold his head down between his arms and wouldn't look, indicating his lack of confidence in my putting. . . .

I carried some candy fruit drops in my bag and ate them frequently for energy. At the start I gave Timmy a share of this candy, but in two rounds he ate all of his and mine too. Finally, after two or three warnings, he was convinced he'd better leave my candy alone.

Below: Carnoustie, 2nd.
Opposite: 3rd.

When the Open returned to Carnoustie, in 1968, Gary Player won. The decisive stroke was a 4-wood over the Spectacles bunkers to the concealed green on the par-5 14th, the ball finishing less than three feet from the hole for an eagle. In 1975 Tom Watson captured the first of his five British Opens when he downed Australia's Jack Newton here in an 18-hole playoff with a 2-iron over the Barry Burn to the home green for a regulation 4.

Ten years went by, then fifteen, and one heard little or no mention of the Open returning to Carnoustie. The shortcomings of the links were not lost on many observers. Once past the 3rd hole, play was on a vast, flattish, and monotonously pedestrian landscape. Holes were often neither arresting nor inviting. There was too much of a dull slog.

And when it came to accommodations and dining for today's traveling golfer—not to mention the thousands of spectators that an Open would attract—the little town's facilities were inadequate. Nonetheless, a number of stalwart locals felt that the situation was not irreparable. First of all, the course had to be improved, markedly. The task got under way in 1992. Second, a hotel of size and substance would have to be built. In 1994 the R&A announced that the Open would return to Carnoustie in 1999, and in 1997 ground was broken for a hotel on the site, squarely behind the 1st tee and the 18th green.

It was in midsummer of 1998, exactly eleven months before the scheduled Open, that, for the first time in ten years, I got back to what was my least favorite Open Championship course. I was bowled over. The new Carnoustie was a revelation. This was Carnoustie reborn—and without any alteration to the routing plan. The holes would go where they had always gone, never more than two consecutive holes heading in the same direction, so that the judgment of wind and distance would still be a consistently provocative business.

In this sweeping makeover, no hole was left untouched. Five greens were totally rebuilt and recontoured, including the 11th, which was moved in the bargain, and the 3rd, which was extended forward to the very edge of Jockeys' Burn in order to imperil the short approach shot. Certain greens were intriguingly angled to the line of flight of the incoming shot. Two new championship tees were built, and some of the regular tees were raised and realigned. Bunkers were filled in on 6 holes; new bunkers were installed on 10 holes; several greenside bunkers were enlarged; and every one of these 118 pits—sod-faced, they range from penal to lethal—was fully reconditioned. As for fairways, they are no longer straight strips. Their widths and perimeters were redefined, so that now they swing a little, narrowing here, expanding there. Complementing all these improvements was new turf, a combination of bent grasses (greens and tees) and creeping fescues (fairways) that makes the entire playing surface the equal of the best in Scotland. Fairway lies are superb; greens are true and beautifully paced. A sow's ear had metamorphosed into a silk purse. This eighteen is the ultimate golfing challenge.

ON THE CHAMPIONSHIP COURSE

Carnoustie puts more pressure on the swing than any course in the British Isles. No hole is a breather. In truth, no shot is a breather. This is the most confrontational golf course we will ever play. Each time we take club in hand, from our drive on the 1st (gorse and boundary left; sand, mounds, and rough right) to our shot to the green on 18 (the broad Barry Burn just short of it, sand right and left of it) there is the threat of danger, tangible, looming. Most hazards are located to punish the shot that is just slightly off the mark. This combination of bunkers (every full shot, without exception, is menaced by sand), boundaries, gorse, thick rough, mounds, and water is relentlessly inimical. Water at the Barry Burn, Jockeys' Burn, and two or three unnamed wet ditches awaits the misguided stroke on 10 holes. Does water menace the shot at Carnoustie as often as on all the other Open Championship courses put together? Club players with handicaps of 2 or 3 tackle Carnoustie in a lively breeze, say, 15 miles per hour, and, their swing in tatters, do not break 85. (How eagerly they retreat to St. Andrews and the comfort of the Old Course!)

Whether we play from 6,100, 6,400, or 6,700 yards, par is 70. The course measured almost 7,400 yards for the 1999 Open; par was 71. There seem to me to be eight incontestably great holes, three going out, five coming in. Following the 380-yard opener, with the rising fairway dropping off to a sunken green in a dell, we face the great 2nd, 395 yards, where the notorious Braid's Bunker, in the center of the tee-shot landing area, stares us down and a channel of fairway (mounds, sand, rough) leads to a 55-yard-deep, narrow, bilevel green corseted by low dunes. The 3rd hole, only 306 yards, is one of the best short two-shotters in my experience: mildly elevated tee (the high point of a course that has otherwise nothing to speak of in the way of ups and downs), rough-clad slope on the right, sand and mounds on the left, Jockeys' Burn running ominously and immediately in front of an irrepressible putting surface with bunkers eating into it on both sides. A wonderful chance at 3 or 6.

The 4th and 5th are solid two-shotters, both curving smoothly right, and the 6th, a 490-yard par 5 from the regular markers, 570 from the tips, is straight almost all the way and is played into the prevailing wind, with the green tucked a smidge right. George Peper and his *Golf Magazine* colleagues chose it not simply as one of the five hundred greatest holes for their book but as one of the very greatest of the great, one of the top eighteen. Short on natural features, it is flat. Skirting the hole its entire length on the left is a boundary fence. In the center of the driving area is a pair of fearsome bunkers, one behind the other. We have three options from the tee: Carry the central bunkers, a very big hit; tack warily out to the right, aiming to avoid a bunker and rough there; challenge the out-of-bounds on the left with the intention of slotting our drive into the 28-yard-wide landing area between the fence and the two bunkers. Ben Hogan owned this third—and most daring—option. In both rounds on the final day of the 1953 Open, he cracked his drive down the fence

line, his customary soft fade drifting the ball perfectly back into the harbor of the fairway, left of the pair of pits. Then, morning and afternoon, he flighted a perfect 4-wood to the green for two-putt birdies.

Jack Nicklaus did not have Hogan's mastery of this hole. "Do you remember," I once asked Nicklaus, "hitting your drive out-of-bounds on the sixth at Carnoustie in the last round of the 1968 Open?"

"Oh, yes," he said, "sure. That shot cost me the tournament. I had a driver with the softest shaft I've ever used. It was an old TTW shaft. The wind was probably the easiest I've ever played it on that hole, because you could get by that right-hand bunker with a good tee shot, so I thought I'd just go ahead and set it out on the right side and turn it by the bunker—and I hooked it out-of-bounds."

The drive on 6 is only part of the story, albeit the most dramatic part. Nudging the right edge of the fairway about 200 yards beyond the two fairway bunkers is Jockeys' Burn. The space between it and the boundary fence is all of 25 yards. As for the green, it is wide but shallow, oblique to the line of play, and defended by five pits. The entire adventure, from tee to cup, has about the same feeling as tiptoeing through a minefield.

Now that the 456-yard 14th, the Spectacles, has been designated a par 4, it strikes me as a truly great one, with a strong forced carry over gorse from the tee to a blind fairway pinched by sand precisely where the hole turns left, then a long and thrilling play over the Spectacles bunkers in the sand hill to the hidden green. The test inherent in this second shot may be the one moment in the entire round that brings a smile to our lips—a wry smile.

Above: Carnoustie, 6th.
Opposite, left: 14th;
right: 15th.

The 15th, 425 yards long, bends left along a hog's-back fairway, crumpled and tumbling, gorse on the left, sand and low dunes on the right, the flagstick (but not the putting surface) visible on the second shot, the green complex full of mounds, sand, slopes, and unpredictable caroms. A perfect hole—better yet, a perfect links course hole. Please take my word for it.

It is hard to make a 3 on the 223-yard 16th (250 yards from the back), played into the prevailing wind. The three bunkers right and short of the green are now of the gathering type and surely attract a lot of customers. The two bunkers short and left are less possessive. The long, narrow green, only a couple of feet above the fairway on its cunning plateau, inclines to shun the ball, thus putting to good use the little falloffs all around. It is a great hole, as witness its selection for the *World's* 500 book, and it is probably an original hole as well.

The 17th is also unique, and it was named one of the top hundred in the 500 volume. Measuring 390 yards (459 from the tips), it takes its name, Island, from the path of Barry Burn, which snakes back and forth across the hole, isolating sections of the fairway and demanding that we traverse this serpentine hazard not once, not twice, but three times.

The 18th, 428 yards long and chosen by Chris Millard for his book *Golf's 100 Toughest Holes*, heads in the opposite direction. Once again that sinuous stream is the riveting element. We must cross it twice, from the tee and then to gain the green, but the second shot here, with the 20-foot-wide waterway no more than a dozen paces short of the green, has always struck me as harder than either shot on 17.

It is impossible to play the last hole at Carnoustie without remembering the 1999 Open and the French farce—or was it *Les Miserables*?—that was enacted when Jean Van de Velde, needing only a double bogey to claim the claret jug, sloshed around in the burn to the tune of 7 and then bowed, along with Justin Leonard, to Paul Lawrie in the four-hole playoff that followed. But the tragicomedy aside, what kind of golf course

was it that flayed this mighty field? In truth, a largely unplayable one made up of dense knee-high rough, unconscionably narrow fairways (a couple of which were, in places, only 12 yards wide), and hard, fast greens, all of which contrived to render helpless the best players in the world. Six-over-par 290 tied for first, the highest leading score in relation to par at a major championship in twenty-five years.

Green superintendent John Philp, the hero of Carnoustie's astonishing restoration, was now the villain of the piece. Many thought he would be—should be—fired. Many thought the Open would never—should never—return to Carnoustie. All were wrong. Philp kept his job. (You've got to love the man who, in the face of the torrent of whining by the professionals, said, "Look, they've got titanium and psychologists. All I've got is nature.") And early in 2004 the R&A announced that Carnoustie would host the Open for the seventh time, in 2007. Expect this championship to be a rigorous but fair examination. And count on this noble muni to reveal itself as one of the very greatest major champi-

Opposite: Carnoustie, 16th.
Above: Carnoustie Burnside, 14th.

give pause. The ground ranges from undulating to hummocky; bounces can be capricious and short pitches tough to control. Two holes are great: the 228-yard 14th, with dunes right and left and a deep swale in front of a green that is surprisingly angled to the line of flight of the shot; and the 473-yard par-4 17th, longer than the celebrated 17th on the Championship Course and also haunted by the Barry Burn.

The third of these municipal layouts is the **Buddon Links**, which was originally a short, artificial, uninspired business. A recent remodeling has considerably improved it.

NEARBY COURSES

Some six miles north on the coast road is the **Arbroath Links**, laid out over undulating linksland and measuring 6,185 yards from all the way back (par 70). Arbroath boasts half a dozen downright delightful holes, their charms generally stemming from greens adroitly sited on knobs or in dells, and ten holes where burns endanger the shot.

No more than a mile or two south of Carnoustie, in Barry, is the **Panmure Golf Club**, which has six excruciatingly dull holes, the first three and the last three. The middle twelve, however, are top-notch. Full of diversity and character, they meander along over low ridges of sand hills. Prior to his triumph up the road in 1953, Hogan did much of his practicing here. He singled out the 6th hole—387 yards, landing area for the tee shot blind and sloping right while the hole itself bends left and drifts uphill—for praise, saying that it could be put on any course and be outstanding.

Next door is the **Monifieth Golf Links**, with its two municipal eighteens. The secondary course, **Ashludie**, measures only 5,123 yards, par 68. The main course, 6,459 yards from the regular tees against a par of 71, is a no-nonsense layout. We get what we hit, and the number of long par 4s sees to it that we are often called to hit full out. The course is a hybrid. With its undulating fairways, modest sand hills, and greens sometimes nestled in dells, it feels like seaside golf. But because of the abundance of mature trees, it looks like parkland golf.

About twenty minutes from Monifieth, on the outskirts of Dundee, lies the **Downfield Golf Club**, with its classic and lovely parkland eighteen by James Braid. The terrain is rolling, a burn cuts through half the holes, the turf is superbly conditioned, and mature trees, both evergreen and deciduous, frame a number of fairways. Testament to its quality is the fact that Downfield hosted final qualifying for the 1999 Open.

onship tests in the world (are Whistling Straits and Bethpage Black its equals?), a course that can stand up defiantly under the assault of the game's finest players, the most forbidding links of all.

OTHER CARNOUSTIE COURSES

James Braid, who has left his mark on the Championship Course, gets sole credit for the second of the town's three eighteens, the **Burnside**. It is a jewel. Par is just 68 on this textbook links course: dunes, gorse, heather, tussocky rough grasses, a few blind shots, and, as is the case next door, bunkers with near-vertical "bricklayer" faces and streams to

Downfield, 11th.

Carnoustie itself is scarcely the place for sightseeing, but Arbroath, Dundee, and Barry all have something that's worth a stop. Arbroath Abbey, in the center of town, is a ruin but a strikingly beautiful one of red sandstone that dates to the twelfth century. On the Dundee waterfront is the *Discovery,* the triple-masted square rigger that was built here and in which Robert Falcon Scott sailed to Antarctica in 1901. And at the Barry Mill, a working mill nearly two hundred years old, we relish the splash of the waterwheel and the sound and smell of real corn being ground.

The **Carnoustie Golf Hotel**, a four-star facility at the Championship Course, has seventy-three double rooms and thirteen suites. Accommodations, some with balconies, have attractive views over the links or the Tay estuary. Both the dining room and the bar/lounge area (informal fare here) can be relied on for good food. The hotel has a number of daily starting times on the great course that are reserved for its guests.

About a mile from the links is **Carlogie House**, a long-established and hospitable sixteen-room hotel on pretty, secluded grounds. Public rooms are inviting and comfortable, but the guest rooms, which are quite spruce and afford pleasant views over the gardens and farmland, are short on charm and space. The cooking has a large local following.

Five Gables House is a simple, homey B&B (all rooms with private bath) perched in its own terraced gardens above the Arbroath eighteen that offers lovely sea views over the links from the lounge and the dining area. It can accommodate eleven people; rooms are small. On the main road leading into Arbroath from Carnoustie— and directly across from the pitch-and-putt course—is an atmospheric old whitewashed pub called **Tutties Neuk**, which is very agreeable for a drink and basic pub food.

Clockwise from above: the ship *Discovery*; on the ship; the sea at Arbroath; and two scenes near the Angus Folk Museum.

MONTROSE

mericans don't bother much with Montrose. Yet in this town of ten thousand, about thirty minutes north on the coast from Carnoustie, a truly ancient links can be found. Part of the Medal Course that we play today actually hosted golfers in 1550, as the diary of Montrose's James Melville, born in 1556, makes clear. Melville tells us that he was taught from the age of six "to use the glubb for goff." Montrose thus takes its place with Leith (Edinburgh) and St. Andrews among the very earliest incubators of the game. And by the middle of the nineteenth century, Montrose was distinguished by the sheer number of its golf holes, twenty-five, probably more than any other single course has ever had.

There are two 18-hole municipal courses at Montrose today: the Broomfield, only 4,800 yards long, and the Medal, 6,451 yards at its longest, 6,231 from the regular markers, par 71. Both eighteens owe much to the hand of Willie Park Jr., in 1903, but Old Tom Morris had provided a number of revisions to the Medal Course twenty years earlier. In the 1960s and 1970s, Montrose hosted the Scottish Professional Championship twice and the Scottish Amateur once. But it's just not long enough anymore.

ON THE MEDAL COURSE

Though a genuine pleasure to play, the Medal Course is not a great links; in truth, it may not offer even one inarguably great hole. There are three or four quite ordinary holes, the bunkering is comparatively light, fairways are generous, and strategic considerations are minimal. Still, this is classic seaside golf, a combination of imposing sand hills, often violently rumpled fairways, gorse, heather, and long rough grasses. Again and again, shots to the green are played along the ground rather than through the air. There is a lot of pure shot-making fun to be had at Montrose.

The first nine is the more appealing of the two. This is signaled at the start as we head uphill into the grand duneland on a delightful 390-yarder. At the sand-free 2nd hole, also 390 yards, the drive calls for a stiff forced carry over wildly broken ground, and at the 152-yard 3rd the shot must carry an overgrown hollow to gain a plateau green that is much wider than it is deep. This is stirring stuff, as indeed are the next five

holes, in the very heart of the dunes, with the 6th, a par 5 of 468 yards, perhaps the favorite among them. The tee here is a tiny platform at the peak of the huge sand hills, with the beach of tawny sand far below on the one hand, the fairway far below on the other.

The 8th, with another lovely falling tee shot, leads us out of this magical golfing country into more open terrain that has little in the way of elevation change.

Paradoxically, the less dramatic second nine is more difficult to score on. Three of the two-shotters are over 400 yards, and one of the par 3s is well over 200 yards. The first time I visited Montrose, I was invited

Opposite: Montrose, 2nd.
Above: 3rd.

on the 14th, a 407-yarder, to join two young men, Martin and Ian Smith, playing just ahead of me. They pointed out that the pair of golfers in front of us were also Smiths, their father and brother. Why, you might wonder, weren't the four playing together? Because the round would be too slow, close to an hour longer than any of them would tolerate.

The four Smiths lived in Oxford. Two of them were studying at the university, and three of them were musicians: a pianist, a violinist, and a trumpeter. They came to Montrose every summer for a golfing holiday. My two companions, who knew the course well, were helpful guides, warning of dangers, explaining subtleties. I earned a "Well done indeed" when I dropped a sliding five-footer for 3 on the 226-yard 16th, with its devilishly contoured green. I also earned a sympathetic "Unlucky" when I just missed from five feet on the 410-yard 17th. The course's best hole,

it curves mildly, gorse on both sides, and only a perfect approach will find the elevated shelflike green carved out of a dune at the left.

They called my attention to a half-timbered house on the periphery of the course, saying that it had been the holiday home of the head of the Secret Service (is it possible, John le Carré, that great deceptions and great treacheries were concocted here?). A widower during the last years of his life, the UK's number-one plotter stayed here with a woman he did not marry, who inherited the property when he died.

I was agog at these revelations. "If you don't mind my asking," I said, "how do you know about this?"

"The piano," Ian replied. "The lady has a concert grand piano in the drawing room, and she likes to stage recitals there. Somehow she learned about our musical bent."

ground, and the long views of the Angus countryside are gorgeous. Edzell measures 6,050 yards from the regular markers, 6,350 from the medal tees; par is 71. There is quite enough sand, including five old-fashioned cross bunkers. Among the better holes, on a course that is solid and testing but rarely if ever exhilarating, are the 2nd, 436 yards and into the prevailing wind, slightly rising at first, then downhill, a boundary close on the right all the way, the shot to the green blind, with bunkers right and left; the 342-yard 8th, swinging right, the approach shot falling to a two-tier green; and the quirky 16th, only 302 yards, cross bunkers short of the sharply elevated plateau green.

Back to the coast and north now, the drive is about thirty minutes to **Stonehaven**, where a first-rate seafood restaurant called **The Tollbooth** sits smack on the harbor and the golf course sits on considerably higher ground. It has been dismissed more than once as "clifftops and railroads." You must come here expecting the unconventional, even the bizarre.

Let me set down some hard facts to guide—or deter—you. Total yardage from all the way back is 5,103. Par is 66. This eighteen is laid out on all of sixty-two acres. There are seven par 3s. The 4th, 5th, and 16th are crisscross holes, but it is the 5th that takes the palm. Here the drive from a hilltop tee sails straight toward the sea and, along the way, *directly over both the 16th and 4th fairways.* The Dundee/Aberdeen railway line features two-car "sprinters" (the locals' term) that race through the middle of the golf course in the middle of your backswing, seemingly five or six times during the round. The holes are laid out in three separate sectors: on the high meadow beyond the tracks, in the narrow neck beyond the railway viaduct, and the majority on the steeply sloping headlands high above the sea. Three of the seven or eight blind shots occur on par 3 holes. Bunkering is light. The greens, which incline to be small, are true, nicely paced, and easy to read. A handful of them are set uncomfortably close to the cliff's edge. The same can be said of four tees on the first nine—at 2, 6, 7, and 8—which are all but cantilevered vertiginously out over the wave-washed rocks far below.

For pure theater, the isolated tee on the 203-yard 2nd rivals the fabled launching pad on the 9th at Turnberry's Ailsa. So totally exposed and so precariously sited is it that I would think twice before going out there in the 30- to 40-mile-an-hour winds that often buffet Stonehaven. And as for that blind 203-yard shot itself, first it has to clear the abyss formed by a cleft in the cliffs, and then it has to carry a humpy ridge in order to gain a wide plateau green bunkered left and right. Inarguably an original golf hole.

"So we've been to the house a number of times and grown quite friendly with her," Martin concluded the explanation.

I never did think to ask whether the Secret Service head was a golfer.

One Montrose golfer, Alex H. Findlay, made a name for himself in America as a course architect (The Breakers, Llanerch, and Basking Ridge, among many others). But his proposal in 1926 to lay out a six-hole course for Pope Pius XI in the Vatican Gardens was rejected. "This was," he would say with a smile, "the only thing I ever failed in."

NEARBY COURSES

Some twenty minutes from Montrose on a northeasterly heading is the pleasant inland village of Edzell and, not far from its center, the equally pleasant eighteen of the **Edzell Golf Club**, dating to 1895. The 1933 revisions of James Braid and the vigorous tree planting to follow give the course its look and quality today. The holes are routed over gently rolling

You will want to have lunch or at least a beverage in the quaintly charming old **Stonehaven** clubhouse, which rambles along the hillside and commands the sea. I remember buying a club necktie, green and white regimental stripes, on my first visit. Though not normally given to such extravagance, I thought it might be useful later to prove that the eighteen at Stonehaven had indeed been real, that I had not dreamed it.

The town of Montrose presents rather too much soot-stained granite to be considered attractive. Nevertheless, the broad High Street has several dignified buildings, among them the Old Church (circa 1832), with its pinnacled square tower and graceful steeple, and the Old Town Hall (1763). Immediately outside town is the Montrose Basin Wildlife Centre, a rich feeding ground for thousands of resident and migratory birds. Unusual displays show how a tidal basin works. Overlooking the basin is the House of Dun, a Georgian residence designed in 1730 by William Adam and featuring superb carved plasterwork. A miniature theater and a Victorian walled garden are charming elements. The **Park Hotel**, in a pretty little park two blocks off the High Street, has a congenial atmosphere. Guest rooms are comfortable, and the cooking in both the brasserie and the dining room will do nicely.

Clockwise from top left: on the boardwalk in Montrose; Dunnottar Castle; Edzell Castle's gardens; the entrance arch to Edzell; Stonehaven. In the center: rapeseed field near Montrose.

BLAIRGOWRIE

ome fifteen miles northwest of Dundee, which would put it about twenty-five miles from Carnoustie, lies the Blairgowrie Golf Club, where the game was first played in 1889. The Dowager Marchioness of Lansdowne leased the land to the club for twenty-five pounds a year, stipulating that this charge would be reviewed after ten years. And so it was, with the result that the annual rent was reduced to twenty pounds!

There are three courses here, the Rosemount and the Lansdowne, both full-length eighteens, and the Wee Course, a par-32 nine. It is the Rosemount, the eldest of the three, that lures visitors.

The course has a remarkable pedigree. Old Tom Morris provided the layout of the earliest holes in 1889. Alister MacKenzie revised the Morris nine and added a second nine in 1923. Then it was Braid's turn, in the early 1930s. He extensively reworked MacKenzie's layout, even siting new tees and greens. Although this is a good course, sometimes very good, it is not great, though many have called it so.

ON THE ROSEMOUNT COURSE

Perhaps those who praise the course immoderately have been overawed by the setting, for this is an extraordinarily beautiful place, reminiscent, in fact, of the heathland courses in Berkshire and Surrey (e.g., Sunningdale, Swinley Forest, The Berkshire) outside London. Each hole on this gently rolling Perthshire tract is played in near total isolation; we stroll along lovely avenues of pine and larch and silver birch, with heather often serving as ground cover in the rough. The tranquillity is exquisite. The springy moorland turf, on a sand-and-gravel base that assures quick draining and a free run on the ball, is a delight to walk on and to hit from. And because the holes are framed by mature trees, the effect of wind on our shots is markedly lessened. Scotland actually has very few courses that look and feel and play like Rosemount.

The holes are nicely varied, and the routing of them is imaginative. Hole after hole strikes off in a fresh direction. And since the fairways are surprisingly broad—75 to 85 yards in the landing areas most times—we

swing away with impunity. The shots to the generous and often passive greens, however, are consistently testing, in large part because of the adroit bunkering that is the legacy of two masters of the art, MacKenzie and Braid.

Rosemount measures just under 6,600 yards from the medal tees (par 72), 6,240 from the regular markers (par 70). The opening three holes and the closing three are Rosemount at its best. The round begins with a strong par 4 rather before we are up to it, a 429-yarder that falls ever so slightly as it curves smoothly left through the trees to a green with a lone bunker, at the left front. Next comes one of the short two-shotters, a straightaway 321-yarder with a raised and heavily bunkered green, where we could pick up a birdie to offset that likely bogey on the 1st. Let us hope

Opposite: Blairgowrie Rosemount Course, 16th. Above: 1st.

so, anyway, because the 206-yard 3rd, its pear-shaped green pinched at the front by sand right and left, calls for something akin to a perfect swing.

Now, skipping over a dozen attractive holes that include a couple of short par 5s where 4 is highly possible, we face the challenge of the last three holes. The altogether excellent 16th is a 435-yarder that begins with a drive over a corner of Black Loch. The fairway narrows (but only by Rosemount standards) in the tee-shot landing area, then bends quietly left. The long second shot must take into account a boundary fence skirting the fairway tight on the left all the way and a green guarded on the right by high mounding, on the left by trees, and on both sides by sand. We need to hit full out, but we find ourselves swinging defensively.

The falling 17th, 165 yards long and one of the *500 World's Greatest*, traverses a valley to an immense bilevel green. Hitting the green is not the problem; hitting the sector that contains the cup is. Failure to do so is inevitably followed by three-putting (or worse).

The 382-yard 18th is a sparkling finisher. As the hole curves right, 200 yards from the tee, the fairway dips sharply and trees on the inside of the dogleg force the prudent drive out to the left. The two-tier green is forcefully defended by bunkers front left and front right.

Thirty years ago, when it was not thought necessary for courses to measure 7,450 yards in order to host a professional tournament, Rosemount was the venue for the 1977 Martini International, won by Greg Norman. This marked the first European Tour victory for the twenty-two-year-old Australian, whose 277 total included a course-record 66.

ON THE LANSDOWNE AND WEE COURSES

It was in 1979 that a second course, called Lansdowne, opened. Designed by Peter Alliss and Dave Thomas and measuring 6,437 yards from the daily markers, it roams through the same woodlands and over the same heathery expanses as Rosemount. But it lacks the shot values of that eighteen, inclining often enough to be both dull and easy.

The Wee Course, on the other hand, is a joy. Braid laid it out in the 1930s. Its length is just 2,327 yards; there are four par 3s and five par 4s. Indicative of the course's challenging nature is the 335-yard 2nd. It doglegs moderately right and drifts downhill in the driving area to leave a pitch that must be landed short of the green and beyond the bunkers well out front, but the shot must come in under two towering firs, one right and one left, whose limbs all but touch as they spread across the line of play before the green. Gaining this green in regulation calls for skillful shot-making.

Be sure to have lunch in the handsome white pebbledash clubhouse, with its large bow windows. If you eat upstairs, in the main dining room, your meal will be accompanied by beguiling views over the start and finish of the Rosemount Course.

NEARBY COURSES

Less than fifteen minutes from Blairgowrie, on a northeasterly heading, lies the **Alyth Golf Club**, founded in 1894. The course, which reflects Braid's extensive remodeling efforts in 1934, measures 6,000 yards from the regular markers, 6,200 from the medal tees. Against the backdrop of pastoral Perthshire—rolling farmland and woodland, grazing cattle and sheep, heather-clad hills—some holes are routed over open ground, others along beautiful allées of evergreen and silver birch. Five or six holes are very good. The 329-yard 5th, for instance, teases us on the tee with a burn we may be unable to carry and then completes the challenge with an angled and elevated plateau green. But the flair inherent in this hole surfaces all too infrequently.

Opposite: Blairgowrie
Rosemount Course, 17th.
Above: 18th.

Left: Kirriemuir, 18th. Right: Forfar, 17th.

At **Kirriemuir**, about twenty minutes farther northeast along the road (the A926), the countryside continues to enchant, croplands alternating with pasture around the perimeter of the course, the Grampian Mountains dominating the long vistas, the course itself gloriously sited above the great vale of Strathmore. An extremely short course (5,553 yards, par 68), it is saved by Braid's irresistible second nine, with its rolling terrain, plateau greens, and sentinel trees. The round concludes with two superb holes. The 17th is a falling 200-yarder called Braid's Gem, where the green, defended by sand and trees, is angled to the line of play. As for the home hole, it is a potent uphill 400-yarder with a deep hidden swale short of the green. At the bottom of this hollow is a voracious sandpit.

Less than twenty minutes southeast of Kirriemuir is the **Forfar Golf Club** eighteen (5,800–6,050 yards, par 69), another inland course properly attributed to Braid. The very ground intrigues us. Though we are a dozen miles from the sea, the fairways are wrinkled, rippling, little short of being a washboard. (How to account for this linkslike feature? "Rig and furrow" cultivation of flax here 150 years ago.) Most holes, though framed by evergreens, are not corseted by them. There is room to open our shoulders. The generous putting surfaces are among the finest and most beautifully contoured in Scotland. In truth, the greens and bunkers are Braid at his best.

Letham Grange Golf Course, in Colliston, a fifteen-minute drive essentially due east of Forfar, hosted the 1994 Scottish Amateur. It measures 6,954 yards from the championship tees, 6,348 from the regular markers. Par is 73. This is big "swing away" golf, with wide fairways, light bunkering, forgiving rough. There is considerable water—ponds on four holes, streams on six others. The topography ranges from rolling to hilly. The first six holes are routed over open terrain, the next four are carved out of the woods, and the last eight reprise the spacious theme. At least half a dozen holes are excellent, including several that are not easily forgotten. The 166-yard 8th, for instance, is framed by tall pines, and a pretty lagoon extends from tee to green. The obvious inspiration for the hole is Augusta National's 16th. The 14th, on the other hand, may be an original. A 480-yard par 5, it edges left as it climbs on a narrow shelf of fairway to a matching shelf of green carved out of a right-hand hill. The muscular hitter senses a chance to get home in two, but a pulled or hooked second shot will miss the shelf and tumble down into the trees. It is a lesson in how a birdie 4 becomes a double bogey 7.

In addition to the agreeable golf, there is another good reason to visit Kirriemuir. It was in this village that James M. Barrie was born and in its hilltop cemetery that he is buried. The creator of *Peter Pan,* not to mention *The Little Minister, Quality Street,* and other plays and novels, was born in "The Tenements," 9 Brechin Road, a small whitewashed stone cottage that today is a museum. It evokes in vivid detail the circumstances in which a linen weaver, Barrie's father, and his large family (the author was one of ten children, and "box beds" were the only answer) lived in Victorian times.

Kinloch House Hotel, set strikingly in 25 acres on a gentle hillside in neighboring Dunkeld, with views to the Sidlaw Hills, is within five minutes' drive of Blairgowrie. The public spaces (antiques, log fires, oriental rugs, oak paneling) and the guest rooms in this graceful country house built in 1840 are enormously appealing, and the cooking is outstanding. A welcome amenity here is the fitness center with indoor swimming pool.

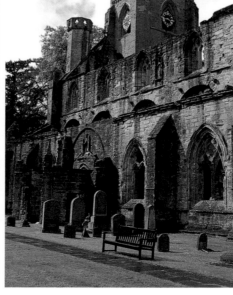

Far left: old bridge in Dunkeld. Middle column, from top: James Barrie's house in Kirriemuir; its interior; on the River Tay; inside Dunkeld Castle. Above: Kinloch House. Left: the exterior of Dunkeld.

GLENEAGLES

At this moment I find myself recalling a piece by Henry Longhurst, golf columnist for the *Sunday Times* long before Americans came to know him as a commentator on televised tournaments. Unfortunately, I'm unable to put my hands on the essay. But I do remember how it began. He wrote of leaving his London office at the end of the working day and of "the anticipatory dinner" at his town club, followed by the cab ride to King's Cross Station, there to fall quickly asleep in his compartment on the night train, secure in the knowledge that when he awakened early the next morning, it would be at one of his very favorite places in all of golf, Gleneagles.

There are about 120 outstanding golf resorts in the world, somewhat fewer that can be termed full-facilities golf-centered resorts. At the top of the list, we instinctively place three at the sea, Casa de Campo, The Cloister, and Turnberry; and three in the mountains, the Greenbrier, the Homestead, and Gleneagles. Judge them for setting, accommodations, cuisine, breadth of activities, service, amenities, and, most important, golf.

On the doorstep of the Highlands, Gleneagles possesses a setting of flabbergasting beauty—at the head of glorious Glen Devon, with forty-mile vistas to the Ochil Hills in the east and south and to the heather-tinged foothills of the Grampian Mountains in the north and west. The openness, the vastness, the grandeur, the shifting patterns of light and shadow on the distant multihued slopes—the forest green of stately firs and pines, the golden beige of hay fields, the gray green of meadows—this is the Scotland of your dreams. And it is there, all of it, with every shot you play on the three superlative eighteens.

The King's and Queen's courses, which opened in 1919, are the work of James Braid and his associate Colonel C. K. Hutchison. Routed dazzlingly over a stretch of wild Perthshire moorland, this collection of thirty-six golf holes, so many of them genuinely arresting, has been painted with bold brushstrokes on a canvas of hills and valleys, ridges and plateaus. Noble hardwoods and equally noble evergreens, bracken and broom and heather and gorse, all contribute to the playability and aesthetic delight of this monumental golf experience.

ON THE KING'S COURSE

Hotel guests will play the King's at 6,471 yards (par 70) or 6,125 yards (par 68). The architects employed the natural folds of the land to give many holes a nice sense not of seclusion or isolation but, if you will, of separateness, which contributes to their individuality. There are a number of elevated tees and some stern forced carries. This is big golf: half a dozen two-shotters ranging from 405 to 466 yards, broad fairways, sprawling greens, deep bunkers (all told, 110 pits), bold elevation changes. There is a magnificence to this eighteen that is exhilarating.

Among the most challenging holes are a couple of par 3s. The 161-yard 5th, called Het Girdle ("hot griddle," or "skillet"), presents one of the great and thrilling knob-to-knob shots. Come up short of this windswept table-top green by so much as three feet and you court calamity in the sandpits far below. No such drama greets us on the 11th, a 221-yarder uphill and over scrub to a closely bunkered green. Most days, anything less than a perfectly struck driver is a losing proposition. The 2nd at Shinnecock Hills is its twin, even to the yardage.

Of the many strong par 4s, two are especially memorable. The 3rd, measuring 374 yards and playing not less than 415, is a good example of holes prebulldozer. It climbs steeply up a fairway full of humps and hollows, the long, blind second shot having to surmount a high ridge far above in order to find a green concealed in yet another hollow. As for the 13th, called Braid's Brawest (*braw* being Scots for "splendid"), it is a 448-yard rollercoaster. A ridge containing a pair of fearsome bunkers blockades all but the stoutest drive; the dispiritingly long second, over a great dip in the early going, must then carry a cross bunker and avoid at the left a steep heather-covered slope and more sand. In all of Scotland there may be no more magnificent two-shotter.

Over the years a number of important competitions have been played on the King's, including the Curtis Cup, the British Ladies', the Dunlop International, the 1977 Skol Lager (Nick Faldo's first victory as a professional), and the Scottish Open half a dozen times in the 1980s and 1990s. In the 1992 Scottish Open, Colin Montgomerie shot 65 on the last day for what

Opposite: Gleneagles King's Course, 1st.

appeared certain to be the win. Not so. The young Australian Peter O'Malley played the final five holes 7 under par—2-3-2-3-3, two eagles and three birdies—for a round of 62, enabling him to beat Montgomerie by 2 strokes. It was surely the gaudiest finish ever in professional golf.

ON THE QUEEN'S COURSE

If the Queen's Course has never witnessed anything like O'Malley's victory, there is still so much golf of a very high standard here that we actually forget the wonders next door. A glance at the scorecard is deceptively encouraging: 5,965 yards, par 68. But a closer look reveals that seven of the dozen two-shotters range from 409 to 437 yards. Two examples are the 9th and 10th, reverse images of each other. The 419-yard 9th climbs steadily from tee to green—playing value a good 460—and bends emphatically right, with the green tucked up and away behind a right-hand slope. The 421-yard 10th—playing value more like 390—falls and bends sharply, but from right to left. This green is also tucked away, below and left, around a corner and beyond a high left-hand shoulder of ground, cloistered in its dell and concealed almost till the very moment you step onto it. An original golf hole—and a beauty.

The last five holes are as rich and rewarding as all that go before them. At 215 yards, and rising gently to a two-tier green with a five-foot difference in levels, not to mention bunkering and a steep falloff on the right down to

Opposite: Gleneagles King's Course, 13th.

water, the 14th is a truly great one-shotter, perhaps the best par 3 at Glenea-gles. The 15th, a mere 252 yards, is one of those bewitchingly driveable par 4s that finds the player coming out of his shoes and maybe going into the trees. And the 378-yard 16th is a straightaway two-shotter from a slightly elevated tee, the green sloping away from front to back and left to right.

The 204-yard 17th is fiendish. The tee is high, the green is narrow and deep (200 feet deep!) and pitches sharply to the right. We would like to bail out left, but three small bunkers lurk there. Still, the shot from

any of them is playable. This is not the case from the mine shaft disguised as a sand bunker below the right side of the green. It is some 12 feet deep and brags of a nearly vertical face. My strongest swing and most precise contact with a sand wedge finds the ball failing to scale the heights by about a foot, then tumbling down this sheer bank to come to rest within a club's length of where I am standing.

The last hole, Queen's Hame, measures 412 yards, but, from the top of a high hill and with the prevailing wind at our back, plays more like

Opposite: Gleneagles Queen's Course, 9th. Above: 10th.

375. The forced carry from the tee over wetlands and gorse is well within our capacity, and the vast green is hospitably open across the front.

The ideal day of inland golf in Scotland? Surely it must be the morning round on the King's, lunch in the Dormy House, and the afternoon round on the Queen's.

ON THE PGA CENTENARY COURSE

Or we could choose the third course in the triumvirate for one of the games. It, too, is a winner. Jack Nicklaus was responsible for the design. My wife, Harriet, and I were on hand for the grand opening, in May 1993. Among the celebrities were Jack and Barbara Nicklaus, Her Royal Highness Princess Anne, Sean Connery, His Royal Highness Prince Andrew the Duke of York, Gene Hackman, His Royal Highness Prince Abdul Hakeem of Brunei (a legitimate 3-handicap), Chris de Burgh (his song "The Lady in Red," no longer high on the charts, is still dear to our hearts), the Duke of Roxburghe (a 9-handicap, given of an

Opposite: Gleneagles Queen's Course, 18th. Above: 14th.

evening and while still in dinner jacket to hitting golf balls over the roof of his ancestral home, Floors Castle), Cheryl Ladd (it is now twenty-nine years since she appeared in *Charlie's Angels*), and Jackie Stewart (the storied racing champion, who has a vested interest in Gleneagles). During the weekend I made a few notes.

Sean Connery, resplendent in tartan kilt and dinner jacket, said grace at the banquet Saturday evening. Reverently he intoned:

We thank Thee for these gifts divine,
For turning water into wine;
Protect us from these foolish men
Who wish to turn it back again.

Cheryl Ladd demonstrated her takeaway for Jack Nicklaus at the bar Friday evening while both were waiting for drinks to be mixed. She appeared to have her hands in the right position at the top of the backswing, but it was not easy for Jack to tell whether the imaginary club was pointing down the line. He did smile agreeably, but he did not nod approvingly.

The Prince of Brunei was the hero of the charity auction. His was the winning bid (a whopping $49,000) on the caricatures of the feature foursome—Nicklaus, Prince Andrew, Connery, Stewart. Then, obviously operating on the principle of noblesse oblige, he promptly bestowed the drawings on Princess Anne so that she might sell them at auction in the future for her favorite charity. Prince Abdul Hakeem's uncle the sultan was widely believed at that time to be the richest man in the world.

Above: Gleneagles PGA
Centenary Course, 1st.
Opposite: 2nd.

It was on Saturday at the Moët & Chandon tent near the 18th green (champagne and smoked salmon were served there all day) that my wife and I hobnobbed with royalty. As we approached the tent door, a middle-aged woman in raincoat, wellies, and kerchief stood off to the side, gathering herself after the walk through the cold, light rain. Harriet preceded me but hesitated momentarily, not certain which way the door opened. The woman now stepped in ahead of me, and I heard her murmur something. The door swung open, and as I reached out to hold it, I recognized the woman between me and my wife as Her Royal Highness Princess Anne. Inside the tent now, I said excitedly to Harriet as we headed toward a table, "That was Princess Anne. I heard her speak to you as you went to open the door. What did she say?"

"She said, 'Pull.'"

The PGA Centenary Course, as the Nicklaus eighteen is called, rolls consistently. There is water but not in excess. Three of the par 5s present the big hitter with that classic risk/reward situation: Go for the green on your second shot, but chance a dunking if you do.

From the championship markers, the course measures nearly 7,100 yards. I suspect that when it serves as the venue for the 2014 Ryder Cup, it will be at least 250 yards longer. Most visitors elect the white markers, at 6,550 yards.

The 1st (394 yards) and 2nd (501 yards) move gently downhill to shelf greens, both holes aiming squarely at breathtaking Glen Devon. They are utterly captivating, and neither is beyond our capacity. The next up a short pitch for a birdie. The 17th, 179 yards, is a falling shot—and an inviting one—to an angled green that is open across the front. And the wiggling home hole, 484 yards, is an uphill double dogleg (maybe triple) par 5 that at no point intimidates us and again is a birdie chance. It's as though Jack Nicklaus were bent on having us walk off his course in a sunny frame of mind.

How does the PGA Centenary stack up against the two "royal" all-world jewels here that have been thrilling golfers for nearly ninety years? As far as test goes, the three are on essentially the same serious level. But perhaps the King's and the Queen's have a bit of an edge when it comes to sparkle and originality—to brio, if you will. Our instinct is to cherish them. And it is a sound instinct, for we shall not see their like again.

AUCHTERARDER

When playing the 15th on the PGA Centenary, you may notice a neighboring golf hole that does not belong to the Nicklaus eighteen. In fact, it is the 6th at the Auchterarder Golf Club, where the game has held sway since 1892. Peter Alliss, Lee Trevino, and Ben Crenshaw are honorary members at this very inviting club. This is a short course—5,800 yards, par 69—with spunk. Though it can in no sense be discussed in the same breath with its neighbors, there are some first-rate holes, the moorland turf is crisp and springy, and the views down Glen Devon are awe-inspiring.

The merits of the course can best be appreciated in the final five holes, which are like no closing cluster I've ever encountered: a par 4, a par 5, and three par 3s. The 214-yard 14th is blind, the high face of a cross bunker hiding a long, narrow green in a little dell. At the very good 15th, 513 yards long and uphill off the tee, a deep dip immediately in front of the green complicates the pitch shot, particularly with the cup cut toward the front of the green. The 16th—great by any standard—is 219 yards long and plays into the prevailing breeze. Gazing down Glen Devon, we play from a knob of a tee across a rough valley to a green that is slightly narrower than instinct tells us it should be and bunkered on both flanks. To hit this green, a string-straight shot, often with a driver, is called for. The 445-yard 17th requires two first-class shots, a drive that carries a vast swale in the fairway and a long second soaring downhill to a big green that is open across the front. The round concludes with a par 3 that measures 188 yards, but, uphill and generally into a left-to-right wind, plays at least 210. Sand at the left and a high hedge tight across the back cannot be ignored.

Above: Gleneagles PGA Centenary Course, 4th. Opposite: 16th.

three holes bring us back to earth with a vengeance. On the 390-yard 3rd, from an elevated tee (Nicklaus is a fan of high tees, confident that golfers are grateful for them) our drive plunks into an opposing hillside, at which point the hole bends right, around a cluster of three bunkers in the crook of the dogleg, and continues its climb to a green pinched at the front by sand right and left. If we can hit it 211 yards uphill (240 from the tips) on the straightforward 4th, carrying an immense bunker at the left front of the green, we have a chance for a 3. At the 5th, a 423-yarder, we drive blindly over the rise in a saddle-shape fairway, then thread the long second shot through trees, uneasily conscious of wetlands just short of the green at the right. It is a great hole, a beautiful killer.

The second nine, also par 36, provides that happy mixture of three par 3s, three par 4s, and three par 5s. What may come as a surprise is that the closing holes give us an opportunity to make up some ground. The downhill 16th, 518 yards, dares us to carry a pond on our second shot, thus setting

Remarkably, it is the not the great golf alone that accounts for the preeminence of Gleneagles. The **Gleneagles Hotel** itself, architecturally more akin to a Loire Valley chateau than a Scottish baronial castle, tellingly calls up the past, specifically the halcyon days of Edwardian country-house luxury. Whether in the public spaces or the guest accommodations, we are struck by the stylish Art Deco–inspired appointments—the fabrics, the furniture, the wallpapers, the floor coverings, the paneling, the light fixtures, the paintings, the objets d'art.

Nor does the display of the decorative arts put the cooking in the shade. A total of thirteen restaurants and bars are scattered about the 850 acres:

- The principal dining room is the immense and sumptuous **Strathearn** (fluted pillars, coffered ceilings, garden views, impeccable service), with its extensive à la carte menu.

Below: Gleneagles Hotel.
Right, top: the Andrew Fairlie;
bottom: a guest room.

- On a considerably more intimate scale—can this room with the velvet hangings seat as many as forty-five?—is the **Andrew Fairlie**, with its Michelin star and six-course *menu degustation*.

Time now to turn away from the cuisine in order to look at the diversions offered here as part of the astonishing tapestry that is Gleneagles. The royal and ancient game certainly gets its due—and rather more—with the three eighteens, to which can be added the Wee Course (nine short holes that provide plenty of fun for family foursomes) and the nine-hole pitch-and-putt course. Also on hand are tennis and squash courts, croquet lawns, a jogging track, a billiards parlor, and a spa (two swimming pools, gymnasium, solarium, sauna, hot tubs, Turkish steam baths, massage and beauty treatment quarters). And there is more:

- At the Jackie Stewart Shooting School, clay pigeons are launched over the heath to simulate the flights of ten different game birds (woodcock, pheasant, partridge, et al). A rustic lodge with an open-hearth fireplace is here on the moors so that marksmen will not have to rough it.
- The Mark Philips Equestrian Centre has three arenas, two of them enclosed and air-conditioned; more than thirty horses available for guests; and numerous activities ranging from dressage to polo.
- For those who have dreamed of tooling across the moors in a Land Rover, the Gleneagles Off-Road Driving School is at the ready.
- For anglers, Gleneagles maintains five beats on the River Tay (salmon and sea trout). Brown trout can be caught in local lochs. Count on the hotel's gillies to know where the fish are biting.
- The British School of Falconry at Gleneagles is an aristocratic experience with a choice. Enjoy it either on horseback (it's called Hawks and Horses) or on foot. Eight Harris hawks are housed here, and two instructors are on hand every day.

Gleneagles has everything you would expect in a great full-facilities golf resort (maybe even a few things you might not expect) and all of it in a setting of surpassing natural beauty. One final point: By most contemporary standards, Gleneagles is not a big hotel. There are 286 accommodations, including 18 suites. The madding crowd is absent. So is the attendant hassle. This is a tranquil place, all the more remarkable when you consider the abundance of diversion. At the time it opened, nearly ninety years ago, the British press saluted Gleneagles as the "palace in the glens" and the "playground of the gods." Both characterizations were fitting then, and they are apt today. Some widely traveled golfers have been tempted to trot out a Scottish phrase: *"heich abune the heick"*—"better than the best." The only way to check the validity of this appraisal is to go there and see for yourself.

The Gleneagles Hotel is not the only place to stay if you want to play its courses. Five minutes from the great resort sits the **Auchterarder House Hotel**.

Dating to 1832 and built on seventeen acres in the Jacobean style, it somehow manages to be stately yet welcoming, grand yet intimate. The explanation lies in the numerous fireplaces, the beautiful old paintings and oriental rugs, and the antique oak paneling. We've stayed in the spacious Maxwell Room, which has a tile-faced Victorian fireplace and captivating views over the hotel gardens to the Grampian Mountains. The cuisine is ambitious, and successfully so.

The unexceptional village of Auchterarder has several antiques shops and the Glenruthven Weaving Mill, which was the last business in Scotland to convert from steam to modern power. Weaving is demonstrated, and a shop sells locally woven products. Not ten minutes north of the village are the Strathallan Aircraft Museum (aircraft and allied equipment dating to 1930) and, rather in an opposite mode, Tullibardine Chapel, a rural fifteenth-century chapel complete and unaltered.

PERTH

One of the rewarding aspects of driving to Auchterarder from Dundee (or from Blairgowrie, Kirriemuir, or Alyth) is that Perth is squarely on your route. You will not want to bypass this city of about forty-five thousand inhabitants, which is spread pleasantly along both banks of the River Tay. Once the capital of Scotland, it is a dignified and prosperous place. Visit fifteenth-century Balhousie Castle, with its Museum of the Black Watch Regiment; St. Ninian's Cathedral, a handsome nineteenth-century Anglican church; and the Fair Maid's House, where a medieval wall may be seen and a gallery with exhibitions by Scottish artists is open daily, as is a shop selling high-quality Scottish craftwork and knitwear. Speaking of commerce, there is a section in the center of town, marked by hanging flower baskets and a total absence of cars, where shopping—or window shopping—in a variety of stores, some old, some new, is most enjoyable.

Mere moments outside Perth is one of Scotland's fabled castles, Glamis. Dating to the fourteenth century and used by Shakespeare as the setting for *Macbeth,* it has turrets and battlemented parapets looking down on a late-nineteenth-century English formal garden and an Italian garden, opulent rooms with a wide range of furniture, porcelains, paintings, and tapestries, and the Grampian Mountains as its backcloth. Glamis was the childhood home of the late Queen Mother and the birthplace of the late Princess Margaret.

Far left: Doune Castle. Middle column, top: the gardens; bottom: grounds of Glamis Castle. Above: Glamis Castle. Left: Scone Palace in Perth.

ABERDEENSHIRE AND NAIRN,
THE HIGHLANDS AND DORNOCH

ROYAL ABERDEEN

I t has taken decades, but American golfers are at last finding their way to Aberdeenshire and its handful of outstanding links courses. Royal Aberdeen itself is the jewel in the crown. Here we find that rarest of combinations: a great and historic club and a great and historic links.

Royal Aberdeen is the sixth-oldest golf club in the world (Royal Blackheath, Royal Burgess, the Honourable Company of Edinburgh Golfers, at Muirfield, the Royal & Ancient, and the Bruntsfield Links Golfing Society are its predecessors). It traces its origin directly to the Society of Golfers at Aberdeen, which was formed in 1780 (and in 1783 introduced the five-minute limit on searching for a lost ball), became the Aberdeen Golf Club in 1815 (annual dues, five shillings), and in 1903, by grace of King Edward VII, was named Royal Aberdeen Golf Club.

During its first hundred years, the club played on common ground within the city. When that links became overcrowded, a lease was negotiated in 1887 on land just north of the estuary of the River Don, at Balgownie, as the links of Royal Aberdeen is sometimes known. Robert and Archie Simpson (Carnoustie brothers, Archie was at one time Royal Aberdeen's professional), Willie Park Sr., and English-born Tom Simpson all took their turn in shaping the superlative golf holes we play today.

ON THE COURSE

The very location of the teeing ground on the 1st hole can prompt jitters, for that swatch of turf happens to be tucked neatly between two large bay windows of the clubhouse's principal rooms, where fellow golfers will be on the lookout for our nervous first swing. Nonetheless, the fairway that awaits below is a generous one, the sea that lies beyond is shimmering, and the prospect of a grand day on the links will never be brighter. So we swing away on this 410-yarder and, avoiding the three bunkers at the landing area, put ourselves in position to reach the green, which, boldly undulating, sits on a rise just beyond a deep, hidden dip and is silhouetted against the sky and the sea. Can the course live up to such an overture?

The answer is promptly forthcoming. Beginning high above the beach on a lonely perch in the sand hills that is the tee of the 530-yard

2nd, the next eight holes weave their way naturally and hauntingly through a landscape of towering dunes and over pure links terrain that ranges from rippling to tumbling to billowing. All the elements are present: gorse, heather, long bents (sometimes dotted with bluebells), tightly textured turf to accommodate the game on the ground, punitive sandpits, an occasional burn, an occasional blind shot, an occasional mischievous bounce, tees atop dunes, greens in hollows, greens on plateaus, forced carries over forbidding country, and ribbons of fairway tracing their cloistered paths along dune-framed valleys.

Opposite: Royal Aberdeen, 2nd. Above: 3rd. Previous spread: Skibo Castle, 11th.

We play this first nine at Balgownie in seclusion. We also play it in awe and something close to rapture. Every hole is an unalloyed delight. The two one-shotters—the splendid 223-yard 3rd, from a top-of-the-world tee to a green far below in a natural amphitheater, and the 147-yard 8th, essentially level, the green ringed by low dunes and ten bunkers—are not easily forgotten. Nor are the two longest par 4s, which are among Scotland's best holes. On the 4th, 423 yards, the drive is launched from another of those lofty tees, with the long second shot menaced by hummocks and dips, not to mention sand at the front, left, and right of the deep, narrow green. As for the finale of this nonpareil nine, it is altogether magnificent. The tee shot on the 453-yard 9th is also fired from on high, this time down over a diagonal ridge of deep rough to an angled fairway well below that turns right. The long second—surely a fairway metal—must climb a goodly hill to gain the well-bunkered, bilevel green. From the medal tees, the outbound nine measures 3,372 yards against a par of 36.

The inbound half, only 3,060 yards but played into the prevailing wind, is routed over less thrilling terrain. The majestic dunes are gone now and with them some of the magic. But the test remains, and the last three holes are especially fine. Gorse and sand on both sides threaten the drive on the 392-yard 16th; sand alone, in five bunkers, patrols the green. Half a dozen pits defend the slightly elevated two-tier green on the 180-yard 17th.

As for the 434-yard 18th, it is one of the outstanding finishing holes in the land (its equals are at Leven, Carnoustie, Muirfield, Loch Lomond, Lossiemouth, Skibo Castle, and Kingsbarns). The platform tee enables us to assess the dangers: Sand awaits the wayward drive, as do gorse and the omnipresent thick rough grasses; a sound drive will stop in a dip. A plateau green now awaits some 200 yards away on the far side of a steep swale. Into the prevailing wind, even a well-struck shot is not likely to chase up the face of this bank. There is a much better chance that it will retreat into one of the gathering bunkers at the bottom. A splendid hole and a fitting climax to

Above, left: Royal Aberdeen, 4th; right: 6th. Opposite: 8th.

a great links, one of the top ten courses in Scotland and the site in 2005 of Tom Watson's second victory in the Senior British Open.

Plan to have a sandwich-and-beverage lunch in the clubhouse's many-windowed lounge, with its views of the starting and finishing holes and the sea. The atmosphere is not stiff, and you will quickly sense the antiquity and distinction of this club. There are old silver and paneling, old pictures and books. Women visitors are welcome in this room, notwithstanding the presence of the charming little black-and-white clubhouse of the Aberdeen Ladies Golf Club, clearly designed in sympathy with the men's, about 150 yards away. Beside it is the 1st tee of the Silverburn eighteen, which the ladies enjoy immensely and which Donald Steel reworked in 1995 to provide a little more spine.

Above: Royal Aberdeen, 9th.
Opposite: 15th.

TOUCHES OF ROYALTY, ON THE LINKS AND OFF

- Play **Royal Aberdeen**, one of Scotland's top ten courses and possessor of the most glorious first nine in the land.

- Make it a point to have lunch in the atmospheric clubhouse of what is the world's sixth-oldest golf club.

- Try to find time for a round next door, over **Murcar's tumbling linksland**.

- Drive west along the Dee to the Queen's **Balmoral Castle**; pop in to see how the other half lives.

- Spend the night—and enjoy dinner—at **The Marcliffe at Pitfodels**, a notable country-house hotel that happens to be in the city of Aberdeen.

MURCAR

Next door—in literal truth, next door—is Murcar Golf Club. Murcar was the only club in Scotland to own a railway, the famous Murcar Buggy, by which members in the early days were transported from the Bridge of Don to the clubhouse for a penny. Its driver, one Jimmy Fiddes, could always be counted on to delay the last run back to the Bridge at night on the promise of a wee dram.

Archie Simpson walked over from his golf shop at Balgownie to lay out the Murcar holes. The 1930s saw a number of revisions by James Braid and his constructor, John Stutt. Together, the three men produced a first-rate eighteen and a very useful relief nine of 2,850 yards.

The terrain here slopes from the high ground, where the clubhouse is situated, to the shore in a terraced fashion, with the result that virtually every point of the course provides views over the water. There is much to engage the eye: south past Aberdeen's busy harbor to the Girdleness Lighthouse, east over the open sea and beyond the oil-drilling rigs to the horizon, and north to the farmlands and coastline at Cruden Bay and Peterhead. But vistas, for all their charm, are not so important as the golfing ground itself. Murcar's is excellent: tall sand hills, springy fairways that range from undulating to violently tumbling, dramatic elevation changes, gorse, heather, long and thick marram grass, and three burns crossing the links and adding substantively to the round's challenge and diversity.

Opposite: Royal Aberdeen, 17th.

The course measures 5,800 yards from the regular markers (par 69), 6,240 yards from the medal tees (par 71). The first couple of holes are unexceptional, but the 3rd, 401 yards, dives off a shelf of fairway into a long gully with a green set in a punch bowl at the far end. Overlooking this green is the elevated 10th tee at Royal Aberdeen. More than once over the years, newcomers to Murcar have been known to putt out on the 3rd hole, climb the hill to the adjacent teeing ground, and hit away, blissfully ignorant of the fact that they were now playing Balgownie.

Even when we do head in the right direction and reach Murcar's 4th tee, in the sand hills above the beach, we are amused to learn that this patch of land belongs to Royal Aberdeen and is on a sort of permanent loan to its good neighbor. In any event, here begins a run of six terrific holes. Again and again we are driving from tees high in the dunes, down into hummocky valleys, then shooting uphill to a green that is good-size, sometimes framed by low dunes, at other times exposed, and always lightly defended by sand. One hole in this skein is unforgettable. Its name is Serpentine; Tom Doak has called it "all world," and it is 423 yards long. Launched from a hilltop tee, our drive must carry two branches of the stream that gives the hole its name. The second one crosses the fairway in the valley far below at about 190 yards. The sliced tee shot vanishes into a ravine, the hook into heavy rough. A straight and sound strike, however, sets up the opportunity to execute a full-blooded second, possibly a 5-metal, up a rising dune-framed channel to a green, bunkered right and left, at the crest of the hill. This is seaside golf at its most natural—and at its best.

The second nine at Murcar, as at Balgownie, finds us turning away from the coastal sand hills into less adventurous terrain. But the holes still sparkle, and getting our figures continues to be a task, albeit an agreeable one.

The **Marcliffe Hotel and Spa** is widely viewed as the finest hotel in the Aberdeen area. A member of Small Luxury Hotels of the World, the Marcliffe is extremely comfortable, furnished partly with period pieces, and characterized by highly personalized service. There are two dining options: the informal and cheery **Conservatory** and the dressier and intimate **The Drawing Room Bar & Lounge**. In both cases the menu is imaginative and the cooking quite good.

Meldrum House, some twenty-five minutes west of Aberdeen, is a rambling stone manor that dates to the thirteenth century. It is filled with antiques, objets d'art, and ancestral portraits. The spacious and charming guest rooms, recently refurbished, provide lovely views over the countryside and/or the golf course. Dining is a matter of superior cuisine in a beautiful room in which you may find yourself at a fireside table. (As for the golf course, it is nine years old. Routed through wood-lands and over meadows, it has water on eight holes, nicely contoured greens, and, on the second nine, pronounced elevation changes and panoramic views.)

Among the attractions of Aberdeen itself are the harbor, St. Andrew's Cathedral (interior with white walls and pillars in sharp contrast to the bright coloring of the coats of arms on the ceiling), and Provost Skene's House (450 years old and containing several carefully re-created period rooms). A half-hour's drive into the country will bring you to Castle Fraser and Crathes Castle, both sixteenth century and in excellent condition. The gardens at Crathes are particularly prized.

Another hour west and you reach Balmoral Castle. When the royal family is not in residence—and they are rarely there for more than four or five weeks, in summer—the public is welcome to visit and gain insight into 150 years of royal living in Deeside.

From left: downtown Aberdeen; Bridge o'Balgownie; Corgarff Castle.

CRUDEN BAY

p the coast, some sixteen miles north of Royal Aberdeen, is Cruden Bay, one of the dozen courses in Scotland that should on no account be missed. Nor is it necessary to play so much as a stroke to confirm this imperative. You have merely to park your car on the heights beside the clubhouse and look down. Below, in all its turbulent splendor, lies one of the most awe-inspiring stretches of linksland ever dedicated to the game. Against a backdrop of North Sea whitecaps stretching away to the horizon, the sand hills rise as high as sixty feet, their shaggy slopes covered with long and throttling golden grasses. For sheer majesty of setting, no Scottish course surpasses Cruden Bay, and only two or three might claim to equal it.

The original holes were laid out by Old Tom Morris in 1899 as the main attraction of an elite resort hotel. However, the course today, while retaining much of Old Tom's basic routing and a number of his green sites, is largely the work of Tom Simpson, in conjunction with Herbert Fowler, in 1926. An English barrister turned golf architect, Simpson was rich, eccentric, dashing. He traveled from course to course in a chauffeur-driven silver Rolls-Royce, emerging from its cosseting interior to tramp the particular tract wearing an embroidered cloak and beret and carrying either a shooting stick or a riding crop. It is said that he hired Philip Mackenzie Ross (Turnberry, Portugal's Estoril, et al.) as his construction boss because Ross showed him how to mount a license plate most becomingly on the Rolls-Royce. Simpson and Fowler were also responsible for the superb St. Olaf Course, a relief nine of 2,550 yards, par 32, laid out over the same marvelous linksland as the principal eighteen.

Though the hotel fell victim to the Great Depression and the Second World War and was razed in 1952, the great course itself survived when an Aberdeen stockbroker, a Cruden Bay hotelier, and a Peterhead solicitor teamed up to buy it. The solicitor, John A. S. Glennie, went on to found the Cruden Bay Golf Club and become its first captain. One of the outstanding amateurs in northeastern Scotland between 1920 and 1960, the brilliantly analytical Glennie was the man who put Scotland's handicap system on a realistic, workable basis. He loved the game as few men do and understood it as do even fewer. My wife and I came to know John and his wife, Edda, who served as ladies' captain for several years, visiting them at both their house in Peterhead and their tiny, picture-windowed chalet above the 1st hole at Cruden Bay, where they lived from June through September. "It's a prefab," John told us. "It cost four hundred and ninety-five pounds back in 1965 and it was put up in a day. We've been using it now for twenty years. If my mathematics is correct, that comes to about twenty-five pounds a year—not at all bad for a long summer holiday."

John Glennie had a rich fund of golf stories at his fingertips, some of them about famous figures in the game. At Mougins, in the south of France, he played a round one winter with Henry Cotton, whom he had known for some time. He asked Cotton what kind of match they might make.

"We'll play even," Cotton said.

"Even it is, then," John replied, "despite the fact that you've won three Opens and I haven't struck a ball in four months."

John continued, "Cotton and I were playing what you call a nassau. Going out he beat me one down, but I had him by a hole on the inward half as we came to the eighteenth. Then he hooked his tee shot out-of-bounds and that was the match. As a matter of fact, he never did play the hole. He simply walked straight to the clubhouse."

Glennie was instrumental in bringing in as head professional, first, Eric Brown, then Harry Bannerman, to Cruden Bay. Brown ran the shop at Cruden Bay from 1963 to 1968, having made his reputation in a series of Ryder Cup Matches in the 1950s, when he won all his singles (then 36-hole contests), in turn downing Lloyd Mangrum, Jerry Barber, Tommy Bolt, and Cary Middlecoff. The Bolt match was downright hostile. The two players refused to shake hands at the conclusion, Brown taunting his vanquished foe: "You knew when the games were drawn that you never had an earthly hope of beating me." In the locker room afterward, Bolt is said to have broken a wedge in half, and he elected not to appear at the presentation ceremony.

Harry Bannerman took the Cruden Bay job in 1976, five years after his only Ryder Cup appearance, at Old Warson Country Club, in suburban

Opposite: Cruden Bay, 4th.

graciously consented when John Glennie asked him to join me for a round. I was familiar with the course, having played it three or four times since my first visit, in 1978. We both carried light bags, though we could have chosen to pull a trolley.

Of average height and a little on the heavy side, Harry smoked a cigar that day with me, just as he had fifteen years earlier in the Ryder Cup. He had those powerful forearms that almost all world-class players seem to be endowed with, and he drilled his drives—no float whatsoever to them—some 275 yards. That put him 60 yards in front of me. Rarely missing a fairway, he hit fourteen greens in regulation.

ON THE COURSE

The course was quite short for Harry (and just about right for me) at 6,370 yards, par 70. The first three holes are spirited par 4s (my companion drove the green on the blind 286-yard 3rd for a two-putt birdie), but they scarcely prepare you for what comes next: four consecutive *great* holes.

The 193-yard 4th is one of Tom Simpson's finest par 3s, as well as a selection for *The 500 World's Greatest Golf Holes*. It plays straight toward the sea (and often straight into the wind) from an elevated tee carved out of one sand hill across a deep, grassy hollow to an elevated green carved out of the facing sand hill. A bunker at the left front in the slope and a steep falloff on the right dictate the need for a well-nigh perfect stroke. The harbor of the old fishing village is visible in the distance.

The 453-yard 5th is doubly demanding. First comes a blind drive from high and deep in the dunes, sighting on the wispy top of some vague hillock. This is followed by a full-blooded metal along the valley floor to a large but ill-defined green (how far short of the putting surface *are* those two bunkers?) in a charming dell. The cloistered quality of many holes, and with it the feeling that we have the course to ourselves, is created by the massive dunes.

The 524-yard 6th, appropriately named Bluidy Burn, is a dogleg left. Once again the tee is well up in the sand hills, but this time the green, feverishly undulating, is tucked away beyond a dune and protected from the birdie seeker's aggressive second shot by a hidden little burn some 60 yards in front. Even Harry prudently chose to lay up.

As for the final hole in this extraordinary quartet, the 7th, 390 yards, commences from yet another beautifully sited tee high in the sand hills. If we somehow find the fairway with our blind drive, we make a 90-degree left turn and face uphill, where the flag beckons from beyond two

St. Louis. The United States won, 18½ to 13½. The twenty-nine-year-old Bannerman teamed with Bernard Gallacher in the foursomes on the afternoon of the first day to turn back Billy Casper and Miller Barber, 2 and 1. The next morning Bannerman and Peter Townsend bowed, 2 and 1, to Jack Nicklaus and Gene Littler in a four-ball match; then, despite a 6-under-par 65 in the afternoon, they lost a heartbreaker to Nicklaus and Palmer when Nicklaus holed a 16-footer on the home green for a birdie. On the final day (singles in both morning and afternoon), the cigar-smoking Bannerman halved with Palmer in the morning (the Scot was 2 up after 12) and beat Gardner Dickinson, 2 and 1, in the afternoon. Dickinson had never before lost in Ryder Cup competition, having won either solo or in partnership nine times.

The future looked highly promising for Bannerman, but a bad back cut short his competitive career, and a series of club jobs followed. On a gloomy but dry and relatively calm mid-November day in 1986, he

Above: Cruden Bay, 5th.
Opposite: 6th.

dunes that stand sentinel at the narrow green like the Pillars of Hercules. Four great and unforgettable holes in succession—par 3, 4, 5, 4.

Then comes the 258-yard par-4 8th, which Tom Simpson called an "outstanding jewel of a hole, mischievous, subtle, and provocative, the element of luck with the tee shot being very high." The hole is set in a confluence of sand hills, a confined territory of hilly, broken ground. The slightly elevated green, a roughly triangular upthrust sloping away sharply on the sides, confounds us; the little pitch calls for uncommon deftness. It is easier to make 5 than 3. John Glennie once holed a 1-iron here. Both of us had to accept frustrating 4s.

Well, I *think* he felt frustrated, but I can't swear to it. I could not tell from his demeanor whether he was making a birdie or a bogey. He was comfortable to be with, but quiet. He volunteered nothing. I commented that his match with Palmer at Old Warson must have been tense.

"Aye," he said, "it was that. I had him, going to the last hole. But I let him off the hook when I missed the green with my five-iron and couldn't get up and in from the heavy grass. The golf was good, but a handshake turned out to be all there was in the match."

The second nine begins at the highest point of the course. The panorama of links, rocks, sea, beach, and ruined Slains Castle is heart-

SCOTLAND

stopping. Ireland's Bram Stoker, of *Dracula* fame—there is no evidence that he played golf, but he came here year after year on summer holiday and regularly roamed the links—was standing on the 10th tee when he envisioned the bay, with its great promontories jutting into the North Sea itself, as the jaws of a wicked monster luring ships to destruction on the rocks.

The next three holes are good but not particularly memorable. Fourteen, 15, and 16, however, are quintessential Cruden Bay, the first two playing from tees above the beach into a very narrow neck of land squeezed by a towering gorse-clad hillside on the left and the dunes that shield the course from the sea on the right. The blind approach shot on the 372-yard 14th disappears over a direction marker into a hollow, where the long green, suggestive of a sunken garden, gathers the ball. The one-shotter 15th borders on the bizarre. On this 239-yarder we stand on an elevated tee and gaze over broken ground down a dune-framed chute. Nothing beckons. Both green and flagstick are hidden. We take it on faith that they await. As it happens, the green falls away toward the back and the well-struck shot creeps inexorably over it into the short rough. But at least you don't have to watch this take place.

The next hole, hillside to hillside and also a par 3, seems almost conventional. *Almost*. The green and its protective bunkers are concealed, but, thankfully, the flagstick is in sight.

The round concludes with a pair of exacting two-shotters. On the 428-yard 17th there is a curious mound—a sugarloaf, really—perhaps 12 feet high and rearing up in the middle of the fairway about where a solid drive finishes. Some believe that it was a burial mound for Danish invaders, who were finally driven out of Scotland when they were defeated right here on the linksland of Cruden Bay almost exactly a thousand years ago, in 1011.

The home hole, 416 yards, presents a broad fairway on two levels, boundary on the left, a burn to snare the cut shot, undulating ground ending in a diagonal ridge just short of the spacious green. We made pars, mine with a chip and a putt, Harry's when a 12-footer for birdie slipped by on the low side. He had struck the ball well but had putted indifferently. I had struck the ball as well as I know how and had putted the ball better than I know how. We had not kept a card, but I was able to account for our strokes. We each shot 73. This parity would have been of no interest to him.

We climbed the very steep slope to the modest clubhouse, since replaced by an impressive edifice with enthralling views over the links to

NOT YET A SHRINE, BUT WELL ON ITS WAY

- Tackle **Cruden Bay**—one of Scotland's ten best—marveling at the majesty of its dunescape.

- Relish lunch in a window of the **smart new clubhouse** that looks down on the links and the sea.

- Play the club's **St. Olaf's Course**, one of the best nine-hole layouts in the world.

- Bunk in the **Red House Hotel**—small, simple, a golfer's haven, with the links mere steps away.

- Dine 20 minutes down the road in Newburgh at the **Udny Arms**—outstanding continental cuisine.

- Be sure to stroll—ideally after dark—past **Cruden Bay's row of fisher cottages** out to the all-but-abandoned old harbor.

Peterhead, 17th.

the sea. For me, it had been one of the half-dozen rounds of a lifetime. For Harry Bannerman, it had been a way to oblige John Glennie, the man who had given him this decent job. There seemed to me to be a hint of melancholy about the Ryder Cupper, or was it simply seriousness? He left Cruden Bay a couple of months later, and I never saw him again.

I recall reading some time ago that Pete Dye had singled out five courses as his particular favorites, making no claim that they were the greatest or the toughest, just that they were the five he liked most of all: Pinehurst No. 2, Pine Valley, Portrush, Camargo (a Cincinnati course laid out by Seth Raynor), and Cruden Bay. The bedrock appeal of this Aberdeenshire links is obvious. What a wonderful time we have playing on this glorious ground, over which are routed truly natural holes—some great, some unique, some nonconformist, all invariably fun. This is links golf to dote on.

PETERHEAD

Five miles north of Cruden Bay lies prosperous (North Sea oil) Peterhead. The Peterhead Golf Club, founded in 1841, has 27 holes. Measuring not quite 6,200 yards (par 70), the principal eighteen is largely a testament to Braid. The first three holes may possess an inland feeling, but beginning with the 4th the course takes on a true seaside character. We now find ourselves in golfing country of knobby greens whipped by the wind, secluded holes framed by tall sand hills, and heaving fairways corseted by tussocky grasses. The sea pops into view every time we climb up to a tee, and if Peterhead is not filled with great holes—although the one-shotter 6th and the 460-yard par-4 15th certainly are great—it is filled with good golf. You will not regret time spent here.

In Newburgh, about twenty minutes south of Cruden Bay, is the well-regarded **Udny Arms**, a homey old inn where some of the rooms can be cramped but the cooking is outstanding. In Cruden Bay itself, the **Red House Hotel** is one favorite of golfers: small, simple, comfortable, quiet, the front bedrooms and the dining room looking directly out over the links to the sea.

Very nearly in the lee of the 4th tee is the **Kilmarnock Arms**, where Bram Stoker used to hole up. Harriet and I still smile at the memory of a short walk we took along the Water of Cruden after dinner in the Kilmarnock Arms nearly thirty years ago. Spanning the stream and leading to the bathing beach, a narrow wooden suspension bridge creaked in the wind, its coat of white paint rendering it eerily ghostlike in the moonlight. Few lights were on in the small, severe cottages—the fisher cottages, they are called—which are built hard against one another and against the sidewalk. Nor was anyone abroad on the darkened street. No boats were tethered in the snug, stone-walled harbor, but a few ill-used fishing smacks were pulled up onto the grass-overgrown quay. The wind, less powerful than during the round that afternoon, was still fresh, and as we approached the high seawall, a wave crashed against it and sent Masefield's "blown spume and flung spray" right over that sturdy barrier and down upon us. We laughed like children in a sun shower and headed back to the haven of the inn.

In the immediate environs of Cruden Bay are the roofless remains of Slains Castle, dating to 1597 and dramatically clinging to the cliff's edge, dizzyingly high above the roiling seas. Quite nearby are the Bullers of Buchan, a natural feature that finds a path tiptoeing along the rim of a sheer two-hundred-foot rock chasm, probably once a vast cave whose roof has collapsed. This is especially compelling in powerful winds, when the waves boil in through the natural stone archway.

The Maritime Heritage Museum, in Peterhead, presents the seafaring past of the people here (building wooden boats, hunting the whale, et cetera) and does so with audio-visual programs, computer touch screens, and hands-on displays. On Kinnaird Head, in Fraserburgh, is Scotland's Lighthouse Museum. Containing a collection of lighthouse artifacts from all over the land, it stands in the very shadow of Kinnaird Head Lighthouse. A museum visit includes a guided tour to the top of the lighthouse. The Lighthouse Tearoom, with its marvelous views, is ideal for lunch.

Just off the A947, some eight miles southwest of Turiff, stands Fyvie Castle. Dating back more than seven hundred years, it boasts an exceptional circular staircase (ascending through five floors), tapestries, arms, armor, paintings (Gainsborough, Raeburn, and Romney, among others), a picturesque lake, a 1903 racquet court, and a bowling alley. A shop sells mementos of your visit to what is one of the stateliest castellated mansions in Scotland.

Top: shoreline at Cruden Bay. Above: the Udny Arms. Left: the Bullers of Buchan.

BOAT OF GARTEN AND GRANTOWN-ON-SPEY

In the northwestern corner of the vast Cairngorms National Park, about a two-hour drive from Cruden Bay, are two of the most beautiful courses in the Highlands. Both go back more than a hundred years.

The River Spey runs through the village of Boat of Garten, where a six-hole course opened in 1898. Three holes had been added by 1910, and the course remained a nine-holer until 1930, when Braid laid out a second nine and revised the first nine.

The setting for the golf holes is exquisite, on the edge of the Abernethy Forest. Almost without exception, the fairways are tree framed but not claustrophobically so. The silver of birch, the deep green of pine, and the royal purple of heather combine to delight us at every turn. Deer are often to be spotted in the thickets, and the osprey wings overhead on occasion. In the distance are the peaks of the Cairngorms, snow-capped for nine months of the year.

ON THE BOAT OF GARTEN COURSE

Curiously, the terrain we trod is linkslike: undulating, rumpled. Perhaps we can attribute it to glaciers. In any event, this extraordinary topography gives the Boat, as it is generally called, considerable character. And when coupled with the hills themselves, the result is a veritable dipsy doodle of a layout, with uphill lies, downhill lies, hanging lies, awkward stances, and the occasional blind shot and attendant bell ringing (the "all clear" sound).

The course measures 5,876 yards from the back tees; par is 70. Among the more memorable holes are the 189-yard opener, which, with a boundary tight on the right, drifts downhill, the shot all but funneled into sand at the left front; and the 437-yard closer (the best and toughest hole on the course) bending right, the long second shot uphill to a plateau green.

The course has an amusing distraction, the bordering railway line. Several times during the round, the Strathspey Steam Railway train (featured in *Monarch of the Glen* on PBS) may hoot and chug along beside us.

ON THE GRANTOWN-ON-SPEY COURSE

Ten minutes up the road from Boat of Garten is Grantown-on-Spey, another place that owes its name to the fetching river. Just a block or two off the wide and decorous tree-lined main street is the Grantown-on-Spey Golf Club, founded in 1890. It is little changed since 1910, when Musselburgh's Willie Park Sr., four-time Open champion, extended the course to 18 holes.

This is another very short course—5,710 yards, par 70. Half a dozen par 4s are under 300 yards; birdie opportunities abound. Bunkering is

Opposite: Boat of Garten, 17th. Above: 18th.

generally light, and the cross bunkers on 2, 3, and 5 give the course an endearingly old-fashioned feel. Water in the form of burns pops up on five holes, and out-of-bounds threatens frequently.

Holes 7 through 12, routed through moderately hilly woodland, provide the most interest. Bunkers seal off the front of the green on the excellent 380-yard downhill 7th; the 161-yard 8th, steeply uphill, has a playing value of 175 yards; the 11th, measuring 190 yards and playing 210, is another stout uphill shot. And the superb 12th, 413 yards long and the best hole on the course, begins on a mildly elevated tee, then calls for a long second shot, with the heather tight left and right, over a crest to a hidden green.

If Grantown is not quite up to the level of the Boat, it is nevertheless agreeable holiday golf in a beautiful setting backdropped by both the Cairngorm Mountains and the heather-clad Cromdale Hills.

A three-minute walk from the golf club in Boat of Garten is the **Boat Hotel**, a four-star facility whose public spaces, with their highly polished hardwood floors, oriental rugs, and marble fireplaces, have style and warmth. The guest rooms are comfortably traditional, and several of them afford beguiling views over the Victorian railway station to the golf course and the mountains. The hotel's **Caper-caillie Restaurant** has a smartly contemporary ambience that is rather in keeping with the cuisine.

Two miles outside the village, on the B970, is a non-golf attraction you may want to take in. The Auchgourish Gardens and Arboretum is full of uncommon and beautiful plants (Himalayan, Chinese, Japanese) as well as rockeries with Alpine flowers and heather beds. Rare white Highland cattle are bred here.

On the northern outskirts of Grantown-on-Spey is Castle Grant, which dates to the fifteenth century and includes eighteenth-century additions by Robert and John Adam. There are a number of Adam rooms with carved plaster decoration in the neoclassical style.

Two moderately priced hotels near Grantown should be mentioned:

- At Dulnain Bridge is **Auchendean Lodge**, built in the Edwardian era. Tastefully furnished, it offers log fires, food with flair, a good wine cellar, and an even better selection of malt whiskies.
- At Ballindalloch is **Delnashaugh Hotel**, comfortable and unpretentious. The decor calls up Laura Ashley; the cooking is simple and satisfying.

Ballindalloch is also the location of the Glenfarclas Distillery. After a guided tour, you are invited to enjoy a dram of single-malt whiskey. A number of other distilleries are also within the Cairngorms National Park and make up the famous Whisky Trail. Among those that welcome visitors are Cardhu, Glenlivet, Glenfiddich, Dalwhinnie, and Royal Lochnagar.

Far left: the Spey River. From top: near Loch Ness; the Strathspey Railroad; inside the Boat Hotel.

NAIRN AND MORAY

L ess than an hour's drive west on the A96 from Elgin brings us to the family seaside resort of Nairn, with its two eighteens: the championship course at the Nairn Golf Club and the Nairn Dunbar layout. The very word *family* reminds me that our first visit to Nairn, thirty-five years ago, was *en famille*—three children and our elder son's high school sweetheart. We had driven up from St. Andrews on Saturday, spending the night at the Huntly Castle Hotel, some forty miles from Nairn. At church the next morning, the pastor announced the banns of marriage for a couple, pointing out that the bride was, of course, known to the entire parish, since she lived here in Huntly. But the groom, from a village in the next valley, was rather an unknown quantity. At first the pastor seemed inclined to provide some details about the young man, particularly concerning his family. Then he threw up his hands, saying, "Well, if I'm not mistaken, none of you know him. But you may take my word for it, he's a fine lad!"

ON THE NAIRN GOLF CLUB COURSE

If there is one course in Scotland that the word *seaside* ought instantly to call up, surely it is the links of the Nairn Golf Club. For here it is entirely possible to slice onto the beach six times in the first seven holes—and, with any luck on the lies, still salvage a couple of pars.

The club was founded in 1887, and it was Royal Aberdeen's Archie Simpson who laid out the course. Old Tom Morris and James Braid each had a hand in revising the Simpson design, with Braid having the last word, in 1926.

The important Scottish championships, professional as well as amateur, have long taken their turns at Nairn, but it was not until 1994 that the British Amateur came here. Five years later, so did the Walker Cup. Great Britain and Ireland, down 7–5 at the end of the first day, surged back in both foursomes and singles, 10–2, on the second day to humble the United States 15–9. Future PGA Tour players who competed were Luke Donald and Paul Casey (for the winning side), Jonathan Byrd, Matt Kuchar, David Gossett, and Bryce Molder.

Visitors are likely to tackle the course at about 6,400 yards; par is 71. This wholly natural links is a lovely walk. The waters of the Moray Firth are always in view, and the dappling effect of sunlight and shadow on the Black Isle, not to mention the beauty of the distant peaks about Strath Conan, makes the round a nonstop aesthetic treat.

The firm and often fast fairways bring even the longest two-shotters within reach. The greens, silken and true, are not difficult to read. On the face of it, we ought to be able to play to our handicap. Then, along about the 6th or the 7th, it becomes clear that we are not getting our figures. Why? For one thing, Nairn is a serious examination in driving. The narrow fairways, undulating, hummocky, and given to the occasional capricious bounce, are hemmed in by heather and gorse. What's more, the approach

Opposite: Nairn, 4th.
Above: 16th.

ON THE NAIRN DUNBAR COURSE

At the opposite (east) end of town is the Nairn Dunbar Golf Club, founded in 1899. Measuring 6,300 yards from the regular markers, this par-72 layout has undulating fairways, gorse, and the occasional elevated tee and plateau green. The first 12 holes are quite satisfying; they provide challenge and a true links feeling. Unfortunately, the next 5 are meadowy and prosaic. Then the vigorous 18th, a short par 5 over heaving ground and with an astonishing rollercoaster green, reminds us all too tellingly of the course's early quality.

ON THE FORTROSE AND ROSEMARKIE COURSE

Forty-five minutes north of Nairn lies the Black Isle's Chanonry Point. Here awaits the short (5,858 yards) but stimulating links of the Fortrose and Rosemarkie Golf Club. Braid—who else?—in the 1930s laid out the golf holes that we play here today. As Malcolm Campbell tells us in *The Scottish Golf Book,* Braid "was able to squeeze 18 holes onto a peninsula that is little more than 500 yards wide at its start and tapers to around 150 yards at the lighthouse end." The wind constantly beleaguers us out on this exposed spit of land, and the sea threatens on 7 holes.

A delightful footnote: Across the water from Fortrose and Rosemarkie lies Fort George. Early in the twentieth century, the club extended honorary membership to the soldiers, among whom was Bandmaster Rickets, who regularly played with his colonel. One day during a round on the links, the bandmaster heard another golfer whistle from an adjacent hole to attract the colonel's attention. Rickets committed the musical notes to memory and later used them in the opening bar of a march he wrote, which he named "Colonel Bogey." It is that same composition that became the jaunty theme music for the Academy Award–winning film *Bridge on the River Kwai,* in which Alec Guiness played the colonel.

CASTLE STUART GOLF LINKS

Nine miles from Nairn and on the Moray Firth, the key figures in the creation of two of Fife's outstanding newer courses, Mark Parsinen (Kingsbarns) and Gil Hanse (Craighead) have teamed up to design and build a new eighteen called Castle Stuart Golf Links. Some holes are routed over linksland while others occupy much higher ground that was formerly cropland. The course, which opened in 2008, looks, feels, and plays like a true links.

shots—to greens that are intriguingly angled or hidden behind dunes (as on the 4th, a wonderful 145-yarder played out to sea) or on troubling plateaus or beyond seemingly innocent little crests—are difficult to judge, even more difficult to hold.

A number of holes are easy to remember, among them the clever 326-yard 8th, where the crowned green wants to shunt off all but the most adeptly struck pitch; the 206-yard 14th, played from on high (the sea view is mesmerizing) down to a green with a deep cleft in it; and the 16th, 417 yards, where a teasing burn just short of the green makes us grateful for the breeze at our back.

But perhaps no hole better typifies the challenge of Nairn than the 337-yard 5th. Here the drive must be fired over the edge of the beach, a pesky Braid bunker awaits in the left side of the fairway precisely where we would choose to land the ball in playing safely away from the water, and the green perches mockingly atop a little plateau. This hole was chosen for inclusion in *The 500 World's Greatest Golf Holes*.

Lunch or a drink in the impressive clubhouse, its broad windows framing glorious views over the Moray Firth to the Black Isle and Cromarty, is not to be missed.

Above: Nairn, 6th.
Opposite: 5th.

MORAY

There are two signs at the 9th tee of the Moray Golf Club's Old Course, in Lossiemouth, an hour east of Nairn. Both get our attention. One, in white letters on a red ground, reads: BEWARE SUDDEN AIRCRAFT NOISE. The other, in red letters on a white ground, reads: BEWARE OF GOLF BALLS FROM THE RIGHT. So, you may wonder, is it worth our life to play this classic links on the Moray Firth, about an hour and a half northeast of Grantown? Nonsense. It's true that the 9th on the Old Course crisscrosses with the 4th on the New Course, calling for alertness and courtesy. And it is equally true that the shrieking jet engines of Jaguar and Tornado fighter bombers from nearby RAF Lossiemouth can terrify the unwary. Please dismiss these distractions. For the game at Lossiemouth is played over rippling and heaving sand-based terrain; and the greens are adroitly sited on low plateaus or in pretty dells or atop teasing ridges; the fairways, burnished in high season (this is one of the driest and sunniest parts of Scotland), play firm and fast, often fiery fast. Old Tom Morris came up from St. Andrews in 1889 to lay out the course, and it is little changed to this day.

ON THE OLD AND NEW COURSES

The regular markers add up to 6,300 yards, with a par of 71. There are 110 bunkers, most of them small. Gorse is plentiful, heather of less concern. Among the outstanding holes are the 3rd, 391 yards, bending right through the gorse and then making a short, steep ascent to a plateau green; the 400-yard 11th, the second shot aimed dead at Covesea Lighthouse, a stream crossing the fairway 50 yards short of the green; the 14th, 398 yards, playing straight toward the sea all the way, the green itself cheek by jowl with the golden beach. Then there is the unforgettable 18th, one of the great finishing holes in Scottish golf: 406 yards long, out-of-bounds down the right, five bunkers along the left, the second shot having to climb over exceedingly restless terrain to reach a deep, narrow green set in a natural amphitheater and defended at the front left by a pair of hellish pits.

As is the case with the Old Course at St. Andrews, Moray's Old Course starts and finishes neatly in town.

It was in 1976 that the New Course, designed by Henry Cotton, opened. Though only 6,000 yards at full stretch, with a par of 69, it has six par 4s over the 400-yard mark. A day at Lossiemouth that begins with a game on the Old, followed by lunch in the sturdy granite clubhouse on the high ground, and then a game on the New is a day to be remembered with affection.

ELGIN

Fifteen minutes inland from Lossiemouth lies the Elgin Golf Club, with its rolling moorland layout and its share of pine, silver birch, and gorse. We are struck at once by the tranquillity of the setting. A couple of rather ordinary short two-shotters notwithstanding, this is a worthy test, nowhere better exemplified than by three par 4s late in the round: the 439-yard 14th, which, uphill all the way, plays more like 480 yards; the downhill 410-yard 16th, both shots blind; and the 18th, 429 yards, the long second shot having to gain an elevated and well-bunkered green below the clubhouse windows.

Opposite: Moray Old Course, 18th. Above: 2nd.

Just across the road from the Moray Golf Club stands the **Stotfield Hotel**, which has been welcoming golfers for the biggest part of a century. Not all rooms are spacious, but some of the larger accommodations enjoy beautiful views over the links and the Moray Firth to the hills of Sutherland. The cooking features the chef's choice of local produce, with the emphasis on fish.

In Elgin, the **Mansion House Hotel**, overlooking the River Lossie, has comfortable guest rooms, good food, and an indoor swimming pool.

Two of the best country-house hotels in Scotland are in the Nairn area. **Culloden House**, a strikingly symmetrical Georgian mansion built in 1788 on forty acres, may be Scotland's single most elegant great house. Every detail of its interior is exquisite, with many one-of-a-kind period pieces, an astounding collection of

crystal chandeliers, splendid fabrics at the long windows of the high-ceilinged rooms, and, above all, beautiful Adam fireplaces and ornately carved plasterwork. The guest rooms, unusually spacious, are appointed to the highest standard, some of them with four-poster beds and fireplaces. And from the kitchen comes a parade of marvelous dishes—for example, marinated scallops wrapped in smoked salmon and a phyllo pastry set on a lemon-cream butter; cutlets of Highland lamb topped with black pudding and peaches, and served on a Rosemary jus; white chocolate crème brûlée with passionfruit sorbet.

Boath House, another graceful Georgian mansion, is set on twenty acres of lawns, woodlands, and water. A suspended spiral staircase leads up to the guest rooms, which are surprisingly—and by no means lux-

uriously—decorated. Dining, solely by candlelight, is a memorable experience. A typical five-course *table d'hôte* dinner: roasted red pepper and plum tomato soup with basil oil; foie gras and chicken liver pâté with an apple and sultana relish; seared medallions of venison on celeriac purée; Howgate brie with an apple and cashew nut salad; and, for dessert, rum *panna cotta* with black currants.

A couple of sister hotels that cater to golfers and to families are within a short walk of the 1st tee at Nairn Golf Club. The **Golf View** has 48 rooms, more than half of them with views of the Moray Firth. Dining in the glass-walled conservatory, which all but hangs over the sea, is a particular pleasure. The castlelike **Newton**, on twenty-one acres of parkland and gardens, provides public rooms and guest accommodations that are smarter

From left: the Golf View Hotel, outside and in-; Culloden House; Inverness.

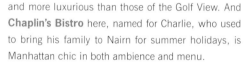

and more luxurious than those of the Golf View. And **Chaplin's Bistro** here, named for Charlie, who used to bring his family to Nairn for summer holidays, is Manhattan chic in both ambience and menu.

There is plenty to see and do within an hour of Nairn, which itself boasts two extensive beaches, not to mention a seafront promenade (a boardwalk without the boards) and a cozy harbor:

- Inverness, divided by the River Ness (the fabled loch is about twenty miles south of the city), makes for a half-day's pleasant outing.
- Cawdor Castle, scene of Duncan's murder in *Macbeth,* is a medieval fortress with beautiful gardens.
- Seventeenth-century Brodie Castle contains carved plasterwork and French furniture, plus a good collection of paintings (seventeenth-century Dutch, eighteenth-century English, French Impressionists).
- Fort George is the ranking example in Britain of Hanoverian military architecture. A polygon with six bastions, the fort, which once housed twenty-five hundred men, today contains the regimental museum of the Queen's Own Highlanders.
- The area's principal sightseeing attraction is Culloden Battlefield, the site of the last land battle to be fought in Britain (1746), marking the end of Bonnie Prince Charlie's doomed cause.

Top row, from left: Lossiemouth dunes; church in Inverness; the town of Cullen. Middle row: Pluscarden Abbey; Boath House guest room; Boath House. Bottom: Cawdor Castle.

SKIBO CASTLE

As guest of members of the Carnegie Club at Skibo Castle, you and your companion are welcome to visit this private enclave on seven thousand acres before applying for a spot at this exclusive private club. The 2010 per diem tariff for guests is £1320 ($2135) per couple and £865 ($1397) for a single, which covers luxurious accommodations in either the castle itself or one of the original lodges; breakfast, luncheon (always at the golf clubhouse), afternoon tea, cocktails, and dinner; all club wines and spirits; as much golf as you can handle (no starting times on the championship-standard links course or the nine-hole parkland course); salmon and trout fishing; canoeing; clay-target shooting and target-pistol shooting; tennis, archery, croquet, and snooker; mountain biking; gymnasium, sauna, and steam rooms; daily falconry display; and swimming in what may well be Britain's oldest indoor pool, a heated marble pool that is the centerpiece of an enchanting glass-roofed pavilion.

A Scot who had emigrated to America when he was thirteen, Andrew Carnegie in 1898—the "Steel King" was now sixty-two and rich beyond the dreams of avarice—bought Skibo, a castle fortress near Dornoch, dating to the twelfth century, that had evolved into a Gothic mansion. He transformed it into a noble rose-tinted baronial castle that would become a haven of peace and tranquillity for him and his wife and their only child Margaret. There are more than two hundred rooms, many of them opulently decorated so that guests such as King Edward VII, Rudyard Kipling, Ignacy Paderewski (the old Bechstein grand piano that he played is in the drawing room for you to play today), Lloyd George, Henry Gladstone, and assorted Rockefellers would feel at home.

In 1899 Carnegie asked John Sutherland, secretary at Dornoch, to lay out nine holes for him and his guests. (Carnegie once said, "Golf is an indispensable adjunct to high civilization," and heaven knows that Skibo was—and is—nothing if not highly civilized.) The Sutherland nine was allowed to go to seed many years ago.

It was in 1990 that Peter de Savary, a visionary English entrepreneur, acquired Skibo for the establishment of the Carnegie Club ("international membership limited by invitation"). He commissioned Donald Steel to

lay out an eighteen. The setting is sublime. The waters of the Dornoch Firth, the River Evelix, and Loch Evelix provide a perfect framework for this contemporary links. The great forests and hills of this corner of the Highlands stretch away as far as the eye can see.

ON THE COURSE

The course can be played as short as 5,540 yards, as long as 6,700; par is 71. A pair of solid two-shotters gets the round under way nicely, the 2nd hole doglegging sharply right, with the shot to the green semiblind. We note that the bunkers are classically links type: generally pot shape and with steep, revetted faces.

At the great 150-yard 3rd, we play from the top of one sand hill across a forbidding rough-clad hollow to the top of another sand hill. There is no margin for error. The same can be said of the 4th (angled,

Opposite: Skibo Castle, 17th.
Above: 4th.

Skibo Castle, 18th.

humpy fairway shedding drive into rough or gorse), the 5th (sea on the right awaiting the errant drive and second shot), and the 6th (a 183-yarder in the dunes with a large, deep pit at the left front of the green).

Loch Evelix is put to good use on the par-4 8th and 13th, tempting us on both to save some much needed yardage by carrying a corner of the water. The 545-yard 12th and 550-yard 14th are husky tests, with sand on the 14th menacing all three swings.

The finishing run is top-notch. On the 186-yard 15th, the right side of the green is no more than a short drop from a tidal inlet. On the 16th, 421 yards, the brave drive out to the right, imperiled by a falloff down to the 18th fairway, is rewarded with an open shot to a green set among low dunes. The last two holes are thrillers. On the seductive 280-yard par-4 17th, the green, from a tee set intoxicatingly high above the Firth, is drivable for some—pro-

viding they are willing to flirt with the sea, which is discomfitingly close along the left, and providing they are able to carry the deep bunkers in the heart of the fairway 30 yards short of the green. On the 545-yard 18th, a long forced carry over a corner of the bay is called for to get the ball in play. The fairway then swings vigorously left as it skirts the shore en route to a slightly raised green on a spit of land, with water just left and beyond. A hidden pot bunker greenside at the right will snare the too safe approach. This is a grand finale, where the big basher can again gamble, this time on both shots, in the hope of getting home in 2.

In 1996 Steel laid out a beguiling nine-hole parkland course that can be tackled as either a par-3 layout (the holes range from 145 to 210 yards) or as a mix of par 3s, 4s, and 5s (2,825 yards). This diverting course wends its way over rolling terrain, through copses, and around ponds and marshes.

Golf at the Carnegie Club, whether on the links or in the park, is a joy. But it is only a part of the Skibo story. The chief attraction here is an elusive lifestyle, at once genteel and luxurious, that has more in common with the Edwardian Age, with 1910, than with 2010. Peter de Savary was at pains to preserve the distinctive quality of Andrew Carnegie's Highland paradise.

Surely the same will be true of de Savary's successor, Ellis Short, of Dallas, the current owner, and Peter Crome, the club's urbane managing director (formerly in charge at St. Andrews's Old Course Hotel and then Hampshire's acclaimed Chewton Glen Country House on the English Channel). They well realize what is irreplaceable here: the ambience of an Andrew Carnegie house party a hundred years ago. As a result, your sumptuous accommodation may well be the Ospis room, where not only the bedroom (26 feet by 16 feet) has a period fireplace but so does the bathroom (26 feet by 10 feet). And your pink gin during cocktails in the drawing room is served by a white-coated butler who will never again have to be told what you are drinking. And the heavy silk draperies and the oriental rugs and the priceless wall coverings (Spanish tooled leather in one area) and the antique furniture and the gilt-framed oil paintings that graced this house while the Carnegies occupied it, in many instances, still grace it today. And when, at 8 P.M. sharp, a bagpiper leads the procession melodically from the drawing room into "Mr. Carnegie's Dining Room" (oak paneled, the blaze from the great hearth and the flames from the great candelabra casting a glow upon the massive dark-stained oak furniture) and each regal detail, beginning with that evening's club host at the head of the table leading everyone in a toast "to Andrew," calls up all the latent Anglophilia within you, then you know, irrefutably, that this is *the* place. And the golf, as excellent as it is, seems almost incidental.

ROYAL DORNOCH

Not ten minutes up the road from Skibo Castle lies Royal Dornoch, ranked fifteenth in the world by *Golf Magazine*. Though golf—or some very rudimentary form of it—has been played at Dornoch for nearly four hundred years, the club was not founded till 1877. John Sutherland, who guided its affairs for almost sixty years after being appointed secretary in 1883, played a key role in fashioning many holes. So did Old Tom Morris. Others to lend a hand were five-time Open champion J. H. Taylor; Donald Ross, the club's professional and greenkeeper in the 1890s; George Duncan, principal architect of Stonehaven; and, in contemporary times, Donald Steel.

ON THE CHAMPIONSHIP COURSE

The course measures 6,732 yards from the championship tees, 6,514 from the medal tees, and 6,229 from the regular markers; par is 70. Since neither the par 5s (496 and 506 yards) nor the one-shotters (177, 163, 147, and 166 yards) call for strong hitting, that requirement must be left to the par 4s. In fact, from the regular tees, eight of the twelve extend beyond 400 yards. And in a number of instances the long approach called for is to a plateau green, occasionally crowned and with sharp and shaven falloffs on the sides. Deft little pitches or chips or scuttles with the putter from somewhere off the green are at the heart of good scoring here. No hole is without challenge or charm; many holes possess both.

The round opens with a short and inviting par 4 to get us going in a positive frame of mind, followed by a tough 177-yarder where the modestly raised and tightly bunkered green tends to shed all but the precisely struck shot. One of the arresting moments in golf comes next: After a brief walk on a path through a shoulder-high tract of gorse, we break into the clear. From the high 3rd tee a majestic vista stretches away hole after hole, seemingly limitless, sea and hills and linksland. The world has been left behind, and as we play on, there is this strong sensation of heading toward land's end. The remoteness is total. We feel that we may outrun the district of Sutherland and penetrate to the very wilds of Caithness on this journey over an ancient landscape where so little is owed to the hand of man.

In *The Golf Courses of the British Isles*, Bernard Darwin wrote: "Those who laid out the older links did not . . . think a vast deal about the good or bad length of their holes. They saw a plateau which nature had clearly intended for a green and another plateau at some distance off which had the appearance of a tee, and there was the hole ready made for them. . . . People as a rule took the holes as they found them and were not forever searching for the perfect 'test of golf.'" We are consistently struck by such a wonderful sense of naturalness as we make our way around Royal Dornoch. Everything simply looks as if it has been this way for centuries.

The 3rd (414 yards), 4th (427 yards), and 5th (354 yards) make up a particularly engaging sequence. Two are played from high tees. There is

Opposite: Royal Dornoch, 4th. Above: 5th.

room on all three to let fly on the drive, but, unless our ball finds the right spot in the landing area, the second shot to the plateau green, sited a bit above us, will be very exacting. It is possible on the 3rd and 4th, where the front is open, to chase our long second shot up onto the putting surface. But in the case of the shortish 5th, with its deep green angled to the approach shot and sand blockading the direct access, the only way on is up and on.

Much the same imperative greets us on the 163-yard knob-to-knob 6th, with sand on the left and the right front, a steep falloff on the right, and a stingy target. In sum, a classic hole that was named one of the 500 *World's Greatest*.

Crowned greens, for which Donald Ross is alleged to have developed a penchant at Dornoch and which find their fullest flower on Pinehurst No. 2, are actually not all that common at Dornoch. Pete Dye, who played Pinehurst No. 2 frequently and got to know Ross, says: "The Pinehurst No. 2 greens were rough Bermuda grass, so they kept top-dressing them to make them smoother. That's how the greens became crowned.

Over the years all that sand-based top dressing built up the middle of the green. Everybody thinks Mr. Ross intended to crown the greens, but he didn't. Many times he told me he was going to cut the crowns off. But he died before he could do it. And the world has been copying the crowns he would have cut off had he lived."

The holes coming in are equally fine. Both par 3s are ringed with sand, the beach-side 10th fully exposed to the wind, the 13th somewhat sheltered in the dunes. But it is the celebrated 14th, called Foxy, that is unforgettable. Completely natural—there is not a bunker anywhere in its 445 yards—the hole breaks left in the tee-shot landing area. Then, after proceeding straight ahead for almost 200 yards, it jogs right, the fairway soon to rise abruptly to chest level and to a wide but shallow green. Both changes of direction on what is a double dogleg are prompted by a long, formidable dune jutting in from the right and covered with bushes and rough grasses. This hole is the very definition of "shot values": The drive must be strong and perfectly drawn; the second shot, perhaps a 5-metal,

ON THE STRUIE COURSE

The championship course is not all the golf to be had at Dornoch. The Struie Course was sweepingly revised in 2002. At nearly 6,300 yards and with newly acquired links terrain for holes 9 through 13, there are good holes here, but we find ourselves wishing for more dash. Perhaps this should be blamed mainly on the absence of elevation change (15 of the 18 holes are dead level) and of feature.

ON THE TAIN COURSE

South on the A9 some ten miles is the royal burgh of Tain and the Tain Golf Club. From the medal tees the course measures 6,207 yards, par is 70. By and large, the undulating fairways on this essentially level tract are spacious, but if we miss them we often find ourselves in dense growths of gorse (lost ball or unplayable lie). Forced carries over heather are also an aspect of the driving. The Tain River makes its bow just short of the green on the 2nd but then is gone until the final three holes. We must carry this broad and sinuous stream twice on the 213-yard 17th and, having done so, also stay clear of it as it edges back toward the right side of the green.

must be high and softly faded. If our long second shot should fail even by inches to gain the table-top green, we are left with a devilishly tricky little pitch or chip—or a rap with a putter for those whose nerves are questionable. In *The 500 World's Greatest Golf Holes*, the 14th has been named one of the top one hundred.

A number of the game's leading players—Tom Watson, Greg Norman, Fred Couples, Nick Faldo, Ben Crenshaw—have made it a point to get to Dornoch. Watson described his three rounds during a twenty-four-hour stay as "the most fun I ever had playing golf." And Crenshaw, in Scotland to compete in the British Open at Muirfield, played a couple of practice rounds there, then seized the opportunity to fly up to Dornoch. When he returned, Keith Mackenzie, then secretary of the R&A, asked him how he enjoyed it. "Let me put it this way," Crenshaw replied. "I nearly didn't come back."

Royal Dornoch, 17th.

CHERISH THE DAY

- Succumb to the spell of **Royal Dornoch**, fifteenth in the world in the 2005 rankings: its compelling golf shots and its heart-stopping scenery.

- Have lunch in the bright and cheery **clubhouse bar**, virtually hanging over the 1st tee.

- Drive twenty-five minutes north on the A9 for the afternoon game at **Brora**, one of Scotland's unheralded yet unforgettable jewels.

- Back in Dornoch, pay homage to **Donald Ross at No. 3 St. Gilbert Street**, the simple row house—still a private residence—where he was born and reared.

- Dine at **Burghfield House**, where the extraordinary cooking has a distinctly Scottish flavor.

- Stay at the **Royal Golf Hotel**, less than 75 yards from the 1st tee at Royal Dornoch.

I can recommend three hotels and one guest house in Dornoch:

- If you stay at the four-star **Royal Golf Hotel**, you will be a mere pitching wedge from the 1st tee. The hotel has style and personality. Bedrooms (several are small) are furnished in a blend of traditional and contemporary. Some overlook the links. Diners can choose between the informal conservatory and the main restaurant. Both provide carefully prepared local game, seafood, beef, and lamb.

- The atmospheric **Dornoch Castle Hotel**, on the town square, also offers thoughtfully appointed guest rooms, some of which have been returned to their original granite walls, dark oak paneling, and high ceilings. Light meals are available in the bar throughout the day; and there is an extensive à la carte menu for dinner.

- On five acres of attractive gardens stands **Burgh-field House**, built more than a hundred years ago. Antiques, oil paintings, open fires, and fresh flowers all contribute to the hospitable feel. The guest rooms are comfortable, and the cooking has a distinct Scottish emphasis (for instance, chicken stuffed with haggis in a whiskey and onion sauce).

- On the aristocratic square in the very shadow of the cathedral is a charming B&B called **Trevose Guest House**. All five guest rooms are appealing, as are the gardens ringing the house. Trevose House was an ideal spot for watching the Madonna–Guy Ritchie nuptials unfold. The ceremony itself (by invitation only) took place in the cathedral, which dates to 1225; the reception was held at Skibo Castle, where the happy couple and their friends were lodged. But the square was the place to see the notables, and paparazzi from tabloids all over the world were on hand to record the event for their respective rags. This triggered a windfall for the natives. In order to gain needed vantage points, the photographers and journalists had to buy stepladders locally. When the ceremony was over, these representatives of the Fourth Estate, rushing now to get back to the Inverness airport, abandoned their newly bought ladders. The townspeople, in the best frugal Scots tradition, claimed them and headed smugly back to their homes, certain that this was indeed *the* wedding of the new millennium.

Across the square from the cathedral, beyond the tall shade trees, bulks what remains of the once imposing Castle of the Bishops, a stone tower that is now part of the Castle Hotel. Next door, in the medieval jail, is the crafts center. And just off the square, behind the cathedral, stands the simple row house on St. Gilbert Street, No. 3, where Dornoch's most renowned son, Donald Ross, and his younger brother, Alex, who won the 1907 U.S. Open, were born and reared. Take notice of the three dormer windows in the roof. They were installed when Donald sent money home to his mother in 1900, after his first year in America, money she used to add two bedrooms upstairs under the eaves.

Dornoch Cathedral.

BRORA

Surely Dornoch, on the same latitude as Juneau, Alaska, ought to be far enough north to spell the end of the line for even the most venturesome golfer. It ought to be, but it isn't. Less than twenty miles farther up the A9 lies the village of Brora, home of an irresistible links. At only 6,119 yards and with a par of 69, it is unlikely to qualify as a great course. That said, it is packed with shot-making demands over as rewarding an expanse of golfing duneland—every natural contour from moderate wrinkling to fantastic billowing—as any golfer could yearn for. With the land everlastingly in motion, stances and lies can be awkward, and flexibility in setup and swing is called for from time to time.

The club was founded in 1891, and nine basic holes were laid out by the Committee. The first golf house was a tiny tin hut that measured 5 feet 4 inches across. A year later the membership was presented with plans for a new and more ambitious clubhouse, 12 feet by 10 feet. These specifications were promptly amended to 15 feet by 11 feet, which, one suspects, allowed for four golfers to occupy it simultaneously, at least if they remained standing. In keeping with what was a continuing expansionist bent, John Sutherland came over from Dornoch to enlarge the links to eighteen holes. Alterations were subsequently effected by Sutherland and J. H. Taylor. Then, in 1924, Braid paid two visits to the club, one in January and one in December. The result was substantive change.

ON THE COURSE

This is as fine an example of James Braid's work at the sea as we are likely to find today. The course was built on a relatively narrow stretch of linksland just two holes wide, the sea on our right all the way out and in view on almost every hole. Cattle regularly graze the links, and sheep sometimes do. A club promotional flyer may exaggerate the case, but it is probably close to the truth: "Eighteen greens as the glacier left them; swings and borrows to gladden the heart." There is gorse but no heather. And the rough is light, which makes the course enjoyable for the high handicapper.

The holes range from good to great, with water in the form of sinuous burns intruding on five holes. The two best holes on the first nine are,

as it happens, also the two hardest, both par 4s. At the 447-yard 3rd, the very long second shot, fired over a ridge as well as hummocky ground, must be held skillfully up to the left because the ground slopes away toward the sea on the right. At the 428-yard 5th, a burn must be crossed on the second shot, and the partially concealed green is defended at the right front by a big sand hill cloaked in long rough grasses. A ravine behind the green discourages the bold second shot. Waves crashing on the rocks behind the green of the 162-yard 9th are an exhilarating distraction.

Now we turn about and head for home, one first-class hole after another, with the final four not likely to improve our score. The fairway on the 430-yard 15th—a blind drive over a high ridge, a boundary edging in unseen on the right, gorse tight on the left—is elusive on what is a strong and original hole. At the 16th, 345 yards, the climb to the putting surface is so steep that the hole plays 385, and the rough hollow, far below green level on the left, is cruelly cautionary.

Opposite: Brora, 17th. Above: 3rd.

Golspie, 12th.

The 17th, 438 yards, is one of Scotland's best par 4s, and it was Braid's favorite at Brora. It is named Tarbatness for the lighthouse down the coast that signals the optimum line of play. Braid designed the hole for two drawn shots, the first being the drive from a moderately elevated tee over rough ground into the neck of the fairway, and the second, also from right to left, to an adroitly bunkered green in a little hollow on the far hillside. It is all there before us and it is all quite splendid, another indisputably great hole requiring two excellent swings.

The final hole is 201 yards long, tending uphill all the way. The depression in the forepart of the green, certainly meant to summon the Valley of Sin, may just be overkill, especially since the clubhouse is all but cantilevered over the green, so that any shortcoming will be duly noted.

Brora is holiday golf at its best—a full measure of Darwin's "pleasurable excitement," a seaside setting of inordinate beauty, and the genuine warmth of the welcome accorded to visitors.

NEARBY COURSES

Founded in 1889, the **Golspie Golf Club**, some six or seven miles south of Brora on the indispensable A9, has a delightful course that is largely seaside. Even shorter than Brora (5,836 yards, par 68) and also with revisions by Braid, it has four first-class holes: the 530-yard 4th, which ripples along as it skirts the beach; the 8th and 9th, each over 400 yards long and rising, where heather constricts the shots and the prevailing wind is against us: and the grand 16th, 176 yards, which, from a lofty tee, plays over a valley to a two-tier green backdropped by the sea. The views at Golspie, mountains and meadows and water, are consistently captivating.

An hour north brings us to **Wick Golf Club**. An authentic links, easy-walking Wick measures almost 6,000 yards against a par of 69 and is laid out along a ridge of dunes, with sandy beach beyond. The small greens, which putt beautifully, make scoring difficult, as does the wind.

There are three attractive places to stay in Brora, all of them on Golf Road and within steps of the links:

- The **Royal Marine Hotel**, formerly a private country house, has handsome fireplaces, a grand staircase and reception hall, and rich paneling. Guest accommodations provide modern comfort at what is a full-facilities hotel: heated indoor swimming pool, sauna, steam room, Jacuzzi, tennis, curling, croquet, and fly-fishing on Loch Brora. The "Taste of Scotland" cuisine is altogether satisfying.

- Two four-star B&Bs here—the three guest rooms in each of these houses have private bathrooms—are also quite comfortable. **Tigh Fada**, a haven for non-smokers, has a large garden with croquet, pitch and putt, and a gate to the golf course and the beach.

As far as nongolf activities are concerned, Hunter's Woolen Mill and the Clynelish Whisky Distillery, both in Brora, nicely repay a visit. However, the outstanding nearby attraction is Dunrobin Castle. Dating to the early 1300s, the ancestral home of the Duke of Sutherland contains impressive period furniture and furnishings, a Victorian museum featuring Pictish stones and wildlife specimens, and magnificent formal gardens, all of it in a setting high above the sea that is an integral part of its grandeur.

From left: Royal Marine Hotel (top) and a view of Brora; the gardens at Dunrobin Castle; the castle (top) and a falconer on the grounds.

LOCH LOMOND AND AYRSHIRE,
KINTYRE AND THE ISLES

LOCH LOMOND

Not thirty minutes north of Glasgow on the A82 lies Scotland's only private golf club in the strict (i.e., American) sense of the term. You cannot play either of the Loch Lomond Golf Club's two courses, one here on the storied lake, the other an hour's drive south, unless you are the guest of a member and in his company. No other Scottish club, not even the Honourable Company or the several "Royals," imposes so sweeping a stricture. Since Loch Lomond's membership is heavily American, it's possible that readers of this book may have a friend or acquaintance who belongs to the club and might be willing to host a game.

In 1992 Tom Weiskopf and Jay Morrish laid out an eighteen here on a six-hundred-acre tract bordering Loch Lomond and near the village of Luss, in Dunbartonshire. Many who had the opportunity to play the course in its early months called it great—and, as it turned out, appropriately so. Weiskopf, scarcely objective, said: "Jay Morrish and I firmly believe that Loch Lomond Golf Club has the best eighteen holes of golf that we have ever created—or quite possibly may ever create."

The course has made its mark in the polls: eighth among the top hundred courses in Britain and Ireland (*Golf World,* a British monthly magazine); sixty-sixth among the top hundred courses in the world (*Golf Magazine*). It is regularly referred to as the "best inland course in the British Isles." It is also kiddingly called—but this is kidding on the square—the "best American course in Europe." In truth, it is very much an American beauty: gorgeously green, lovingly manicured, pristine, its style of bunkering owing nothing to the birthplace of the game.

Beginning in 1996, the European Tour has stopped annually at Loch Lomond. Ernie Els has won here twice (2000 and 2003). Among the other victors have been Retief Goosen, Colin Montgomerie, Tom Lehman, Lee Westwood, and Thomas Bjorn. In 2000 the Solheim Cup was held here.

ON THE LOCH LOMOND COURSE

The course measures 7,100 yards from the championship tees, 6,350 from the regular markers. Par is 72. The first nine has little in the way of elevation change; the second nine is rolling. A single hole may well display

oak, copper beech, silver birch, maple, chestnut, larch, holly, Scotch pine, and Douglas fir. A tree in this veritable arboretum sometimes dictates the line of play, as on the par-4 15th, where the green is defended on the left by an immense silver birch.

The holes fall with perfect naturalness on the terrain; nothing is forced or gimmicky here. The demands on the swing are fair, shot values are of a high order, and the holes are attractively varied. The bunkering is consistently functional but nonetheless elegant, often with peninsulas of turf breaking up the expanses of sand. No revetted pots here. As for the

Opposite: Loch Lomond Course, 5th. Above: 6th. Previous spread: Loch Lomond Dundonald Course, 9th.

greens, they are brilliant—endlessly varied in size, shape, and contouring, spacious when the shot to them is long, less generous when it is short, swift and silken surfaces for a ball to skim across. Fairway lies delight the pure ball striker (they are tight), and the overall condition of the course is impeccable.

No hole at Loch Lomond is less than good, and at least half a dozen are genuinely great. The 5th, 6th, and 10th have been selected for *The 500 World's Greatest Golf Holes,* and it might be well to focus on them. The 5th, which we play at 152 yards and the professionals at 190, is essentially level. It is also breathtaking, presaging the full majesty of Loch Lomond. The tightly bunkered green is set against the shimmering backcloth of the lake, with low hills looming on the far side of the water. Weiskopf's words of caution are in stark contrast to the beauty of the setting: "Never, ever miss this green in the bunkers left or you are as good as dead."

The next hole is called Long Loch Lomond. In both senses of the word *long* is this true, for the hole is a 500-yarder (625 yards from the tips and as such the longest hole in Scottish golf) and it plays along the loch. An energetic slice on any stroke will find the water. Determined to make

Opposite: Loch Lomond
Course, 10th. Above: 9th.

It is at the 10th that we enter new territory, a lot of it quite rolling and much of it with water squarely in the center of things—a stream here, a pond there, wetlands here and there. The second nine may possess a little more pepper, a little more flair and surprise and zing, than the consistently excellent but a shade more passive outward half. The loch itself is now at a considerable remove, but great golf continues to be much at hand.

Hole after hole glitters, perhaps none more so than the 14th, a sharp right, 310 to 345 yards. The player who believes he can carry his drive an honest 270 yards will be tempted to go straight for the flag across a bog. The rest of us will play safely out to the left, leaving a ticklish little pitch to an elevated green on the far side of a stream and beyond a deep bunker. This hole almost cost Tom Weiskopf his life during construction. Shortly after dawn one morning, when there was no one within hailing distance and he was reconnoitering the green site, he lost his balance and was sucked down into the bog. Very slowly sinking, he fought desperately for several hours to get free, finally gaining hold of a root and painfully inching his way out of the clutching muck, minus Wellington boots, socks, and trousers, but alive and able to bring the great course to completion.

ON THE DUNDONALD COURSE

In 2003 the club acquired a second eighteen, this one a links course an hour south of Loch Lomond in an area dominated by Prestwick, Royal Troon, and Western Gailes. Called Dundonald, it is another example of the skill of Kyle Phillips, architect of Kingsbarns, who has fashioned here a second modern links. Sand-based, it has low dunes covered in fescue and gorse framing many of the fairways, steep-faced revetted bunkers, and an assortment of exquisitely sculpted greens that are actually more natural than many at Kingsbarns. A burn meanders across half a dozen holes. The waters of the Firth of Clyde are rarely in view; not so the Isle of Arran. Admittedly, there is not the majesty of Kingsbarns—the views are altogether more ordinary—but the golf holes themselves sometimes approach that masterpiece in terms of originality and shot values.

Dundonald measures 7,300 yards from the championship tees, 5,580 yards from the forward markers, and 6,410 yards from the middle tees. Two level par 4s on the second nine are especially fine: the 365-yard 13th, out-of-bounds tight all the way on the left; and the 400-yard 17th: sweeping dogleg left; three bunkers at the inside of the bend to swallow the overly aggressive tee shot, low runoffs at the left and right sides of the green that demand deft chipping—or putting.

this hole a legitimate three-shotter, Weiskopf and Morrish have plunked down a large and fanciful cross bunker smack in the center of the fairway 120 yards short of the green.

The third and final contribution to the seminal book is the 10th— richly scenic, rigorously exacting, 405 yards from the daily markers, 455 from all the way back. The tee is elevated, and our drive toward Glen Fruin hangs suspended against the wooded mountainside. Said Tom Lehman, "You face a tough downhill tee shot with 'stuff' both left and right—bad 'stuff.'" Moreover, crossing the fairway on the diagonal in the driving area is a burn. How much risk will we assume on the tee in order to shorten the long second shot? A pond lurks at the left of the green, which slants from the front right, where there is sand, to the back left, where the water is. It's not surprising that this hole was named one of the one hundred greatest in the 500 *World's Greatest* book.

Above: Loch Lomond Course, 18th. Opposite: Dundonald Course, 9th.

Top-notch also are a couple of the par 5s, both for the same reason. On the level 3rd, 510 to 560 yards, a burn haunts us much of the way, to devour first the pushed drive and then the weak or pulled second shot. On the 18th, 550 to 585 yards and also level, low dunes flank much of the hole, but in the end it is a waterless burn, a ditch, edging in from the left to cross just short of the green and then skirt the right side of it, that gives the hole its sting. That leaves only the one-shotters, and what a quartet they are! A dune boldly intrudes at the left front of the 170-yard 4th; a burn unnervingly close on the left guards the spectacularly contoured green of the 6th; a marsh must be crossed to gain the elevated green on the 125-yard 11th; and on the 15th, 190 yards, the elevated green is defended by two "in-over-your-head" pits at the front and at the left, and the railroad track is not far behind the putting surface. A very demanding test, Dundonald is, I suspect, more than most of us can handle in a 30-miles-per-hour wind.

The members of Loch Lomond now have a choice of exceptional courses, parkland or links. There will be occasions when rain at the one will send them scurrying to the other. And occasions when they will play one in the morning and the other in the afternoon. Now that's a *day* of golf.

By the time this book is published, the club's third eighteen should be well along, though probably not open for play. Jack Nicklaus has designed a course on Loch Lomond to take its place beside the Weiskopf-Morrish jewel. When I followed the proposed routing in mid-2004, the tees, greens, and center lines were clearly marked. But I'm not about to advance an opinion based on what I could make out. I will say that Tom and Jay did not lay claim to all the trees on the property—not by a long shot—and that Jack may intend to incorporate the great loch into his layout even more extensively than they did. At any event, count on it to be a worthy companion.

Opposite: Loch Lomond
Dundonald Course, 3rd.
Above: 18th.

We cannot leave Loch Lomond Golf Club, however private it may be, without a word or two about **Rossdhu House**, the eighteenth-century manor that is the clubhouse. It is magnificent. An imposing and symmetrical Georgian structure built of a warm beige sandstone, it is a procession of noble spaces, virtually all with fireplaces: the main hall, the drawing room, the cocktail lounge, the library, the spike bar (just the place for breakfast as well as lunch), the dining rooms, the locker rooms, and, up the grand staircase out of the main hall, the six accommodations, which vie, in luxury and comfort and style and view, with the accommodations at Skibo Castle. As for the cooking, it is marvelously creative and contemporary. Presentation, service, and wine list are also exceptional, in a period setting that calls up an age of opulence.

Set on the southern shore of Loch Lomond and not five minutes from the golf club is one of Scotland's foremost country-house hotels, **Cameron House**. Traditionally decorated, this nineteenth-century former residence is noted for its elegance, warmth, and cuisine. The hotel has long had a nine-hole golf course, the Wee Demon, which measures just 2,266 yards. However, in 2007 Cameron House built a new full-length eighteen on land bordering Loch Lomond: The Carrick on Loch Lomond, a name that

takes its cue from this Carrick area of Scotland, not from the architect, Doug Carrick. He is the designer of twenty-four courses in his native land, including Osprey Valley, northwest of Toronto, which, with its echoes of North Berwick and Prestwick, is a hymn to old-style British golf. Several holes here run right beside the grand loch, and 14 holes provide generous views of it. An effort is being made to see to it that this course plays firm and fast, with vigorous roll on the ball that brings the game along the ground much into play.

Opposite: Kilchurn Castle. This page, clockwise from above: Rossdhu House; Loch Lomond; Cameron House; Balloch Castle.

THE MACHRIE

S ingle-malt whiskey and traditional links golf—no more need be claimed for the Isle of Islay (pronounced eye-la). Islay lies eighteen miles off the southwestern coast of the Scottish mainland. It is the home of eight distilleries and The Machrie Hotel and Golf Links.

Regularly scheduled flights from Glasgow take us there in thirty minutes. Or we can drive and use the car ferry. This will require a good five and a half hours, but what a rewarding trip it is! The run south on the A83 through Argyll is endlessly beautiful—the great fjord Loch Fine, the starkly rugged mountains and lonely wooded glens, the inviting lochside villages of Inverary, Fornace, and Lochgilphead. At Kennecraig we board the ferry for a nonstop two-hour cruise on a commodious and comfortable ship (bar, cafeteria, lounges, gift shop) to dock at either Port Ascaig or Port Ellen. The latter is only a few miles from The Machrie.

For golfers, the question is a simple one: Is this links worth getting to? The answer is equally simple: Yes. Oh yes, indeed.

The course was laid out in 1891 by Willie Campbell of Musselburgh. Ten years later, in an effort to attract attention to this western outpost, the owners held a professional match-play tournament with an unignorable first prize of one hundred pounds. Many leading players made the arduous two-day trip to The Machrie immediately following the Open Championship at Muirfield. J. H. Taylor nipped James Braid in the final on the last hole to pocket the winnings.

ON THE COURSE

The word *unforgettable* is likely to surface with some frequency in a book of this nature. It is an adjective that can fairly be applied to The Machrie, which is riddled with blind shots. Par is 71. The low-handicap golfer thus gets to play 35 full shots. And of these 35, at least 18, probably 19, will be blind. The Machrie is truly unforgettable. You may be inclined to insist that it must also be unknowable and unmanageable. I urge you to play here and make your own judgment.

To begin with, this is splendid golfing country. The grass-cloaked dunes, which constitute the dominant feature of this 260-acre tract, are

often colossal. Within this turbulent landscape are a number of obvious green sites: amphitheaters, plateaus, ridge tops, punch bowls. An architect might start by identifying the eighteen best green sites, then work out a route back to the potential tee for each. Given ground of The Machrie's exuberance and, 115 years ago, given the absence of equipment for altering this topography, the result would necessarily be blind shots. For between tee and green, sand hills, whether modest or mighty, would intervene again and again to produce a series of holes that are marked by the thrill of the unknown. Concealed targets would be the order of the day.

The Machrie wastes no time in making this clear. The first hole on this 6,292-yard course is a mere 308 yards, but since the ground rises in front of the tee and since a hollow at the foot of a ridge hides the green, both drive and pitch turn out to be blind. Only the drive is blind on the

Opposite: The Machrie, 7th.
Above: 8th.

508-yard 2nd, which doglegs abruptly left as it skirts the bank of a fast-flowing stream. On the climbing 3rd, 319 yards, with its tee commanding our first view of the broad, tawny beach, both shots are blind, the hole climaxing in an outlandishly terraced green just beyond a ridge. The 390-yard 4th plays from an elevated tee, our back to the sea, down to a fantastically billowing fairway that, somewhere in its abundance of hummocks and hollows, contains a landing area, then up and out of this secluded spot to a green concealed beyond yet another ridge. A marvelous hole by any yardstick, and a suspense-filled delight.

We are not prepared for the 5th. Why? Because all 163 yards of it, from the pulpit tee down over broken ground to the green, is in full view. The putting surface is defended by a large bunker and a small one. Bunkers are in very scarce supply at The Machrie. There is a grand total of six, with

Below: The Machrie, 9th.
Opposite, top: 13th;
bottom: 15th.

two of them spent recklessly here on the short 5th, one each reserved for the 1st, 11th, 13th, and 17th. Willie Campbell and Donald Steel (Steel revised the course in 1979) were both reluctant to dig holes, preferring to rely on the natural contours of the greens themselves, which are generally undulating or wildly sloping (some are both), to say nothing of the green surrounds, which almost always contain cunning little folds and creases.

A stretch of four outstanding two-shotters completes the nine. Only the 7th will be described. A candidate for the title "Blind Hole of the World," it goes beyond the merely theatrical. The tee is tucked away in a tiny hollow on low ground. The fairway is nowhere to be seen. Then our perplexed gaze happens to light on an overgrown footpath working its way up the dune that towers some 40 to 50 feet above us, a good 150 yards out from the tee. The fairway, we conclude, must be somewhere on the far

side of this shaggy pyramid. A brief walk around its base confirms our instinct. The forced carry up and over has a value of not less than 185 yards (in the calm). Into the wind, the shot required to surmount the pinnacle is very like 220 yards. Fail to pull off this drive and we find ourselves—that's assuming we can find the ball—in deep and clinging grass on a slope so precipitous as to preclude any chance of making a swing.

Ah, but the drive that does clear this "Alps" plunges into a broad, rumpled fairway along and above Laggan Bay, where miles of deserted sand sweep away toward the horizon. Beyond the Rhinns of Islay, five or six miles across the bay to the west, lies the open Atlantic. To the northeast, the Paps of Jura soar twenty-five hundred feet above the water. What an inspiring amalgam of beauty and solitude, of tranquillity and spaciousness and freedom.

Now, having surmounted the giant sand hill, surely we deserve a clear shot at the green. No such luck. The green is out of sight, just over a low ridge. Nor do we catch a glimpse of the flag. We have no choice but to make our best guess and attempt our best swing.

The inbound nine, though at a slight remove from the sea, is nonetheless routed over characteristically heaving linksland, a patch of bracken here, of heather there, fierce rough flanking the broad fairways. The two par 3s could scarcely be less alike. The 156-yard 10th plays from a raised tee in low dunes beside the beach down to a green guarded by wetlands on the right and the wide Machrie Burn on the left. On the other hand, the 174-yard 12th is exposed and windswept, rising gently on a suggestion of ridge to a green that falls off to the left. Beyond this slope is a peat moor—Islay's whiskeys are noted for their distinctive peaty flavor—that stretches away toward dark low hills. The remoteness is palpable.

High tees continue to present compelling seascapes and landscapes. Blind shots—on the 13th, 14th, 15th, and 16th—continue to befuddle us. By now the disbelieving shake of the head may even be accompanied by a rueful smile.

Which brings us to the 352-yard 17th, almost certainly inspired by the 17th at Prestwick. Following a drive that must clear rough rising ground, we launch our 6- or 7-iron over a high dune, the shot disappearing out of sight toward a green far below in a pretty dell, a green defended in front by sand.

Now home at last, on a 374-yarder that, you will have guessed it and braced yourself, culminates with a totally blind approach shot. But this time, the green, in the lee of a broad ridge, welcomes our shot.

The Machrie, 17th.

If it is excessive, this nonpareil eighteen at The Machrie, it is an excess born of naturalness, an excess that produces more than its share of pure golfing joy. Could a claim for greatness be made? Probably not, though this links can usually be found in a ranking of the top seventy courses in Britain and Ireland. Still, there is perhaps too much of the dicey. More than half the shots are a lottery. But what should be kept in mind is that there is not a single prosaic hole, that there are four or five great holes (4th, 6th, 9th, 14th, 16th), and that Darwin's "pleasurable excitement" is present in full measure—all in a setting of uncommon beauty.

One other thing: Here is a course that is very rarely crowded. The five times I've played it, on three separate trips, I simply walked over to the 1st tee and hit off. Nobody ahead of me, nobody behind me, nobody with me, no starter. The Machrie may require a journey, but when you do make the effort, it's all yours and, even more to the point, it's terrific.

The hotel and the golf course are now owned by Graeme Ferguson Lacey, who seems to have a penchant for islands. He is also the owner of the admirable Castletown Golf Links and attendant hotel on the Isle of Man. Here at The Machrie he has a minor (possibly silent) partner, Peter de Savary, of Skibo Castle fame, the owner of the Bovey Castle country-house resort, in Devon, England.

The hotel dates to 1745, when it was built as a farmhouse. Guest rooms, each with private bath, have been freshly decorated. While in no sense fancy, they are comfortable. Public rooms are cheerful and relaxing. An open fire and a pool table make the Golfers' Bar inviting. As for the cooking, the seafood, beef, lamb, and game, all from Islay itself, are reliably flavorful. And the scallops on our last visit were as delicious as any we've eaten.

I spoke with the estimable Ian Brown, general manager, who is a sound golfer (almost a prerequisite for running The Machrie), about possible changes now that Mr. Lacey has the bit in his teeth. I expressed a concern that the very character of this plain-vanilla, get-away-from-it-

all place, this simple haven for golfers, might be altered to give it an upmarket look and feel (and tariff). He assured me that such a transformation was not in the plan.

If you can tear yourself away briefly from the wonderful links, keep in mind that five single-malt distilleries are still in operation on Islay. Guided tours can be arranged by the hotel. There is a distinctive flavor and hue and character to each of these whiskeys, to say nothing of distinctive names such as Bruichladdich, Bunnahabhain, Caol Ila, Lagavulin, and Laphroaig.

Also worth a visit is the Museum of Islay Life, on the shores of Loch Indaal. The collection contains some sixteen hundred items, dating from 8000 B.C. to the 1950s. Among the displays are those showing life in a simple cottage and in a farmhouse bedroom during the Victorian Age. One other place might be mentioned, the Round Church, in the village of Bowmore. Built in the 1760s, it is said to have been designed so that there would be no corners where the devil could lurk.

MACHRIHANISH

Machrihanish is less than an hour's drive south from Kennecraig, the port on the mainland for the Islay ferry. If you are making the long land or over-the-sea trip to The Machrie, you will want to visit Machrihanish. But then, you will want to play Machrihanish (a twenty-five-minute flight from Glasgow, a four-hour drive from St. Andrews) regardless of your intentions regarding Machrie.

One thing is certain: The opening hole at Machrihanish is superior to its counterpart at The Machrie. It may also be superior to just about every other 1st hole in the world. The tee on this 423-yarder, tight beside the curving beach, is elevated 10 feet above it. Our drive is fired on the diagonal across the Atlantic's waves to an undulating fairway that skirts the shoreline. How much of Machrihanish Bay have we the courage to bite off on our first swing? The beach—perhaps with an oystercatcher strutting about on it—is very much in play. This is a thrilling, tempting, tantalizing business. So we pick a target, probably a low dune, and if our swing be rhythmic and unrushed, away we go on a round that will give us enormous pleasure not only as we play it but as we hark back to it again and again.

It was on March 20, 1876, here near the bottom of the Kintyre Peninsula, that four men (including a Presbyterian minister) laid out a ten-hole course and "cut the first sod." Then, having handled the easy part in the morning (i.e., designing and building the course), they got down to playing it that afternoon, and playing it a second time as well that same day!

Over the years that followed, the task of shaping or reshaping the course fell to Prestwick's Charles Hunter, then to Old Tom Morris, J. H. Taylor, and, following the Second World War, Sir Guy Campbell. Machrihanish today, though chiefly attributable to Sir Guy, still contains a few reminders of Old Tom and J. H. Taylor.

ON THE COURSE

The links measures 6,225 yards from the medal tees; par is 70. After the unique opener, the 2nd, 395 yards, is no letdown. The approach shot must first clear a very broad stream called the Machrihanish Water and then a bluff with two large bunkers in its face. The ball comes to rest out of sight—

in the best Machrie tradition, Machrihanish has seven or eight blind shots of its own—on an astonishingly large and shapely putting surface. On the 3rd hole, the green swoops through a dune-framed dell to a length of 144 feet. By whatever yardstick—novelty, artistry, fascination, test, smoothness, pace—the Machrihanish greens rank with the very best in Britain and Ireland.

Now we are deep in the duneland: platform tees with intoxicating views across soaring and shaggy sand hills; fairways tossing and tilting or

Opposite: Machrihanish, 3rd.
Above: 7th.

doglegging around pyramidal dunes or twisting along snaking dune-lined valleys; now a hidden punch bowl green, now an exposed green on a ridge, now a breezy plateau green with steep falloffs right and left. We are called upon to draw the ball, fade the ball, knock it down into the teeth of the wind that comes funneling along a valley floor, lift it up to sail with the wind in order to gain a green high on a knob. The game here is inordinately rich and complex and involving. The sea is sometimes in view, at other times shut off by the massive sand hills, but the sound of it, which may range from a murmur to a roar, is always with us.

Though it steadily challenges the scratch player, Machrihanish does not discourage the high handicapper, who is not being overpowered (the last six holes on the outbound nine measure 122 yards, 385, 301, 428, 339, 353) or intimidated. The game here is joyous in this rough-and-tumble, enticingly natural—in truth, this magical—expanse of linksland that is the first nine.

If the inbound half lacks the grandeur of the huge sand hills, it still provides the vigorous movement of sand-based terrain. And the prevailing wind seems to be perpetually hostile: Virtually every stroke is played into it or across it. Among the numerous outstanding holes are the 513-yard 12th (a pair of deep bunkers hidden in a swale just short of the green awaits the aggressive second shot that just fails to get up) and the 231-yard 16th, a brutally long one-shotter that must traverse broken ground and rough country.

The record must show that the home hole, a 313-yarder over dull ground to an ill-defended green, disappoints, but let's just be grateful for

Opposite: Machrihanish, 5th.

this birdie chance and say no more about it. Besides, we may take the opportunity on the green to turn around and see just where we've been, perhaps even spotting the tilled land on higher ground immediately beyond the links. For a number of years the second farm belonged to Beatle Paul McCartney, whose attachment to this corner of Scotland—the sea, the lovely green hills of Kintyre, the panoramas that include the islands of Islay and Gigha and Jura—was powerful. In 1977 he composed a song called "Mull of Kintyre," and recorded it with the Campbeltown Pipe Band. Wistfully evoking this idyllic place, it enjoyed worldwide success.

Of all Scotland's notable golf clubs, Machrihanish must be the most egalitarian. So don't be surprised if your caddie is a member, is a first-rate player with a keen knowledge not only of the golf holes but of the club's history, and is an unpaid officer in the club administration, perhaps even captain. He might also be a philosophical humanist. I recall being caught once in a pitiless rain here, a downpour so drenching that our heaviest waterproofs utterly failed to be waterproof. One of our caddies muttered, "The rain can only go so far—it has to stop at the skin."

I was not surprised to find my friend Michael Bamberger writing in his classic *To the Linksland,* "If I were allowed to play only one course for the rest of my life, Machrihanish would be the place." I might not go quite that far, but taken all in all, links and club and remote, appealing Kintyre, Machrihanish has also gained an enduring hold on my affections.

It's worth noting that golf and lodgings at Machrihanish are soon to get a big boost. Next door to the much-loved eighteen, golf photographer Brian Morgan is building an upscale hotel and a links course designed by Kyle Phillips. Both are scheduled to open in 2007.

DUNAVERTY

All of fifteen minutes south of Machrihanish is the appropriately named Southend, a holiday village on the Mull of Kintyre. Northern Ireland, often in full view across the North Channel of the Irish Sea, is only twelve miles away.

Tiny Southend has its own tiny golf course, Dunaverty, measuring just 4,597 yards and playing to a par of 64. It is a cow pasture—literally: The first time I played it, more than twenty-five years ago, I had to nudge two Ayrshires aside in order to begin the round. They were chewing their cud squarely between the markers on the 1st tee. Sheep contend with the cattle for pride of place.

You get a good idea of the golf at Dunaverty simply by reading the local rules on the scorecard: "SUNKEN LIES. A ball lying in a rabbit scrape, rabbit hole, sheep path, hoofmark, or cart road [the reference is not to a golf cart] may be dropped without penalty. . . . When a ball lies in or touching DUNG, or if dung interferes with a player's stroke or stance, the ball may be lifted and dropped without penalty. The ball may be cleaned. . . ."

The views, of Dunaverty's Rock and the island of Sanda and the coast of Northern Ireland, are enormously winning. The course has no hole as long as 400 yards, but several holes are testing, including the 240-yard 6th, a stout par 3, and the 387-yard 17th, where the green is fronted by a fifty-foot-wide stream. The club's lone greenkeeper mows the greens twice a week and the fairways about ten times a year. It is a beguiling primitive, this links, and there's a chance you would get a kick out of it.

Opposite: Machrihanish, 8th.
Below: 6th.

The lower end of the Kintyre Peninsula, for all its natural beauty, is not full of important sightseeing opportunities. The village of Machrihanish is little other than the golf club, though there is good windsurfing near the RAF base at the end of the long beach. In nearby Campbeltown, which has a population of about seven thousand, the waterfront is a pleasant place to walk. Facing the harbor is the fifteenth-century Campbeltown Cross, with its elaborate ornamentation. In the bay lies Davaar Island, where a cave painting of the Crucifixion, which was completed in 1877, can be seen. Back in town are the Campbeltown Museum, with its geological and archaeological exhibits, and the Campbeltown Cemetery, of necessity somewhat less lively but still intriguing, situated as it is at the end of a row of grand houses (once occupied by merchants and ship owners now buried next door) and rising up the terraces of a steep overhanging bank.

A hilly, winding, and scenic coastal road runs from Campbeltown to Southend. Beyond Keil Point, a minor road across the Mull of Kintyre leads to Mull Lighthouse, built in 1788. As from Dunaverty, the views across the sea—this is the meeting place of the Atlantic Ocean, the Firth of Clyde, and the Irish Sea—to Northern Ireland are enthralling.

I'll suggest a few places to stay in Kintyre:

- Overlooking the golf links and Machrihanish Bay is **Ardell House**, a B&B with eleven bedrooms, eight in the sturdy Victorian stone dwelling, three in the converted stables. Those in the house itself are more spacious and have the views.
- In the center of Campbeltown is the **White Hart Hotel**, more than 150 years old. The rooms are decently appointed, and the cooking on our most recent visit was exceptional, particularly the seafood dishes and most particularly mussels in a cream sauce. A sign near the reception desk is worth quoting: THE GROUND FLOOR OF THE HOTEL IS A MAZE OF EATING AREAS. PLEASE FEEL FREE TO WALK AROUND AND VIEW AT YOUR LEISURE BEFORE CHOOSING A TABLE.
- Five or six miles north of Campbeltown lies the hamlet of Saddell, its ruins of a Cistercian abbey dating to the twelfth century. But, for us, it is not the abbey ruins that are the lure; **Shore Cottage** is. This Landmark Trust property is one of more than one hundred eighty structures of historic interest or architectural importance to which the Trust has given new life and a future by restoring them and making them available to vacationers. Almost all are in the United Kingdom, though there are a few outlanders, in Rome, Venice, Florence, and even four in Vermont, one a house where Rudyard Kipling lived for a time.

From left: the Kintyre Peninsula; Shore Cottage (top) and the White Hart Hotel; the shoreline.

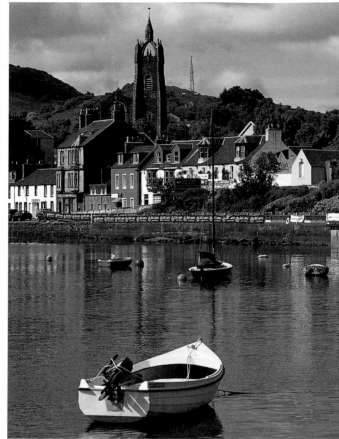

A number of years ago, Harriet and I occupied Shore Cottage on two occasions. It was built in 1870 and sleeps six. In Saddell, we drive briefly along an embowered lane, past Saddell Castle (it dates to 1508 and sleeps eight; in a cove perhaps a quarter of a mile farther on is Cul na Shee, a pine-paneled bungalow that sleeps four), and proceed through a low stone archway in a garden wall. Directly ahead, no more than 150 yards away and at the water's edge, sits Shore Cottage. Thanks to the surrounding trees and rocks, the whitewashed house, with its slate roof, has a sheltered look, this despite its situation on a spit of land where Saddell Bay meets Kilbrannon Sound. The Isle of Arran lies just six miles away across the water.

It is not easy to imagine a finer day than the morning and afternoon rounds at Machrihanish, followed by a home-cooked meal with a good bottle of wine in front of the fireplace at Shore Cottage. On one of our stays here we were joined by our second son, John, then twenty-three and working in Belfast to bring a little cheer into the lives of the ghetto children there, Protestants and Catholics. At our urging, he related some of his experiences. The contrast between serene Kintyre and deadly Belfast was stark. After he went off to bed and the glow of the last embers had died away, I pulled Alisdair Kilmichael's *Kintyre* from the bookshelf and read for a while. Then I put the book down and went outside. A few steps took me to the water's edge, beside the rivulets and the rock pools. There was no breeze, no moon, and only a scattering of stars. I looked across to Arran, its pastures sloping down to the sound. There was no sign of life, but I could make out the ghostly silhouette of its peaks. Or was I imagining them? I went back inside. Machrihanish and Shore Cottage: No combination in this book of a place to play and a place to stay could hope to surpass them.

Above: The town of Tarbert in night and day. Left: fields near Campbeltown.

SHISKINE

I f you are heading for the Isle of Arran from Ayrshire (Troon, Prestwick, Irvine, and the like), you will take the ferry from Ardrossan over to Brodick, a fifty-five-minute crossing. Arran is sometimes referred to as "Scotland in miniature," with its mountains, heather-clad glens, rolling farmland, sea cliffs, and rock-ribbed beaches.

The delightful old 12-hole Shiskine links is the best—actually, the best and only—12-hole layout I've ever played. And of the seven courses on the island, only Shiskine is a links. The club was founded in 1896, and St. Andrews–born Willie Fernie (1883 Open champion, architect of the original Ailsa and Arran at Turnberry) was brought in to design nine holes. In 1910 and 1912 a total of nine more holes were laid out by Willie Park Sr., but six of them, wearyingly high on Drumadoon Hill, fell into disrepair during the Great War and were abandoned. Thus the 12-hole course.

The Shiskine Golf & Tennis Club today, located at Blackwaterfoot, is a reflection of the two Fionas. Fiona Crawford is the club manager; Fiona Brown runs the golf shop, collecting green fees and telling you when to hit away. The manager's office is up at the clubhouse, opposite the 18th green. Fiona Crawford is a gracious and kindly woman and an avid golfer. She will be most pleased to make your acquaintance and, if she has the time, to take a cup of tea with you in the clubhouse tearoom (the club has no liquor license), calling up the early years of Shiskine and spelling out the makeup of its membership today. She may tell you that there used to be three tennis courts, but that some fifteen years ago one of them was converted into a bowling green. (I'm a little surprised that this move did not call for a change in the club name: Shiskine Golf & Tennis & Lawn Bowling Club.)

The irrepressible Fiona Brown, in her simple quarters beside the 1st tee, will accept your modest green fee and, beyond congeniality and hospitality, exude nothing short of delight about the pleasure in store for you. She will put in your hands a hole-by-hole commentary, which she wrote, and then review it with you. A typical entry: "8th. Hades. Don't let the name put you off! . . . you can see the green from the tee. (Just pretend that the big hollow is not there)!!"

ON THE COURSE

The course, on its broad seaside shelf, measures 2,996 yards from the tips; par is 42. There are seven one-shotters, ranging from 128 to 243 yards; four two-shotters, ranging from 249 to 391 yards; and one long hole, the 506-yard 9th. Clearly, power is not the point. With the ball on this firm and rolling—and sometimes hilly—terrain often seeming to have a mind of its own, control is everything. There are boundaries and burns and blind shots (by the time we put behind us The Machrie and Machrihanish and Shiskine, we will surely have the blind staggers) but no crisscross holes. The seascapes are stunning and Kintyre itself is often in view across Kilbrannon Sound. And if your instinct is to think that the game here is not

Opposite: Shiskine, 4th.
Above: 2nd and 3rd.

to be taken all that seriously, you are doubtless right. Still, it is just possible that there are three great holes: the 243-yard 5th, a one-shotter along and above the sea from a giddily high perch to an ill-defined green on somewhat lower ground; the 275-yard 6th, a par 4 with the sea slamming into the rocks beside the tee, the blind drive gently downhill and the second shot seeking the hollow where the green is hidden; and the blind 209-yard 11th, improbably up and down from tee to concealed punch bowl green, a case of having to trust your swing and your luck.

I should mention the winds, anything from the sweet caress of a zephyr to the savage battering of a gale. The last time I played Shiskine—and while I was still out on the course—the greenkeeper stopped at Fiona Brown's shop to advise her that some madman (me) had driven from the pinnacle tee on the 5th with the anemometer at the equipment shed registering 72 miles per hour. In relaying this news to me, Fiona laughingly added, "I could only hope you wouldn't find yourself back on the mainland sooner than you'd planned."

Opposite: Shiskine, 6th.
Below: 11th.

We've not stayed in Blackwaterfoot, where Shiskine is situated, but we've looked at two places there, both attractive:

- The **Kinloch Hotel**, within paces of the sea, is a nicely decorated modern hotel with plenty of leisure facilities: heated indoor swimming pool, sauna, solarium, squash, and snooker.
- The **Greannan**, on the other hand, is a five-room B&B in an elevated position that affords panoramic views over the village to the Mull of Kintyre. All rooms have private bath and color TV.

The finest hotel on Arran is 17th-century **Kilmichael Country House**, just outside the port of Brodick and a very beautiful twenty-five-minute drive from Blackwaterfoot. The oldest house on the island, it is the only Arran hotel to merit five stars ("world class, exceptional") from the Scottish Tourist Board. Each of the seven accommodations is luxurious and tastefully appointed. Fresh flowers and fruit welcome you on arrival. We occupied the Garden Suite, whose bright yellow sitting room overlooks the garden (giant sequoias here courtesy of California). And the island's premier hotel is its premier restaurant as well. Coffee and petits fours are served in the antiques-filled drawing room with its log fire and baby grand piano.

Roughly twenty miles long and ten miles wide, Arran is mainly moor and mountains. The best way to experience it is simply to get in the car and roam. It is boundlessly scenic. Worth seeking out are Brodick Castle, which dates in part from the thirteenth century and contains much in the way of fine furniture, silver, and paintings. Goatfell, at 2,866 feet Arran's highest peak; Corris, a sweet seaside village; Glenashdale Falls, a series of cascades in a rocky gorge (swimming is paradise), about three miles from Whiting Bay; and the plain village of Shiskine, which claims to be the burial place of St. Malaise. Pious legend has it that despite deliberately contracting thirty diseases in order to make amends for his sins, the good man managed to live to the age of 120.

Above: the view of Holy Island, from Lamlash. Right: Brodick Castle. Opposite: the Mauchrie Stones, on Arran.

WESTERN GAILES

Of approximately 170 genuine links courses in the world (seaside, sea level, undulating terrain, sand-based turf), 14 of them are to be found an hour south of Glasgow along the Firth of Clyde, on a twelve-mile stretch of Ayrshire coastline between the city of Irvine and the town of Prestwick. Two of the 14, Prestwick and Royal Troon, are world renowned, and they tend to overshadow most of the nearby courses. Most, but not all. Western Gailes is the exception.

The club was founded in 1897 by four Glasgwegians who had been playing parkland golf in the city. To attract golfers who, like themselves, were already members of other clubs, they set the annual dues at ten shillings and sixpence and, for those who took the long view of things, lifetime dues for just one payment of five pounds.

The new club leased a long, narrow strip of linksland between the Glasgow and Southwestern Railway line and the Firth of Clyde. The club tells us in its "Strokesaver" booklet that it was the first greenkeeper who laid out the course.

ON THE COURSE

For the habitual slicer, it is entirely possible to bend northbound drives onto the railway tracks and southbound drives onto the beach. And for all of us tackling this great and classic links, there are dunes and heather and gorse and long, spiky marram grass. The overall elevation change can hardly be twelve feet; the walk itself is an easy one. There are raised tees, and greens in dune-framed dells and on plateaus exposed to the wind. Burns give pause, as do bunkers—one hundred of them, steep-faced revetted pots where, in most instances, a stroke is lost. The course can be stretched to more than 6,700 yards; the regular markers come to a bit under 6,200. Don't be put off by the shortness of Western Gailes—this test is very real.

Three of the first four holes are short par 4s, all with quite enough going on in the lively green complexes, but perhaps still offering the opportunity for a birdie. The 2nd, 412 yards, offers no such opportunity. It curves left, and the long second shot presents an appreciable drop to a blind punch bowl green. This is a tough-as-nails beauty, and we dearly love it.

Now we walk over to the shoreline and do an about-face. If the wind is out of the southwest—and that is the prevailing wind—we play the next nine holes dead into it. Like the first four holes, these nine are routed over what can fairly be called perfect linksland for golf: undulating, full of hillocks and hummocks and hollows, rising here, tumbling there, the greens strikingly sited, the fairways uncomfortably narrow at times but always neatly defined by the low dunes and the wild grasses

Opposite: Western Gailes, 7th. Above: 6th.

and the heather. Superb—and superbly natural—holes pop up again and again: the short par-5 6th, doglegging right, its second shot fired through a broad "cartgate" in the dunes, the fairway dipping at the last to a green in a hollow; the 7th, 145 yards from a pulpit tee to a green in a dune-framed amphitheater; the 8th and 10th, a pair of shortish two-shotters, each defended by a burn across the face of the green; and the 11th, 415 yards, curving smoothly right to an exposed plateau green. The 13th, a short par 3 down at the end of the property, its green ringed by seven bunkers, marks the end of what is probably the longest straight run along the strand in Scottish golf.

Another 180-degree turnabout and it's time to head for home, inside, along the railway, on the 525-yard 14th, 562 from the medal tees. One of the chosen in *The 500 World's Greatest Golf Holes*, it often plays downwind, tempting big hitters to open their shoulders in order to get

home in two, but ten bunkers spread over the final third of the hole encourage prudence. The short and level 15th is also stoutly defended by sand, and the 16th, 364 yards, is crossed by a burn about 30 yards short of the green to swallow a flubbed second shot. Seventeen, 404 yards (443 from the medal tees) is the course's final feature hole, and what a memorable one it is! A long diagonal ridge, six or seven feet high, dominates the driving area. If we can place our tee shot on top of it, we have a clear view of the flag on a green tucked away among hillocks and hollows. On the other hand, forced to play from the base of the ridge, we not only have a blind shot to contend with but we must get our fairway metal or long iron up very quickly. This is an original golf hole and a great one.

Over the years, Western Gailes has hosted the Scottish Amateur, the Scottish PGA, the British Seniors, and both the British and Scottish Boys' Championships. It was also the venue in 1972 for the Curtis Cup

Below, left: Western Gailes, 9th; right: 10th. Opposite: 17th.

Match, which the U.S. team, led by Hollis Stacy (who would go on to win three U.S. Women's Opens) and Laura Baugh, won in a squeaker, 10–8.

The graceful clubhouse, white and with a red tile roof, has exactly the interior we would expect: old paneling (the lockers have a wonderful antique patina), old leather, old pictures, old silver. And the view from the clubhouse is the same captivating panorama one enjoys from the elevated tees at 6, 7, and 9: across the Clyde to the hills of Arran and to the bold outline of Ailsa Craig. The course was ranked thirty-eighth by the UK's *Golf World* in its most recent list of the top one hundred courses in the British Isles. The late Sam McKinlay, long Scotland's most astute commentator on the game, coined a simple encomium for this superlative, links. It is, he said, "full of golfing goodness."

NEARBY COURSES

Glasgow Golf Club's Gailes Links, on the other side of the railway line, is a basically level and straightforward course with views of the Arran hills but no sight of the sea. Visitors are likely to play it at 6,300 yards; par is 71. Five par 4s, ranging from 409 to 425 yards, call for hitting. Gorse and bunkers, all of them revetted, must be avoided; even more so the vast acreage of fierce calluna heather. Among the best holes are the 530-yard 5th, with its shrinking fairway and its green in a dell just over a rise; and the 18th, 409 yards, sand at the four corners of the green but open across the front. In recent years this worthy test has been the venue for the Scottish PGA Match Play and the Scottish Amateur.

The **Barassie Links of Kilmarnock Golf Club**, also next door to Western Gailes, has plenty of gentle ups and downs. This links measures just under 6,500 yards from the regular markers; par is 72. The beautifully contoured greens look quite natural. Gorse, heather, revetted bunkers, low dunes, old stone walls, and stands of pine all lend character. So do burns, which threaten to snare the mis-hit on half a dozen holes. Memorable is the double-dogleg 8th, 519 yards, dunes and gorse corseting the sinuous route as we get closer to the green.

Nearly 120 years old, the **Irvine Golf Club**, **Bogside**, is packed with sport and spine from the tough rollercoaster opening hole (418 yards, blind second shot) to the delightful finishing hole (337 yards, stiff forced carry from the tee over two of the deepest boarded bunkers we're likely to encounter outside of Royal West Norfolk). And in between are sixteen diverse holes, not one of them dull.

The course measures 6,408 yards (par 71) or 5,687 yards (par 72). The collection of par 4s is sterling. The 289-yard 4th, for instance, is a quirky little gem: a mildly elevated tee, a narrowing fairway with gorse tight on the right, a railway embankment (OB on the tracks) even tighter on the left, a stone wall so close to the left edge of the green that it could impede your takeaway when putting, and a stream at the foot of a sharp falloff behind the green. The 465-yard 11th, on the other hand, is textbook: gently rising and curving smoothly left, four pits in the crook of the dogleg to catch the pulled and underhit drive, sand right and left at the green to menace what is a very long second shot. This links owes much of its distinction to the design work in 1926 of none other than James Braid.

Opposite: Western Gailes, 18th. Above: Barassie Links of Kilmarnock Golf Club.

ROYAL TROON

Like Western Gailes, Royal Troon, with its championship course and its Portland eighteen, occupies linksland between the railway line and the Firth of Clyde. All the holes along the sea belong to the championship layout. The club was founded in 1878, and Prestwick's Charles Hunter laid out the first golf holes, just five of them. It was Willie Fernie, in 1900, who lengthened the course to eighteen.

Royal Troon has hosted the British Amateur and the British Ladies' Championships five times each, and it has served as the venue for the Open Championship eight times. England's Arthur Havers won the first Open at Troon, in 1923, edging defending champion Walter Hagen by a stroke. Hagen seized this occasion to dramatize his distaste for the treatment too often accorded golf professionals, particularly Americans, by British private clubs. He recounted the moment in his autobiography, *The Walter Hagen Story*:

> *After my bunker shot missed and Arthur Havers became the new British Open champion, the secretary . . . insisted that I come into the clubhouse with Havers for the presentation of the trophy. . . . At the doorway I stopped and turned to the enthusiastic gallery.*
>
> *"I'm sorry I didn't win," I told them. "I've been asked to come to the clubhouse with Arthur Havers for the presentation. . . . But at no time have we Americans been admitted to the clubhouse, not even to pick up our mail. At this particular time I'd like to thank you all for the many courtesies you've extended to us. And . . . I'd like to invite all of you to come over to the pub where we've been so welcome, so that all the boys can meet you and thank you personally. If the Committee likes, they can present the trophy to the new champion over there."*
>
> *I turned and walked away with . . . the gallery following me to the pub, leaving only the Committee and Arthur Havers at the clubhouse.*

In 1950 South African Bobby Locke won the second of his four Opens with a final-round 68 here for a 279 total, the first time 280 was broken in the championship. In 1962 Arnold Palmer captured the claret jug for the second straight year—he had won at Royal Birkdale in 1961—with a record-setting aggregate of 12-under-par 276 (71-69-67-69) that left second-place finisher Kel Nagle 6 strokes back. Only six rounds under 70 were shot in the entire championship, and three of them were by Palmer.

Eleven years later, Tom Weiskopf, on record for disliking the course, tied Palmer's 276 and finished 3 strokes to the good on Johnny Miller and Neil Coles for what would be his only victory in a major. In 1982 Tom Watson's 284 total gave him the fourth of his five Open Championships as twenty-five-year-old Nick Price, up by 3 shots with six holes to play, stumbled to a pair of bogeys and a double bogey. And in 1989 Mark Calcavecchia beat Greg Norman and Wayne Grady in the Championship's first four-hole playoff by completing the four extra holes 2 under par. In the final round of the 1997 Open, Justin Leonard uncorked a glittering 65 to wipe out Jesper Parnevik's 5-stroke lead and win by 3 with 272 (69-66-72-65). And in 2004 an American won here for the sixth consecutive time as Todd Hamilton, a thirty-eight-year-old PGA Tour rookie, edged Ernie Els in a four-hole playoff by a stroke after they had tied at ten-under-par 274.

ON THE COURSE

Troon is as classic an example of links golf as is to be found: an out-and-in design with rumpled fairways, grass-covered sand hills, punishing rough, gorse, and remorseless revetted bunkering. Just under 7,200 yards for the 2004 Open, the course is likely to be set up at just over 6,200 yards for visitor play; par is 71. The prevailing wind, which can be counted on about 75 percent of the time, helps going out and hurts coming in. This is another way of saying that we need to get our figures on the first nine, because the second nine is downright hostile.

Having tried to provide a general picture of this links in the preceding two paragraphs, I have little choice now but to spell out a basic aspect of

Opposite: Royal Troon, 11th.

it that will come as an unpleasant surprise for many: Troon is too frequently dull. The first six holes, more or less level, march straight out. The last six holes, also more or less level, march straight in. Despite the necessary differences in length (the 6th, chosen as one of the 500 *Worlds Greatest*, measures 601 yards from the tips), the holes are too much of a piece. There is a sameness about them that borders on monotony. Understand, they are challenging, rigorously so more often than not. But exhilaration is hard to come by.

As for the "middle six," ah, they are another matter altogether. Here we find originality, character, drama. In a couple of instances, they are unnerving simply to look at. But even more to the point they are a delight to play.

At the 355-yard 7th, after six holes paralleling the shore, we turn our back to the sea and, from a raised tee, drive inland. Pot bunkers and a sand hill in the elbow of the gentle right-hand dogleg dare us to cut the corner. Then our second shot must carry a dune and a deep dip to gain the elevated, sand-defended green.

The 8th, called Postage Stamp, measures 123 yards from the back (113 from the regular markers) and is the shortest hole on any Open course. It is honored in *The 500 World's Greatest Golf Holes* as one of the top one hundred. Isolated in the dunes, it has a sharply plateaued, mesa-like green. Birdies are common, but so are double bogeys. The extremely narrow putting surface, about 11 paces wide at the middle, is guarded by five cavernous pits, one at the front, two at each side. The wind may require us to play any club from a 5-metal to a sand wedge. When he triumphed in 1962, Palmer had to go with a 5-iron in one round. In 1997, after just making the cut, Tiger shot 64 in the third round to climb back into the competition. On Sunday, birdies at the 4th and 5th further brightened his chances, but a triple-bogey 6 on the Postage Stamp sent him reeling to 74 and a tie for twenty-fourth. On the other hand, at the age of seventy-one Gene Sarazen came back to Troon for the 1973 Open, fifty years after his initial appearance in the championship, which was also at Troon, and in the opening round notched a hole-in-one here. But my favorite 8th-hole tale is the one about the woman who hit her driver into the bunker short of the green. Even as it plunked into the pit, she wrathfully denounced her caddie: "You underclubbed me!"

Both 9 and 10 measure about 370 yards from the daily markers. Two bunkers threaten the drive on the 9th. Because of high sand hills, only a patch of the 10th fairway is visible from the tee and the shot to the

Opposite: Royal Troon, 8th.

green is blind. There is no greenside sand on either of these sporty and inviting holes, but low dunes flank the putting surface at 9, and gaining the 10th green, with its embankment of gorse on the left and steep falloffs on the right, is a demanding task. In the third round of his Open, Weiskopf was relieved to escape the 9th with no worse than a double bogey after hooking his drive nearly 100 yards off line into a stand of gorse and choosing to drop the ball 125 yards behind the spot where he found it. Later, claret jug safely in his clutches, he laughingly called this strategic decision "one of the longest drops in history."

Play the 11th at 357 yards (regular markers) and you may wonder what all the hullabaloo is about—after all, the 11th is one of the top hundred among "the world's 500," where it is also singled out as one of the 18 most difficult holes and one of the 18 most penal holes. But from the medal tees (421 yards), both danger and drama rear their heads, and from the championship markers (490 yards), well, it can be said that there it takes courage even to place your ball on a wooden peg, not to mention taking a swing at it.

This hole is a story of railway and gorse. The railway runs ominously close along the right for the length of the hole, warning that a slice means a 2-stroke penalty. Our drive, from a small tee up the hillside, involves a fierce forced carry of at least 185 yards over a sea of strangling grasses, heather, and gorse to an angled fairway about 30 yards wide, where gorse awaits both left and right to wreck our card. The drive is blind and claustrophobic. We incline to aim left, away from the cruel combination of railway and gorse. And we incline to steer the tee shot, ideally with a view to a soft fade. The fade may not materialize. So if, in fact, the ball hangs left when it should slide right, it now vanishes, horrifyingly, into what may well be the densest thicket—no, jungle—of shoulder-high gorse in the game.

As for the long second shot, the need to slot it between gorse and railway continues, only now the railway's encroachment is even more pressing, for the green nestles in the very shadow of the low stone wall that separates it from the tracks.

When Palmer won here in 1962, the 11th was a par 5. It is the same length today, 490 yards, but now it is a par 4 in the Open. In the course of the 1962 championship, Palmer posted one eagle, two birdies, and a par here. Nevertheless, he called the 11th "the most dangerous hole I have ever seen." Jack Nicklaus probably agreed. He flew into Troon on the wings of his victory at Oakmont in the U.S. Open, where he had defeated

Opposite: Royal Troon, 12th.

Palmer in a playoff. In the first round Nicklaus took a 10 on the 11th. He finished 29 strokes behind the "champion golfer of the year."

The last of Troon's marvelous "middle six" is the 380-yard 12th. There is the merest suggestion of bending right. The fairway pitches and heaves characteristically. A sand-hills ridge renders the drive blind. Every foot of the way is menaced on both sides by throttling rough. The slightly raised green is defended by a bunker tight on the right and a sharp little falloff at the left, where another bunker lurks. It is a superb hole.

Now we head home, essentially on the straight and level and, sad to say, too often on the prosaic. The holes—there are two one-shotters, one par 5, and three par 4s—are testing enough, particularly into the prevailing wind. Sand threatens almost every stroke. A burn crosses the fairway on the par-5 16th, but it should be of no consequence. There is little of an arresting or inspiring nature.

Colin Montgomerie, whose father was club secretary from 1987 to 1997, knows the course better than any other top player. "Royal Troon," he has said, "is more difficult than good." It is a carefully phrased—and pointed—assessment. Troon is solid stuff, offering all the basic ingredients of championship links golf. It is honest, straightforward, stalwart. Over more than eighty years, it has hosted eight Open Championships, so you will certainly want to tackle it. But if you do so in the knowledge that it is not full of flair and fascination, you will probably get more pleasure out of your round.

The club's second eighteen, called Troon Portland, measures 6,274 yards against a par of 70. Laid out by Willie Fernie in 1906, it has not been greatly altered. It offers the challenge of traditional links golf, especially when it comes to the importance of the game along the ground. And the inbound nine has the attractive diversity of three par 3s, par 4s, and par 5s.

Ayrshire is chock-a-block with rewarding places to stay, and Troon is particularly rich:

- **Lochgreen House**, set amid thirty acres of woodlands and gardens, has public spaces with paneling, period paintings, fine furniture, and log fires. Its guest rooms are individually and stylishly appointed (lovely floral chintzes, king-size canopy beds, rugs in the Aubusson manner), and the table d'hôte dinner is superb.
- Overlooking the 18th hole of the championship course and providing marvelous views across the Clyde to Arran and Ailsa Craig, the **Marine** is a golf hotel in the Scottish baronial style. Renovations and redecoration in 2003 and 2004 have upgraded the hotel's appearance and comforts (families particularly appreciate the leisure center with indoor pool), and the menu in the **Fairways Restaurant** is extensive.
- Just across the road from Royal Troon's clubhouse is **Piersland House Hotel**, built in 1899 for the grandson of Johnnie Walker (of Scotch whiskey fame). The original features remain, including oak paneling, stone fireplaces, carved millwork, and a Jacobean

embroidery frieze worked by the tapestriere to King George V. The exquisitely landscaped grounds contain a Japanese water garden, and the guest rooms, decorated in period styles with muted colorings, retain their Edwardian charm. **The Redbowl Restaurant**'s cuisine is imaginative.

If by some chance you're looking for a Troon pub where golf is king, drop into the **Anchorage Hotel**. When it comes to talking the game, customers compete with bartenders—no amateurs here.

At the Scottish Maritime Museum, in Irvine, the history of seafaring and boat building in Scotland can be explored. Also to be seen here are historic vessels, including the oldest clipper ship in the world, a shipyard worker's tenement home, and a shop where engines were built. In nearby Kilwinning is the Dalgarven Mill, a restored water mill that houses a museum of Ayrshire country life, with costume displays.

PRESTWICK

Next door to Prestwick International Airport lies the Prestwick Golf Club, twenty-seven years older than Royal Troon. It was founded in 1851 by men of means and leisure, many of them landed gentry. More than a century and a half later, there is still a somewhat elitist aura about the great Ayrshire club, although, paradoxically, there is also a notably hospitable attitude toward the unsponsored visitor.

Within weeks of the club's founding, Tom Morris—he was not "Old Tom" then, being all of thirty—was induced to leave St. Andrews and take the post of professional and greenkeeper at the fledgling club. His first assignment was to lay out a twelve-hole course. (The final six holes, also his work, were not added till 1882.)

Here at 12-hole Prestwick, in 1860, was born the Open Championship, the world's first national golf championship and still the most important of all golf competitions. Musselburgh's Willie Park Sr. won the 36-hole event, three rounds of 12 holes, with a 174 total (55-59-60), two strokes better than Tom Morris's.

The championship was played solely at Prestwick through 1872, when St. Andrews and Musselburgh began to take their turns. Prestwick hosted the Open twenty-four times. Among the winners here were, in addition to Park, who also won in 1863 and 1866, Tom Morris Sr. (four times) and Tom Morris Jr. (four times); Willie Park Jr.; Hoylake's celebrated amateur John Ball (eight-time winner of the Amateur Championship); Harry Vardon (three of his six Open victories came at Prestwick); and Jim Barnes, Cornish-born but by 1925, when he won the last Open played at Prestwick, a U.S. citizen. It was the conduct of that championship that spelled the end of the premier event at Prestwick. Carnoustie-born-and-bred Macdonald Smith, the crowd favorite, teed off in the final round with a 5-stroke lead over Barnes. But Smith's thousands of unruly fans (there were no marshals then)—cheering and whooping and rushing about uncontrollably, crowding their hero so that he scarcely had room to take the club back and was rarely in position to see a shot finish—so disturbed him that, as Herbert Warren Wind memorably phrased it in *The Story of American Golf,* "they killed old Mac with their ardor." Smith collapsed to an 82 and a fourth-place finish,

3 strokes behind Barnes, who had closed with a solid 74. It was not long after this tragic debacle that Prestwick was deemed too confined and too short for the Open championship.

ON THE COURSE

Prestwick currently can measure as much as 6,678 yards, but we will play it at 6,544, with a par of 71. The 1st is one of the game's truly lethal opening holes, portentously named Railway. Level, straightaway, and only 346 yards long, it presents a high stone wall running tight along the right side of the fairway from tee to green, the Glasgow–Ayrshire train tracks immediately beyond it. Intruding from the left in the driving area as the fairway narrows sharply is low duneland full of sand, gorse, and heather. The green, with a bunker at the left front, actually extends to within two feet of the wall on the right. There is no breathing space here on the drive or the approach. A fade on either—the wind off the sea encourages just such a miscue—sends our ball over the wall and onto the rails. A pull or hook will not trigger penalty strokes, merely a plunge into penalizing vegetation or sand. This may *not* be a place to trust your swing. At any rate, Railway surfaces in the *500 World's Greatest Golf Holes* book as one of the top hundred and one of the eighteen most penal. You may be amused by the story—very probably apocryphal—of the woman who sliced her tee shot and hit a passing train's engine, the ball then sailing back over the wall and onto the fairway. Leaning out of his cab, the engineer called to the woman, "If it will be of any help to you, I'll be here at the same time tomorrow."

Well, this is only the beginning of a seaside golf experience that offers towering sand hills, fairways that call up a moonscape, dramatically undulating greens, perhaps the world's two most storied blind holes, and a fabled burn, not to mention one of the game's truly astonishing bunkers. There is so much to defy and delight us here that sometimes we have to remind ourselves how studded with superlative golf holes Prestwick is.

Following the dropping 167-yard 2nd comes a par 5 of only 482 yards that was named one of the five hundred greatest holes. The infamous Cardinal Bunker is its centerpiece. It is a tripartite business: first

Opposite: Prestwick, 11th.

some 200 yards off the tee, a pair of good-size pits side by side crossing the fairway, then an island of turf, and finally a vast excavation of sand at least forty yards wide and some ten feet deep, its forward ramparts "paneled" with huge timbers standing on end and stretching from one side of the hole to the other. Harry Vardon called this bunker "an ugly brute that gives a sickening feeling to the man who is off his game." There is no way around this hazard—it must be carried. Into a stiff wind, clearing it on our second shot cannot be taken for granted. In the 1908 Open, Braid took eight on the hole after, as Bernard Darwin described it, "playing a

game of rackets against these ominous black boards," but somehow pulled himself together and went on to win the fourth of his five Open Championships. Blame the Cardinal for the railroad ties that Pete Dye installed in bunkers on some of his courses after he first saw this old-world feature here in 1963.

The Pow Burn edges scarily close to the right side of the Cardinal Bunker (as though that blackguard needed reinforcement!), and it sticks with us even more adhesively for the entire length of the 382-yard 4th, which curves gently right. (Some golf historians point to it as having introduced the principle of the dogleg.) The wind off the sea will send even the mildest fade into the Pow on both drive and approach.

The 5th, called Himalayas, is another of Prestwick's legendary holes. For sheer suspense, there is scarcely anything quite like a blind 206-yarder over a twenty-five-foot-high sand hill smothered in wild grasses. Optimistic—perhaps foolishly so—that our shot will scale the Himalayas and float down somewhere onto the concealed putting surface, we have no choice but to swing away. Six greenside pot bunkers—one at the right front, a second at the left front, and four along the left side—make the obstructing sand hill seem almost incidental.

Five consecutive rolling and sternly demanding par 4s now follow: 362 yards, 430 yards, 431, 444, and 454. Sand imperils every swing. That 454-yarder, the 10th, is another of Prestwick's great holes. It plays

directly toward the sea. Our drive, launched from the Himalayas ridge of sand hills, must first clear the Pow Burn. The rather spacious uphill landing area is defined by pits left and right. The hole continues to climb into the prevailing wind as sand brackets the fairway and we struggle—most of us in vain—to reach in two an elevated green that, appropriately, has no sand, just steep falloffs. This is a hole not simply of character but of majesty.

There is no elevation change on the 11th. This 195-yarder plays over broken ground beside the beach to a green ringed by six deep pots. A well-nigh perfect stroke is called for.

The 12th also parallels the beach, but the 513 yards play along a little valley where we are slightly sheltered from the sea winds by low dunes on the right. Despite the string of bunkers down the left, a birdie is pos-

sible here. Which is more than can be said about the par-4 13th. One lonely pot bunker, hidden in the middle of the fairway about 240 yards from the tee, is all the sand there is. But there is length and to spare here, 460 yards, routed over uneven ground. The small green, angled to the fairway, is marked by convolutions and falloffs that make it unreceptive even to a short pitch or chip, to say nothing of an all-stops-out fairway metal. An inarguably great hole of both style and distinction, the 13th is, for many, the finest hole on the links.

Fourteen, 15, and 16 are all short or shortish two-shotters, but none of them is a snap. The 15th (falloffs, low dunes, sand right and left) and

16 (this 288-yarder can be driven by the prodigious hitter willing to run the very real risk of finishing in the Cardinal Bunker) create equal opportunity for birdies and double bogeys.

The 17th may be Prestwick's most unforgettable hole. Going back many decades, world-class players who conquered it, even in merely companionable games, pointed proudly to their achievement. In 1912 Philadelphia's Johnny McDermott, the first American-born-and-bred U.S. Open champion and at that time the holder of the crown, made his initial visit to Britain. In a letter home to fellow Philadelphian A. J. Tillinghast, McDermott boasted of having birdied the "Alps."

down. Our astonished gaze encompasses a vast and cavernous sandpit, with the green on the far side of it. This first view from the pinnacle of the Alps down to the depths of the Sahara Bunker—how would any club dare employ the names of two famous topographical features on one hole?—is one of golf's indelible moments.

The 18th is anticlimactic, a 284-yard par 4 where we aim on the clubhouse clock and strive to stay clear of the sand that awaits right and left 215 yards out as well as greenside. The chance of making a birdie here is obviously a good one. But the green is 141 feet deep, and the indifferent little pitch that meanders away can result in a three-putt bogey.

Little changed over more than a century, Prestwick may indeed be old-fashioned, a "museum," a monument to the era of the gutta percha ball. But say what you will, on this marvelously natural golfing terrain, the game is still vital. In truth, you have not played golf in Scotland unless you have played this great and inimitable course.

NEARBY COURSES

No distance down the road is the **Prestwick St. Nicholas Golf Club**, only four months younger than what some have taken to calling Old Prestwick and counting among its twenty-eight founding members none other than Tom Morris himself. It was an artisan club (caddies were members here from the outset), and the links, laid out between the railway and the sea by Charles Hunter, is the authentic undulating and sand-based stuff, just under 6,000 yards, par 69. Fairways that incline to be narrow and framed by gorse and heather add up to a stern test of driving. Bunkers are not easily avoided. This is a sporty layout that plays firm and fast and offers unimpeded views over the Clyde to Arran and Ailsa Craig.

Some seven or eight miles south, in Ayr, lies **Belleisle**, a very beautiful parkland course laid out by Braid in 1927 and widely viewed as one of Britain's finest inland public courses. Somewhat sheltered, it can be an attractive alternative to windswept links. It is long on the card (6,540 yards, par 70) and long underfoot (relatively little run on the ball). Only two of the par 4s are less than 400 yards. The remaining nine two-shotters are not only more than 400 yards, but, in most instances, much more. And the four par 3s are challenging, particularly the long uphill 3rd and the tricky 17th, played across a burn. Belleisle is all the golf most of us can handle.

This 391-yarder is blind. The green is not in sight on either the drive or on the second shot. There is a big forced carry from the tee over rough ground to a liberal fairway flanked by sand hills. A steep mound about 220 yards out gives way to another level stretch. And then the fun begins. The fairway now climbs abruptly and, along the way, shrinks scandalously, becoming little more than 25 feet wide as it crests this immense sand hill. All we can be sure of is that the green is somewhere on the far side. To have any chance of successfully executing this blind second shot, we must climb the hill and, gaining its peak, look down, straight

Belleisle, 3rd.

Worthy accommodations all but crowd in upon Prestwick Golf Club:

- The **Parkstone Hotel** is on the Esplanade, with wonderful views to Arran. The twenty-two guest rooms in this modern three-star facility are nicely decorated, and the hotel, a member of the Taste of Scotland association, prides itself on its cooking.
- The **Golf View Private Hotel** on Links Road is an intimate four-star guest house with coastal and golf-course views from generous windows; breakfast is the only meal served.
- The **North Beach Hotel**, also on Links Road, has thirteen rooms, many of them with views over the links to the Firth of Clyde. The cooking has a reputation for consistent quality.

A number of sightseeing attractions are distinclty worthwhile. Ayrshire is the land of Robert Burns, Scotland's national poet ("O my Love's like a red, red rose, / That's newly sprung in June: / O my Love's like the melodie, / That's sweetly play'd in tune."). Among the most important sites on the Burns Heritage Trail are the thatched-roof cottage in Alloway where the poet was born in 1759 and which contains the foremost collection of Burns manuscripts and memorabilia; Alloway's Auld Kirk, where he was christened; the Brig o' Doon, scene of Tam o' Shanter's dramatic escape from the hellish witches; the

Burns House Museum, in Mauchline, where Burns lived after his marriage to Jean Armour; Souter Johnnie's Cottage, in Kirkoswald; and the Mount Oliphant, Lochlie, and Mossgiel Farms, where at various times Burns eked out a living.

Shopper alert: Little known to traveling golfers is the Begg of Scotland Mill Shop, in the town of Ayr, which offers a large selection of high-quality ladies' and men's cashmere knitwear at factory prices. The Scots themselves find bargains here.

Clockwise from above: near Mauchline; the Mauchline parish church; beach near Alloway; the Robert Burns birthplace.

TURNBERRY

It could be claimed that the Royal & Ancient club was dilatory in waiting till 1977 to assign the Open to Turnberry's Ailsa Course for the first time. The majestic links had for twenty-five years been conceded to be the best course in the west of Scotland. In any event, the Ailsa finally got its due, however long overdue, and the result was the titanic Watson-Nicklaus mano a mano (they were paired on both the third and fourth day) that produced one of the very greatest Open Championships in history. Watson was twenty-seven, Nicklaus ten years his senior. Remarkably, the two posted the same score in each of the first three rounds, 68-70-65. Watson fired another 65 on the last day. Nicklaus, missing a breaking downhill four-footer on the 71st hole, had to be content with 66. Michael Corcoran's book *Duel in the Sun* is the definitive and enthralling account of this open.

Greg Norman, the only player to equal the par of 280 in a championship cursed by vile weather for the first three days, left the field behind in 1986 to win by 5 strokes. There was no runaway in 1994, as Nick Price birdied 16, eagled the par-5 17th (a fifty-foot downhill curler somehow found its way to the cup!), and parred the home hole to post a 268 total that nipped Jesper Parnevik (bogey on 18) by a stroke.

Some fifty miles south of Glasgow on the A77, Turnberry is the only golf resort on the British Open rota. Of the other eight courses that serve as venues for the championship, two are municipal (St. Andrews and Carnoustie) and six belong to private clubs (Royal Birkdale, Royal Liverpool, Royal Lytham & St. Annes, Royal St. George's, Royal Troon, and the Honourable Company of Edinburgh Golfers, Muirfield).

Golf has been played at Turnberry for a hundred years. Concrete runways to accommodate military aircraft scarred many of the holes on both eighteens (Turnberry long had a relief course called Arran) during the two World Wars. Philip Mackenzie Ross (Royal Guernsey and Club de Campo de Malaga are two of his better-known courses) was hired in 1949 to undertake the restoration, which in the case of the Ailsa might better be thought of as a resuscitation, so near to expiring was it. Using modern earth-moving equipment such as the bulldozer, he rerouted a number of holes on the Ailsa, preserving its natural features and bringing boldly to the fore the range of sand hills skirting the shore. The result was a links with a nobility and challenge it had never possessed.

ON THE AILSA COURSE

The Ailsa measures 6,976 yards from the championship tees (par 70), 6,440 from the regular markers (par 69), and 5,757 from the forward tees. The first three holes (358 yards, 381, 409) are a bit of to-and-fro-ing, with minimal elevation change. There is sand right and left at the green on all three and sand in the driving area on the 1st and 2nd.

The next eight holes are strung out like a necklace, along and above the sea. If there is any other links course where eight consecutive holes are able to produce challenge of this level and pleasure of this depth, I don't know where it might be. For what we are talking about here are golf holes so splendid that they actually measure up to the splendor of the scenery. Consider the setting first, as the Firth of Clyde at long last melds into the Irish Sea, with Arran's mountains looming across the water to the north, the curving outline of the Mull of Kintyre due west, and, popping out of the deep in the foreground to claim our attention, rocky, turtle-backed Ailsa Craig, the plug of an extinct volcano. It is a panorama of surpassing fascination and one made all the richer when the day is crystalline, for then we are able to make out, on a southwesterly heading, even Northern Ireland's Antrim Coast, by the Giant's Causeway.

The parade of great golf holes accompanying this riveting seascape begins with the 165-yard 4th, "Woe-Be-Tide," a witty play on words that stems from the presence of the beach along the left. The shot is played uphill across rough ground to a small and strikingly sited plateau green with a long, steep falloff left and a bunker backed by a sand hill at the right. Any kind of wind is a mischief. This is one of the best medium-length one-shotters you will ever play.

The 415-yard 5th curves left along a dune-framed valley, the tee shot falling, the second shot rising, all of it difficult—greenside bunkers front, left, and right—and all of it beautiful. Another great hole.

Opposite: Turnberry Ailsa Course, 9th.

The 6th is the second of the Ailsa's four superlative short holes. It is 221 yards long, hill to hill, three pits tight on the left, a big bunker out front in a sharp rise, a steep falloff right. The shot is all carry. Into a headwind or a left-to-right crosswind, few ordinary mortals can make it. Unveil your best swing and pray! Greatness yet again.

The great 7th is a cousin of the 5th, only a much longer par 4: 475 yards, turning emphatically left ("roon the ben") through the tall sand hills, down off the tee, up to the green. From the championship markers it is a par 5 of 529 yards. Watson hit driver/driver to reach the green and make 4 in the last round of the 1977 Open.

Eight, 431 yards, runs steadily uphill to a sand-defended green that is one of the highest points on the links. Played with a fairway-metal or a long iron, this is one of the most taxing second shots on the course: It must be perfectly struck—line, power, trajectory—or it will fail. The views over Turnberry Bay from the green are entrancing.

The same can be said of the spectacle that awaits at the 9th, which measures 411 yards from the regular markers, 454 from the tips. I urge you to walk out to the championship tee, unless you are subject to vertigo. The teeing ground is a mere scrap of turf atop a crag that towers above the rocky shore. For all the thrill, it is a lonely spot and so starkly exposed to the wind that there will be days when it will be all we can do to hold our position at the ball. The drive from this perch must carry 200 yards over the abyss, past the landmark white lighthouse and the remains of Robert the Bruce's castle, to reach the haven of the far slope. Glorious indeed, but how fierce! The green, subtly angled to the fairway and sand-free, with humpy shoulders on both sides, inclines to shunt away our long second shot. From tee to cup, a powerful experience. You will not be surprised to find this hole one of the top hundred in *The 500 World's Greatest Golf Holes*.

Now comes one final display of seaside grandeur coupled with drama, on the 429-yard 10th. From the headland heights, the drive floats down to a generous fairway, the sea thrashing at the base of the cliff on our left. The long second shot must traverse a large bunker in the center of the fairway, this hazard containing an island of turf ringed by sand.

This magnificent coastal run, which inevitably summons images of Pebble Beach, concludes with the 161-yard 11th, playing along the cliff top to a mildly raised green, sand right and left. A left-to-right crosswind off the water raises hob with any stroke that is less than solid.

Time to turn inland now and surrender the pleasure of shot-making along the shore but not the rewards of tackling first-rate golf

holes all the way home. Two of the remaining seven are among the world's five-hundred greatest. The green at the 380-yard 16th—the hole is called Wee Burn—is fronted by a deep, precipitously sloping swale with a trickle of water at the bottom. There is no penalty-stroke hazard on the preceding hole, the last of the par 3s, which measures 170 yards from the regular markers, 210 from the championship tees. The cavernous drop at the right into broken ground must be avoided at all costs. It was on this hole that Watson, trailing Nicklaus by a stroke in their epic Sunday-afternoon struggle and electing to use a putter from just off the green and 60 feet from the hole, gave the ball a characteristically crisp rap. Off the hardpan it skipped, over the collar, true to the unattended flagstick, and, miraculously, into the cup.

"Was it," I asked Nicklaus three years later (and two years before Watson holed the little pitch of perhaps half that distance on the 17th at Pebble Beach to steal the 1982 Open from Jack), "the most unexpected shot ever hit against you at a critical moment in a major championship?"

"Well," he replied, "that one was a big surprise. I thought there was a chance I might add to my lead, and suddenly we were even. But I got an awful lot out of my short game that week. I'm not sure I hit the ball all that well. Watson obviously played fantastically, and he played one stroke better than I did."

For me, the Ailsa is one of the three best courses in Scotland. And from the standpoint of pure delight in the game, it may well provide the single most satisfying round in the game's birthplace.

Opposite: Turnberry Ailsa Course, 8th. Above, left: 10th; right: 11th.

ON THE KINTYRE COURSE

The Arran Course was reconstructed in 2001—so sweepingly, in fact, that it was even given a new name: Kintyre. Donald Steel was the man behind this wholesale makeover. There are six new holes; there are twelve new greens; the bunkers, all of them revetted, have been carefully reworked. From the championship tees, the Kintyre measures 6,861 yards. (It was used for final qualifying in the 2004 Open, held at Royal Troon.) It is set up regularly at about 6,370 yards, par 71.

The old holes, down their well-remembered channels of menacing gorse, have been freshened, and the new holes are bona fide sparklers. Two of the newcomers, the 8th and 9th, are routed over Bains Hill. The 8th is mysterious. It plays straight out to sea and measures only 298 yards. The tee is high, but there is no sign of the green. It turns out to be hidden, just over a narrow ridge and down in a cove that seems to merge with the rocky strand beyond. This green can be driven, provided you are willing to take on the two nasty pot bunkers that, like the putting surface they defend, are totally concealed. I can't think of a hole that either looks or plays like the Kintyre's 8th. It is an original, and the degree of golfing fun that it provides is incalculable.

The stimulating tee shot on the 9th, a short par 5 playing from high ground into the prevailing southwesterly, actually crosses the approach to the 8th green as it wings away against Turnberry's two symbols, the lighthouse and Ailsa Craig. The fairway, running parallel to the coast on land that had just been waiting to be pressed into service, is at first well above the water; then it drops, by way of a grassy buffer zone, to the shore.

Make no mistake about it: The Kintyre is a treat. It will be interesting to see whether, like the New Course at St. Andrews, it finds a place in the top hundred courses of the British Isles.

Opposite: Turnberry Kintyre Course, 8th. Below: 9th.

Remarkably, the hotel itself at Turnberry—the long white Edwardian structure stretched out on the crest of a hill, monarch of all it surveys—manages the difficult feat of living up to the superlative golf. It is luxurious yet relaxed, the epitome of Old World graciousness. Public rooms are welcoming, stylish, comfortable, and blessed with those nearly incomparable land-and-sea vistas. Much the same can be said of the guest accommodations, which reflect a thoughtful attention to detail (heated towel racks, terrycloth slippers to match the robes). Rooms on the front, looking out over the links to the sea, are especially bright and spacious, and it is not uncommon to find two crystal chandeliers, one over the beds, the other over the sitting area.

The spa boasts a glass-fronted indoor swimming pool more than 60 feet long that embraces the sea views. There are also steam rooms, sauna, a plunge pool, the latest fitness equipment, twelve treatment rooms, and a staff trained to provide hydrotherapy, aromatherapy, massage, mud wrap, and holistic ministrations.

The hotel's cooking is sublime. Among the dishes served regularly at **1906** are a haddock and saffron risotto with poached egg, fennel cream, and Parmesan; smoked and seared medallions of Scottish beef with mushrooms, creamed spinach, caramelized butter onions, and a malt whiskey jus; and, for dessert, warm apple *vol au vent* with cinnamon cream, honey syrup, and Calvados ice cream. The wine list is carefully chosen, comprehensive, and provocative to peruse (just under a thousand dollars for a bottle of Château d'Yquem, 1983, a very good dessert wine indeed). But as though to prove that the best things in life are free, we find ourselves mesmerized by the magic of a pink-tinted golden sunset suffusing the western sky beyond Ailsa Craig.

For more informal and less expensive dining, the **Tappie Toorie** at the clubhouse presents a selection of lighter dishes, with captivating views of the Ailsa and Kintyre courses.

About a hundred yards from the hotel building itself is the outdoor activity center. Among its offerings are trout fishing in the resort's own loch, clay-target shooting, archery, falconry, off-road driving, mountain biking, and horseback riding (gallop down the beach in the very shadow of those seaside holes on the Ailsa's first nine, where pars are so dearly bought).

What it all adds up to is a transcendent golf resort, a cornucopia of the good life with the game as its soul. Turnberry is without peer at the sea, not simply in Scotland but anywhere in the British Isles.

Virtually next door to Turnberry and high above the sea on tree-clad cliffs is **Culzean Castle**, a magnificent late-eighteenth-century castellated mansion designed by Robert Adam that is now a museum open to the public. General Eisenhower occupied it as his headquarters prior to the Normandy invasion, and the top floor was later presented to him for his lifetime use. This large accommodation has been converted by the National Trust for Scotland into six beautifully appointed guest apartments. We've not stayed here, but friends who have say that it was a unique and thoroughly enjoyable experience.

A few miles east of Culzean Castle, on the A77, is Crossraguel Abbey, whose ruins evoke the life of Cluniac monks here from the thirteenth through sixteenth centuries. More intact and extensive than most such ruins,

Crossraguel includes a turreted gatehouse, a dovecote, and a rectangular chapter house with groined vaulting.

Purely for fun, and nearby, is a section of the road to Danure that is famous for an optical illusion known as the Electric Brae. You would wager your favorite putter that the car you're driving is heading uphill, when in truth it is going downhill.

Top row, from left: Girvan shore; Crossraguel Abbey arch. Bottom row: Culzean Castle views and a gatehouse at Crossraguel.

J ust where is the Lanark Golf Club? In Strathclyde, southeast of Glasgow and a very pretty two-hour drive from Turnberry across meadows and over hills. A good forty miles from the sea, Lanark is a moorland course. It is built on washed glacial sand and gravel, which produce not only terrain that drains quickly but topography full of hummocks and wrinkles and ripples. Fairways in season are firm and fast, encouraging us to play much of the game along the ground. As at Boat of Garten and Edzell, you would swear this is links golf.

Founded in 1851, Lanark is among the twenty-five oldest golf clubs in the world, the same age as Prestwick and Prestwick St. Nicholas. It was in 1851 that Old Tom Morris laid out an eighteen here, charging the club £3.50 for his services. North Berwick's Ben Sayers lengthened and toughened the Morris design fifteen years later. The course we play today, however, is largely the offspring of the ubiquitous Braid and his partner John Stutt, who in 1927 substantively modified the layout, even building new holes at the 13th and 14th.

In 2001, to mark its 150th anniversary, the club published an addendum to the history of its first hundred years. Here are a few of the moments that lightened this new chronicle: In 1953 the club considered removing the sheep from the course, but this would have meant giving up annual income of £85 for grazing rights. . . . Watering the greens in 1953 was a matter of persuading the local fire department to carry out a hose exercise on the golf course. . . . Sunday golf was turned down in 1960, but the vote to permit it carried by a large majority the next year. . . . In 1981 the club bought its first TV set, with the stipulation that "it was only to be used for important occasions." . . . In 1985 there was consternation when the need to renew the club liquor license was overlooked by the secretary, precluding the sale of whiskey for almost a month.

ON THE COURSE

Gently rolling Lanark insists that we keep our wits about us or pay the price exacted by bunkers and burns and boundaries, thick, tussocky rough, spinneys of pines and stands of gorse, and the characterful greens.

The imaginative routing plan sees to it that consecutive holes never run in the same direction, thus introducing again and again the element of surprise into the round, not to mention the constant adjustments needed to combat the wind. And speaking of surprise, there are three pairs of crisscross holes: 1 and 18, 2 and 15, 9 and 10.

Don't expect greatness here, where the back tees add up to a length of 6,428 yards (par 70). There are a couple of humdrum holes and a handful of birdie opportunities. But nine or ten holes are very good, including four strong two-shotters. The 459-yard 2nd calls for both hitting

Opposite: Lanark, 14th.
Above: 4th.

and control as it doglegs nicely right, presents frustrating fairway hummocks early, middle, and late, and serves up a green defended by sand, falloffs, and mounds. The 4th is almost as muscular, 446 yards, a case of down, up, down, and up to an elevated green. The 12th, 357 yards, bends smoothly right (sand tight at the right in the tee-shot landing area) to reveal a beautifully sited narrow plateau green bunkered at the left and with steep falloffs at the front and the right. Our approach shot has to be perfect. On the 388-yard 14th, a rising drive is followed by a shot that must carry a deep hollow just short of another plateau green.

The 18th is a tester and, as it happens, also a charmer. It is that rarity for a finishing hole, a one-shotter, in this instance 207 yards long and downhill ever so slightly. What makes the hole memorable is the location of the stone clubhouse, no more than 20 feet from the right side of the green. Twenty feet is close—seven paces. Still, I was assured that the clubhouse is not struck by a ball as often as twice a year and that never has a window been broken.

You will enjoy a game at Lanark, with its panorama of distant hills, some of them wooded, some of them farmland in shades of beige and green. The linkslike topography so far from the sea is a delight, and the club is most hospitable. Be sure to look at the trophies, particularly the Silver Claret Jug, remarkably similar to the Open Championship claret jug and, dating to 1857, actually fifteen years older.

If you are overnighting in Lanark, a good bet is **Cartland Bridge Country House**, an imposing structure little changed since its days a century ago as the home of a rich Clyde shipbuilder. Though the hotel is not luxurious, public spaces and guest rooms have a stately air about them. Fireplaces, paneling, old gilt-frame oil paintings, and intricate plasterwork all contribute to the feeling of a more tranquil age. Views over the wooded and hilly property are enchanting. As for the cooking, the menu is likely to be limited—such staples as salmon, chicken, and beef, prepared simply—but the ingredients are fresh and the net of it on our stay was satisfying.

Unlike Ayrshire, Strathclyde is not full of tourist attractions, but it does boast the Falls of Clyde, dramatic waterfalls in a long gorge of the Clyde River, and New Lanark. In 1820, with the Industrial Revolution shifting into high gear, factory owner Robert Owen, a visionary humanitarian, recognized the need for safe working conditions complemented by decent housing. So on the Clyde River he built New Lanark, a then pioneering industrial town that provided a school system (including the world's first nursery school) and free health care. New Lanark, with its uniform look, is today a living museum and a UNESCO World Heritage Site. You would find a visit memorable.

Below: in New Lanark.
Right: the Falls of Clyde.

MUIRFIELD AND
THE EAST LOTHIAN COAST

MUSSELBURGH

A level, slightly scruffy, somewhat weedy, and largely feature-less nine-hole course inside a racetrack is not why we cross an ocean. Yet Musselburgh Links, The Old Golf Course (its formal designation), should not be ignored. For this is truly sacred ground: Six Open Championships were contested here, between 1874 and 1889, on holes akin to the ones we play today.

The course is six miles east of Edinburgh, in East Lothian. Mary Queen of Scots is said to have played on the Musselburgh links in 1567. James VI of Scotland (James I of England) is supposed to have played here in 1603. Rather more important, the first golf tournament strictly for women was held at Musselburgh in 1810, when the town's fishwives teed off, the prize being a new creel (a small fish basket) and scull.

By 1875 the nine-hole course was shared among four clubs—Mus-selburgh (later Royal) Golf Club, the Honourable Company of Edinburgh Golfers, Bruntsfield Links Golfing Society, and Edinburgh Burgess (now the Royal Burgess Golfing Society of Edinburgh)—to say nothing of the general public. For roughly half a century, Musselburgh—with its presti-gious clubs, its wealth of outstanding local players (most of them profes-sionals/caddies), its golf equipment makers (the Gourlay family for balls and the McEwan family for clubs), and its role as a six-time venue for the Open Championship—could claim to having eclipsed mighty St. Andrews.

Musselburgh's Mungo Park, Willie Jr.'s brother, won the first Open contested on his home turf, in 1874, with a 36-hole total of 159, two strokes better than Young Tom Morris. Bob Ferguson, also of Musselburgh, won the Open there in 1880. Like most of the leading players of the age, Ferguson was a professional/caddie, so I suppose we should not be sur-prised to find Bernard Darwin writing in 1910, thirty years after Ferguson's first Open victory: "At Musselburgh there is a right line and a wrong line [for shots] and if we are very fortunate, or very highly hon-oured, we may have it pointed out to us and our clubs carried for us by Bob Ferguson, who won the championship three times running. . . ."

It was fitting that the final Open at Musselburgh, in 1889, was won by perhaps the town's most illustrious golfing son, Willie Park Jr. This was his second Open victory, his first having come two years earlier at Prest-wick. An accomplished putter—it was he who said that "the man who can putt is a match for anyone"—Willie Jr. also carved out a reputation in golf course architecture on both sides of the Atlantic. Among his outstanding courses are Sunningdale's Old Course, Formby, and Huntercombe, all in England, and the North Course at suburban Chicago's Olympia Fields, the venue for the 2003 U.S. Open.

ON THE COURSE

Having shamelessly managed to pass by Musselburgh over a period of thirty years, I finally could live with myself no longer. Shortly before ten o'clock on Thursday, July 26, 2001, I presented myself, alone, at the golf house, which contains small and spartan changing rooms and a space for the green-fee-collector/starter to do business. I teamed up with two local ladies, Felicity (short and well into her seventies) and Joan (tall and in her early sixties). They vowed to show me the way, though it would not be easy to go off the prescribed path on this straightforward and very com-pact layout that appears to be routed over less than thirty acres.

The mile-long racetrack has been here since 1816. Today only four shots begin or end outside the white rails. All others take place within the infield. The par-35 course measures 2,808 yards.

It was a pleasure to play with the ladies, who seemed to relish my good shots every bit as much as their own. Joan got the ball airborne with some regularity and probably scored in the low 50s. Felicity's efforts were not so, well, felicitous, and she did not break 60. Still, both enjoyed themselves.

The nine begins with a par 3 named, aptly, the Short Hole. It is 160 yards long and simplicity itself. A matched pair of pot bunkers, one at the right front and one at the left front, make clear the requirements of the shot. Almost all the bunkers are penal: steep-faced and revetted, in the classic links tradition. The rough, often fiercely thick, is also penal.

There are no trees, gorse is scarce, and holes often lack definition. The fairways on this sand-based terrain were weed infested, but we did not play preferred lies. The greens, small to medium and with little

Opposite: Musselburgh, 4th.
Previous spread: North
Berwick East Course, 13th.

some complex contouring has to stay clear of the sand right and left. Strong stuff, indeed, like Mrs. Forman's libations.

If you do make it a point to play The Old Golf Course, consider using a set of hickory-shaft clubs, which you can rent right here.

NEARBY COURSES

While we're within hailing distance of the capital, a light once-over of a handful of Edinburgh courses and two other Musselburgh courses might be in order. **Royal Musselburgh**, designed by Braid in 1924, is a solid, tree-lined layout with five long par 4s. What may be most memorable here is the mansion that is the clubhouse, one of the most impressive in the United Kingdom. Less than fifteen minutes away is the **Musselburgh Golf Club**, at Monktonhall. Another worthy test, the eighteen here is laid out over ground ranging from level to gently rolling. There is plenty of room off the tee, but sand consistently threatens the shots to the green.

Ronnie David Bell Mitchell Shade, a five-time Scottish Amateur champion and a four-time Walker Cupper in the 1960s, grew up at **Duddingston Golf Club**. The uncanny straightness of his shots prompted one journalist to suggest that the initials R.D.B.M. really stood for "Right Down the Bloody Middle." This kind of accuracy is essential at Duddingston, where the bunkering is almost as menacing as the burn, which comes between player and target eleven times in the course of the round.

Unlike Duddingston, **Dalmahoy**, three miles from Edinburgh Airport, is not a golf club; it is a full golf resort with two eighteens and 151 accommodations. The golf on these gently rolling meadowlands courses is good but, by and large, lacking in excitement. The par-68 West Course is only 5,200 yards long. The par-72 East Course, however, laid out by Braid in 1926, is 6,670 yards. There is a good birdie opportunity on the wide-open 505-yard 1st hole and an excellent chance to follow that illusory start with bogeys on the 2nd (435 yards), 3rd (446 yards), 4th (430 yards), and 5th (461 yards).

The upper echelon of Edinburgh private golf clubs consists of the **Royal Burgess Society of Edinburgh** and the **Bruntsfield Links Golfing Society**. Founded in 1735, Royal Burgess may thus claim to be the oldest continuously established golfing society or club in the world; Bruntsfield incorporated in 1761. Both clubs first played their golf on the Bruntsfield Links itself, a common not far from the city center, and then, in the last quarter of the nineteenth century, at Musselburgh. But the explosive popularity of the game forced another move, shortly before the

character, were slow. A sprinkler plagued us at three of the greens, but I had to smile: This was not the kind of problem that Bob Ferguson or Willie Park Jr. ever had to deal with. Nonetheless, the day was sunny and warm, the company was convivial, and the game was golf. I was delighted to be abroad on this storied links.

The 2nd and 3rd holes, a pair of short par 4s, play in front of the grandstand, reminding us that 150 years ago the Honourable Company found a couple of rooms somewhere in the back to serve as a makeshift clubhouse, and also reminding me that when the Thoroughbreds are running and the crowds are cheering, the golfers are sidelined.

The nine has four good holes: 1, 5 (called the Sea Hole, though the Firth of Forth, once quite near the back of the green, has by now retreated more than the length of a football field), 6, and 9. And there is one hole that is terrific, the 424-yard 4th. (It is called Mrs. Forman's, the name of the old whitewashed tavern right behind the green. For decades, a pass-through cut out of a wall in the pub saw to it that the game could proceed apace even while the players savored their pint. Now you have to use the door if you're thirsty.) The hole doglegs right, around the race-track starting gate, and the long second shot to an angled green with

turn of the nineteenth century. With Royal Burgess taking the lead, the clubs each bought ground in Edinburgh's Barnton district, built fine clubhouses, and, for the first time, constructed golf courses. Both clubs radiate an atmosphere of welcome and warmth and well-being. The two eighteens are pretty parkland layouts: rolling, tree-studded, manicured, each with its quota of good holes. Strategically sited trees and an innocent-looking low-cut rough that will snuff a thin hit—it is these elements that give Burgess and Bruntsfield a measure of test. Like the clubs themselves, the two courses can be viewed as gentlemanly.

And then there is **Braid Hills**, specifically Braids No. 1 (the No. 2 Course is too short and too altitudinous to be taken seriously). Hundreds—perhaps thousands—of trees have been planted here in recent years, threatening to spoil this treasure. It is doubtful that the philistines can be forced to retreat, but meanwhile, with their depredations not fully in flower, we continue to play what has long been one of the world's grandest municipal courses, where Tommy Armour and James Braid won club championships; where the length from the back tees is all of 6,172 yards (par 70) and the green fee is not all of £18; where the views of the capital, including the castle on its crag, are of breathtaking grandeur; and where the round inevitably calls up Royal Dornoch and Ballybunion and Royal County Down. There are narrow plateau fairways to be hit—and held; gorse-covered hillsides (à la Dornoch, a golden blaze in May) to be given a wide berth; the occasional rock outcropping; the more than occasional humps and hillocks and hollows and mounds and swales; tees high and cruelly exposed to the winds (after all, this is the "breezy Braids"); greens in wonderfully natural dell-like settings that call for precisely struck irons or, failing that, highly creative chipping; and, it need hardly be said, feature holes aplenty.

I think of the 202-yard 13th, which rises modestly over broken ground to a tightly bunkered green where nothing less than a perfect swing, sometimes with a driver if the wind is at us, will suffice. Be prepared to repeat that perfect driver swing immediately. Reminiscent of the 9th at Royal County Down, the 378-yard 14th calls for a long forced carry from an elevated tee across a gorse-covered hillside to the safety of a blind landing area in the valley below. Accomplish that and you are left with a medium-length iron over another expanse of gorse to the shelter of the green. The great James Braid (this facility, dating to 1889, is not named after him) once characterized Braids No. 1 as "absolutely rich in sporting quality . . . scenery from every point that is romantically beautiful, and air that makes one feel a good few years younger while playing."

Opposite: Braid Hills
No. 1, 16th.

Vibrant and graspable and fascinating Edinburgh is full of things to see and do that need scarcely be noted in this book (with the possible exception of the vast putting green at the heart of the sunken gardens in Princes Street). The city also offers an assortment of outstanding hotels, including:

- The **Balmoral**, luxe in every respect and towering over the Waverly Street train station, in the center of town.
- The **Caledonian Hilton**, also five star, around the corner from the Castle and boasting a bar that is a popular meeting spot and a spa that is a rare amenity.
- **Channings**, quiet and stylish, five period town houses cheek-by-jowl in the West End.
- The **Howard**, a five-minute walk from Princes Street, fifteen generous rooms and three suites, no bar or restaurant.

There is one other accommodation, in truth not all that comfortable and not actually in the city. But it is unique.

Long ago we spent a week no more than twenty minutes' drive from downtown in a fragment of a fifteenth-century castle. It sleeps seven. There was and is no housekeeper, no cook, no help of any kind. Still, it is wonderfully atmospheric, isolated on a wooded and rocky promontory high above the River North Esk. Next door, on even higher ground, is a striking stone church, also dating from the fifteenth century. We rented the castle from the Landmark Trust, proprietor of Kintyre's Shore Cottage. Over the years since, our thoughts have gone back to this extraordinary accommodation, but it was never in the forefront of our minds. Not until some seventeen years later, that is, when we read the novel that all the world seemed to be devouring, *The Da Vinci Code*. Imagine our astonishment at finding this high-speed potboiler ending in Rosslyn Chapel, mere paces from **Rosslyn Castle**, where we had stayed in 1986. Our Christmas card that year had shown the hauntingly beautiful church.

Views of Edinburgh, including the castle from West Princes Street Gardens (above), Rosslyn Castle (bottom), Doune Castle (right), and the Royal Mile buildings (opposite).

NORTH BERWICK

About thirty minutes east on the coast road from Musselburgh lies North Berwick, with its two widely curving bays, its little sheltering harbor, and its two seaside eighteens. The West Links is for me one of the seven or eight best courses in Scotland and one of my very favorites in all the world.

It was in 1850 that the railway first reached North Berwick, from Edinburgh and via Musselburgh. With the trains came vacationers, many of them people of means and prominence, so many that fashionable hotels and handsome villas sprang up right and left in the latter part of that century. Golf was a principal element in the town's appeal, and two individuals were in the forefront of the boom.

A.J. (Arthur James) Balfour, a Member of Parliament whose ancestral home was in nearby Whittinghame, would serve variously as Chief Secretary to Ireland, Home Secretary, and Prime Minister. Balfour seemed at times to live for golf, which he took up at the age of thirty-six. He was captain of North Berwick Golf Club in 1891 and 1892. In his excellent history *Golf: Scotland's Game*, David Hamilton quotes from the prime minister's memoirs:

> *I spent each September at North Berwick, at the Bass Rock Hotel, or in later years at Bradbury's, in rooms which looked down on the seventeenth green and the first tee. . . . I lived a solitary and well-filled life, playing two rounds of golf or more a day, and in the evening carrying on my official work, and such philosophical and literary undertakings as I happened to be engaged on. Each Friday after my morning's round I drove to Whittinghame . . . in a brougham, with a pair of horses, and spent the weekend with my family and guests.*

In 1898 *The Times* noted with a touch of sarcasm Balfour's role in the game that had fairly recently become so popular in England: "Mr. Balfour has insensibly attained to a sort of grandmastership of golf players in this country. . . . A new golf club can hardly be satisfactorily set on foot without his assistance.

The correct thing to do is either to make him President [of the new club] or . . . an honorary member and then induce him to play over the new course, or to make a little speech to the players or better still to do both."

The other man who helped put North Berwick front and center was Mr. Balfour's frequent foursomes (alternate stroke) partner, Bernard "Ben" Sayers. All of five feet three inches tall and 130 pounds, "Wee Ben" made golf clubs and balls, gave lessons, and played in every tournament of consequence (winning 24, in Scotland and England), to say nothing of big-money challenge matches. It is said that he once worked in a circus as an acrobat, and there are accounts of his executing a series of cartwheels and handsprings on the green after holing a 45-foot putt. He also climbed 40 feet off the ground to the roof of Wemyss Castle, club in hand, to fire a recovery shot 150 yards down the fairway.

Sayers was consistently sunny, his cheerful disposition laced with a ready wit. Often partnered in foursomes with Andra Kirkaldy, Ben also faced off against the dour St. Andrean in high visibility "brag matches." In one such contest he wore an unidentifiable contraption over his shoulder and attached to the grip of a pitching club. When asked afterward how much this curio had helped him, he replied, "Not a bit. I just used it to frighten Andra." And when he sent a postcard to Andra from the United States (Sayers was visiting his son George, then the professional at Merion), he addressed it "Andra, Hell Bunker, St. Andrews, Scotland." It did reach Kirkaldy, who at the next Open buttonholed Ben to ask what he meant "by sending a postcard like that." Ben answered, "I lost your address and this was the only one I thocht on."

Nothing contributed more to Wee Ben's celebrity than his role as golf professional to the royal family. He gave lessons, sometimes playing lessons, at Windsor Castle to King Edward VII, King George V, Queen Alexandra, Princess Victoria, and others. He also made a set of clubs for King Edward, whom he had first met at North Berwick. The king asked him on that occasion how Grand Duke Michael of Russia, one of Ben's pupils, was progressing. The ever candid Sayers replied, "I am sorry to inform your majesty that he is one of the keenest and one of the worst."

Opposite: North Berwick West Course, 15th.

ON THE EAST COURSE

North Berwick has continued to thrive chiefly because its courses have steadily attracted golfers from all over the world. The East (or Glen) Links is the lesser of the two. It is strictly holiday golf, but that in no sense detracts from the pleasure—if not the challenge—in playing it. Total yardage is just under 6,100 yards; par is 69. It was Sayers who designed the first nine, in 1894, and it was he and James Braid who collaborated on the second nine in 1906. Following the Second World War, Philip Mackenzie Ross made certain revisions.

Laid out on clifftops high above the sea, the East presents enthralling views. Into the prevailing wind, half a dozen of the par 4s are quite testing. And in any kind of breeze, so are all four of the one-shotters: the 4th (190 yards), 9th (250 yards), 13th (a blind 146-yarder with the green in a hollow a good 100 feet below the tee), and 16th (200 yards).

ON THE WEST COURSE

It is the West Links, however, that has drawn knowledgeable golfers to North Berwick for 150 years. The combination of authentic links golf, inarguably great holes, and ravishing sea views—Bass Rock, the islets of Fidra, the Lamb, and Craigleith, and the coast of Fife—makes the game here a joyous occasion every step of the way.

Though we're inclined to think of this course as having simply evolved over many decades, one individual ought to be given a measure of credit for it. David Strath, a St. Andrean, accepted the greenkeeper job here in 1876. In less than three years, as Geoffrey Cornish and Ronald Whitten relate in *The Architects of Golf,* he formalized the course, extended it from nine to eighteen holes, and so thoroughly revised the 14th (Perfection) and 15th (Redan) that these holes gained worldwide renown. In years to come, first Tom Dunn and then Sir Guy Campbell would make limited revisions, but for well over a hundred years the best holes have been very little changed. Like Prestwick, the West Links is, if you will, a museum of the game, taking us back to the latter half of the nineteenth century.

The course, measuring 6,317 yards against a par of 71, is laid out on undulating linksland that lies 10 to 30 feet above sea level. Dunes, beach, burns, long rough grasses, blind shots, and stone walls are all critical elements. Thanks to the elongated figure-8 design, both the outbound and inbound nines have their share of seaside holes. There is a beguiling unpredictability about the routing plan, but then, the West Links has rather more than its share of surprises, beginning with the opening hole.

Called Point Garry Out (the 17th is Point Garry In), the 1st measures just 328 yards. The breeze, however, is generally into us, and the beach is unsettlingly close. The anticipated flow of the hole is interrupted about 190 yards from the tee by a vast sandy area that isolates the well-elevated green from the fairway. We have no choice but to lay up, then play a little longer approach than we would like, the green perched 20 feet above us. The concealed green, which can be counted on to be fast, slopes perilously toward the rocks and the sea. This is an entirely natural hole and a nonpareil. It is also potentially lethal. Once, in an important medal competition, Mr. Balfour took 8 here.

The next two holes, both great two-shotters (more like three-shotters into a west wind), are straightforward. The 435-yard 2nd, named Sea, begins from an elevated tee. The shoreline eats into the fairway on the right; the merest push or cut sends us down onto the beach, a hazard from which the ball may be played but in which the club may not be grounded. The left side of the fairway is studded with giant hillocks that sometimes obstruct our view to the green. On the 3rd, 460 yards, the beach is less magnetic, but the long second shot, almost always a fairway metal, must clear a low stone wall. A thin hit here rebounds from the wall or, worse, huddles in its shadow. To play this pair of par 4s, into the prevailing wind, in a total of 8 strokes is beyond dreaming.

The next six holes head inland, and though not so thrilling as the opening trio, are very testing. Two of them were chosen for the 500 *World's Greatest Golf Holes* book. At the 353-yard 7th, the Eil Burn fronts the green, which is also tightly bunkered on the right, bounded by a wall on the left, and backed by high grass. On the 496-yard 9th, it is the drive that teases. The hole turns left in the tee-shot landing area; an out-of-bounds wall on the left forces us right, where two bunkers, solidly in the fairway, await. The daring player who can slot his drive into the gap between wall and sand has a chance to reach the elevated green in 2. Boldness and accuracy on this classic risk–reward hole can produce a birdie.

Following three good holes near the sea—the 161-yard 10th, played from high in the sand hills, is particularly worthy—the inbound nine unveils a fine and thrilling long run home.

Opposite, top: North Berwick East Course, 13th; bottom: 16th. Above, left: North Berwick West Course, 1st; right: 4th.

The 355-yard 13th doglegs smoothly left to a green that is shoehorned into a hollow, one blockaded by a low stone wall and backstopped by a high sand hill. Delicately clearing the wall, which is less than three feet short of the putting surface, on our 125-yard approach shot—almost like a high-jumper slithering over the bar!—calls for very pure ball-striking.

On the 14th, 382 yards long, both shots are blind; the drive is into wickedly choppy terrain with sand right and tousled rough left. Our iron is then fired over a high diagonal ridge, the ball disappearing downhill toward a bunkered low-plateau green scarcely two paces from the beach. We are hitting straight out to sea on this second shot, desperately hoping that somewhere down there we will find a safe harbor. Just choosing the right club—never mind swinging it well—prompts fearful indecision. A brilliant and unique hole.

We now putt out, ring the all-clear bell, and proceed to the 15th, Redan, a military term that refers to a type of guarding parapet. This is one of the most copied holes in the world, and in the 500 *World's Greatest Golf Holes* book it is one of the top one hundred. On this 190-yarder, the flag can be seen but not the green. Angled away beyond a deep bunker under its left

front flank, the green also slopes downward to the left and the rear. More-over, there is a high shoulder at the right front of the green, plus three pits awaiting the shot that misses on that side. On a given day, depending on the wind and the location of the cup, the shot called for may be a draw, a fade, or a low, straight "chaser" that dashes onto the green.

There is a lot going on here, and that is surely the chief appeal of this great one-shotter. Charles Blair Macdonald simulated it—he may even have improved on it—at the 4th hole of the National Golf Links of America, in Southampton, New York, the first great American course. And next door, at Shinnecock Hills, a close look at the 7th (which caused calamity in the final round of the 2004 U.S. Open) reveals another Redan hole, this one the effort of William Flynn and Dick Wilson, which was also inspired by the granddaddy of them all, the 15th at North Berwick.

Macdonald comes to mind again at the next hole, where our drive on this level 403-yarder must clear a stone wall and, about 200 yards out, a ditch. As for the green, is there another quite like it in the British Isles? This long, narrow surface is divided into three discrete parts, from front to rear: plateau, trough, plateau. Fail to place your second shot on the

part where the hole is cut and the likelihood of three putts is imminent. This green obviously prompted the even more eye-popping 9th green at Macdonald's great Yale University course.

The 17th has always seemed to me to be one of the very best holes on a course that has more than its share of "very best holes." At 422 yards, level for the first half and uphill for the second, it is long. We can well employ the frequently helping breeze. The broad and tumbling and naturally sculpted fairway makes a grand platform for the long uphill second shot. The green cannot be seen, but the flagstick can.

The 18th, a 275-yard par 4 and in that respect similar to the last hole at Prestwick, is the best birdie chance on the course. Today's power hitters can easily reach the large, bunker-free green, a plateau with a hollow in front and gentle falloffs at the sides. The only hazard is the road bordering the right side of the fairway, which is always lined with parked cars (St. Andrews). Hundreds of dents must be incurred here in the course of a year. Still, there is ample room to drive left (St. Andrews again). Backdropping the green is the handsome and comfortable stone clubhouse of the North Berwick Golf Club, where visiting players are welcome for a drink or a meal or some good talk about this sublime links.

For pure golfing pleasure—a pleasure bred of diversity, challenge, unpredictability, proximity to the sea, and the satisfaction of true links shot-making—few courses can equal North Berwick's West Links. Is it a candidate for the one course to play, day in and day out, for the rest of your life? Oh my, yes.

Opposite: North Berwick West Course, 14th.

The hotel choices in East Lothian are nearly limitless:

- The **Marine**, just off the 16th fairway of North Berwick's West Links, was extensively refurbished in 2005 and 2006. A stately turreted pile, it offers eighty-three rooms and suites (half of them with sea views), a sauna, heated outdoor swimming pool, tennis, and billiards. The bar is especially welcoming and the cooking is creative.
- **Blenheim House**, a small hotel that caters to golfers, is a two-minute walk from the 1st tee of the West Links. It is quiet, professionally run, moderately priced. Room 15 is a spacious accommodation (double bed and single bed) with a large bay window overlooking the municipal putting green, the strand, the harbor, the 1st tee and 18th green of the West Links, and the Firth itself.
- **Glebe House**, a centrally located Georgian mansion behind a garden wall, lacks the views provided by the Marine and Blenheim House, but its furniture (many antiques) and furnishings are superior. It is almost certainly North Berwick's best B&B and surely an excellent value.

Roughly halfway between North Berwick and Gullane on the coast road lies Dirleton, one of the prettiest villages in Scotland. There are two triangular village greens and a ruined thirteenth-century castle that encompasses a garden and a seventeenth-century bowling lawn. Guest rooms at the **Open Arms**, though smallish, are tastefully decorated, and some have a view of the ancient castle. A particularly delicious entrée in the inn's intimate **Library Restaurant** is the saddle of wild venison wrapped in pancetta and presented on a bed of chive mash with roast parsnips.

Another dining spot worth keeping in mind is the **Waterside Bistro**, in Haddington, an atmospheric pub and restaurant that serves bar snacks as well as complete meals. Go for lunch on a lovely day, when you can sit outside, on the bank of the River Tyne and in the lee of an old triple-arched stone bridge, gazing idly across the water at fourteenth-century St. Mary's Collegiate Church and enjoying a toasted ham and cheese sandwich and a pint of lager. Such an idyllic setting, which calls up Constable or Turner and which surfaces with considerable frequency across the face of England, is a rarity in Scotland.

Opposite: Dirleton Castle. Left: Bass Rock. Middle column, from top: the Open Arms; Tantallon Castle; the Marine. Above: Tantallon Castle.

DUNBAR

L ess than twenty minutes east along the coast road from North Berwick, lies the seaside resort of Dunbar, a historic fortress-port and royal burgh where once again we find that the game, or some rudimentary form of it, has been played for more than 350 years. As early as 1640, a local clergyman was disciplined and held up to public disgrace "for playing gowfe" on Sunday.

The Dunbar Golfing Society was formed in 1794, but it had disappeared from the scene by the time the Dunbar Golf Club was organized in 1856. The new club's founders immediately called in Old Tom Morris to lay out fifteen holes. In 1880 Willie Park Sr. added three holes to bring the links up to what had become the accepted standard. Like North Berwick, Dunbar is little changed since then.

ON THE COURSE

The course is set up for daily play at about 6,200 yards, par 70. The start of the round is not promising: a couple of level and humdrum short par 5s that run back and forth beside each other, with the result that we soon find ourselves where we began: outside the golf shop. These two holes are inland in character, as is the 3rd, a falling 170-yarder to a heavily bunkered green by the spiffy white clubhouse. But it plays straight toward the sea, and we know without being told that the golf we have come for must be just around the corner—or, more precisely, just on the other side of the stone wall that backdrops the green.

The 4th hole marks the beginning of what might be called the real Dunbar. This shortish two-shotter and the thirteen holes that follow are laid out—sometimes squeezed in—between the wall and the sea. On the inland side of this fieldstone barrier lay for many decades the Duke of Roxburghe's deer park. Since the seaward side also belonged to him, whoever succeeded to that eminence became president of the club.

The slicer must negotiate these fourteen holes warily. The boundary wall nags all the way out on the right, and the rocky beach threatens virtually all the way in on the right. The net of it is out-of-bounds on ten holes and the sea a worry on nine. The round can be stressful.

This long strip of land beside a crescent bay has a pleasantly rolling character. Bunkering is light; gorse imperils the shot on occasion. And the deceptively short rough turns out to be penal.

The 386-yard 7th, one of the two best holes on the first nine, doglegs smoothly right to follow the wall and calls for a semiblind second shot over rising ground down to a green set between the wall and a beautiful old barn called Mill Stone Den. Following the uphill 8th, 365 yards long and with a large green sloping emphatically down from back to front, comes the other top-notch hole, the 9th, 507 yards long. A blind

Opposite: Dunbar, 7th.
Above: 9th.

Ironically, however, it is possible that the beauty of the setting rather than the rigors of the test may be what colors the memory of most visitors. It is difficult to call up any stretch of holes in Scotland with lovelier views than those at Dunbar. On a sparkling day, the blue of the sea is a brilliant reflection of the blue of the sky, the fishing smacks slowly ply the waters not a mile offshore, the chatter of the oystercatchers as they hop, stiff-legged, from rock to rock delights our ear, and Bass Rock and May Island and the distant outline of the Fife coast all vie for our attention. And on the way in, the spires and roofs of the town extend the same warm invitation to us as do those at St. Andrews.

NEARBY COURSES

There is a second eighteen in Dunbar, at the opposite end of town. It is also seaside. Only 5,200 yards long and with a par of 64, **Winterfield**, atop the cliffs, is nothing if not sporty, or so it looks to me. I say *looks* because I must confess to never having played it. But I've stood on the 1st tee, and if that hole is any indication—an unnerving shot over a deep, grassy swale—this little course has to be fun.

Located midway between North Berwick and Dunbar is the **Whitekirk Golf Course**, which opened in 1995. A public course that welcomes everybody at all times, it was laid out by a Scot, Cameron Sinclair, whose design experience had previously been confined to the Far East. Whitekirk measures 6,200 yards from the regular markers, 6,420 from the medal tees; it wanders over 160 acres of high, hilly, and treeless land. Though laid out several miles from the coast, this delightful eighteen has a linkslike feeling, thanks to its openness, its panoramic sea views, its broad and undulating fairways, its festive greens, and the naturalness that imbues it all. The holes are never less than good, and one hole can fairly be called great: The 420-yard 5th climbs, bends left in the driving area (three bunkers here), and then plunges into a hollow only to rise almost vertically to a shelf of green angled to the line of the long second shot. The numerous lofty tees at Whitekirk provide 360-degree views of the world of East Lothian, with rich farmland ringing the course, an occasional village catching our eye, Berwick Law and Bass Rock in the middle ground, and, as ever, Fife on the horizon across the broad Firth. And as we stand on the noble 18th tee, Tantallon Castle (built in 1375 and reduced to ruins in 1651 by twelve days of Oliver Cromwell's bombardment) lies far below on our left, Dunbar off in the distance to our right.

uphill drive puts us on the flat and within sight of the distant Barus Ness Lighthouse. A solid 3-metal now, sailing high above the sloping fairway, should get within a short pitch of the green far below.

The excellent 200-yard 10th brings us to the far end of the links. Six of the remaining eight holes play along and modestly above the sea. Seven of them often play into a westerly wind, which for most of us means a losing battle, since four of the two-shotters measure 417, 459, 433, and 437 yards. And three of those are perilous, with the greens at 12, 14, and 15 perched in lonely splendor above the rocky strand. The pitch on the short par-4 17th must carry a burn, and the 437-yard home hole (we are now back inside the great wall) is one of those par 4s that calls for two stout blows into the wind if we are to have any chance of gaining the green in regulation.

Dunbar's ivy-clad **The New Bayswell Hotel** gets a lot of repeat business from golfers. Guest rooms are comfortable but in no sense luxurious, the clifftop setting affords spectacular sea views, the food is good, and the tariffs are reasonable. At nearby **Creel Restaurant**, in an old smuggler's house, the emphasis is on locally caught fish.

Difficult as it may sometimes be to believe, there is much more to East Lothian than the royal and ancient game. Twenty-six miles of beaches beckon (some locals insist that the water reaches 60 degrees at least twice a summer!). Among the beguiling harbors are those at Dunbar and North Berwick, with the latter town offering antiques shops, art galleries, and, on the outskirts, Berwick Law, an extinct volcano.

Dunbar may lack the refinement of North Berwick, but this ancient fortress port and royal burgh has witnessed important moments in British history. In 1295 England's Edward I suppressed a Scottish revolt here. And it was outside the town in 1650 that Oliver Cromwell, whose forces had been encamped on the links for six weeks, crushed the Scottish supporters of Charles II. Since Cromwell then used the castle stones to reinforce the harbor, there is little of this once imposing structure to be seen today.

The steepled seventeenth-century Town House, Scotland's oldest civic building in continuous use, is of interest. Also, John Muir, father of America's national parks, was born in this town. His birthplace is a little museum on the High Street. Not far outside town to the north is the John Muir Country Park. South of Dunbar, on the coast, are picturesque Cove and Eyemouth, where the harbor, stretching up the river, is a bustling scene. The Eyemouth Museum, in Market Place, presents informative displays about fishing and farming in this district.

At the foot of the hill over which many of the Whitekirk golf holes are routed is the hamlet of the same name, with its large fifteenth-century church and its two-story sixteenth-century barn, both built of a rust-brown stone. In pre-Reformation times Whitekirk possessed a miraculous crucifix and a holy well, which attracted thousands of the faithful annually, including the man who became Pope Pius II. The future pontiff is supposed to have walked here barefoot from Dunbar, thus contracting the rheumatism that would plague him the rest of his life.

Lenoxlove House, home of the Duke of Hamilton, and Gosford, the residence of the Earl of Wemyss, are two stately homes open to visitors. For a change of pace, pop into the Myreton Motor Museum (a knockout collection of vintage cars), just outside Aberlady, and the Museum of Flight, in East Fortune, with its Concorde, the supersonic jet that's no longer in the skies.

In addition to Dirleton (page 231), the county is dotted with endearing villages such as Preston (here are Preston Tower, a fifteenth-century fortress house, and Northfield House, a sixteenth-century tower house with turreted stairs); East Linton, site of Preston Mill, a working water mill, and of a six-hundred-year-old stone bridge that spans the Linn River; Gifford, a planned estate village that is the gateway to the Lammermuir Hills; and a trio of old stone-walled villages, Garvald, Morham, and Saltown. It is quite possible that a stay in East Lothian would turn out to be golf in the morning and sightseeing in the afternoon.

Along the shore, Dunbar.

GULLANE

Touring golfers are sometimes surprised to find that Muirfield is just one of five 18-hole courses in Gullane. The other four in this small town given over entirely to the game (its population is about 4,200), are Gullane Golf Club's three eighteens and Luffness New. All five are endowed with the crisp sand-based turf of a true links, and three of them—Gullane No. 1, No. 2, and No. 3—play up and down, over and around Gullane Hill.

In his charming book *Golf on Gullane Hill,* published in 1982, Archie Baird celebrates the game here, and on the opening page he singles out the unlikely heroes: rabbits. It was rabbits that cropped the grass "to a lawn-like smoothness." Perhaps even more important, "If they found a succulent new shoot of hawthorn or buckthorn had taken root, they applied their sharp little incisors and 'nipped it in the bud.'"

Golf was played over the Gullane links as early as 1650, probably on three or four very rudimentary holes near the ancient church, which dates to 1150. A close look at one of the headstones in the graveyard there will reveal—if revelation be needed—the value placed on the services provided by those who work for golfers:

ERECTED BY THE GULLANE GOLF CLUB
TO THE MEMORY OF JAMES DOBSON 1853–1924
IN GRATEFUL APPRECIATION OF THIRTY YEARS
OF FAITHFUL SERVICE AS STARTER ON THE LINKS

Two golf clubs were formed in 1854, but it was in 1882, spurred by the need to improve the course ("in very poor order, mole hills being numerous and grass very rank"), that Gullane Golf Club was formed and Willie Park Sr. was called in for extensive revisions. By 1898 play was so heavy that a second eighteen was fashioned by Willie Park Jr. Eleven years later, he also laid out Gullane No. 3. So Gullane Golf Club has had three eighteens in play for very nearly a hundred years.

I first played over Gullane Hill in 1971. On my many visits during the years since, I have been conscious of almost no change (except for the construction of a handsome clubhouse specifically for visitors) in this timeless place—not to the town nor to the golf club nor to the courses. In more recent years, most of my games on Gullane No. 1 have been with Archie Baird, an RAF pilot in the Second World War and a practicing veterinary surgeon from 1954 to 1980. Captain of Gullane Golf Club in 1976 and 1977, Archie is also a member of the Honourable Company of Edinburgh Golfers and of Kilspindie Golf Club, in his home village of Aberlady, some three miles west of Gullane. Of compact build and a shade under average height, he is easily met, and you sense at once that the twinkle is never far from his eye. His handicap, once as low as 6, has crept up over the years, but he continues to make an aggressive pass at the ball, fearlessly employing his driver "off the deck" ten or twelve times in a round with the hope of reducing the mileage on those two-shotters that he now needs three shots to reach.

Archie's wife, Sheila Park Baird, a retired veterinarian as well and a former ladies' captain at Kilspindie, is the great-granddaughter of Willie Park Sr. Sheila and Archie used to visit the United States during the winter to play golf in Florida, but they no longer do. They stick to East Lothian, with its dozen links courses. Archie now plays only links golf, even declining to join his son-in-law, a member at nearby Haddington, for a game at that perfectly acceptable parkland course.

Archie's faithful golfing companion of more than a dozen years, an obedient Border terrier named Niblick, died in 2001, to be replaced by an equally endearing Border terrier called Brody, whose conduct is also impeccable.

Over the years, Gullane No. 1 has been the scene of the Scottish Amateur, final qualifying for the Open Championship when it is held at Muirfield, and, on three occasions, the British Ladies' Championship.

ON THE NO. 1 COURSE

The No. 1 Course measures 6,466 yards from the medal tees and 6,100 yards from the regular markers; par is 71. The level and straightforward opening hole, all of 287 yards from the regular tees, is a likely par or better. But the 2nd, warningly dubbed Windygate, is a likely bogey or

Opposite: Gullane No. 1, 9th.

worse. The card says 334 yards, but I have never known the 2nd to play less than 400. It climbs straight up Gullane Hill every foot of the way. Don't be misled by the sheltered look of the hole, which follows a natural cut in the hillside. The prevailing wind funnels so powerfully down this cut and into us that climbing is a chore and standing solidly over the ball on our second shot can be difficult. What's more, the fairway is narrow, the rough is throttlingly thick, and the skimpy sand-free green is cunningly framed by little falloffs. Two very straight and cleanly struck shots will do the job, but nothing less.

Now, having jotted 5 on the card, we hoist ourselves up onto the tee of a shortish three-shotter that, even into the prevailing breeze, should be manageable. The elevated tee reveals a good deal of the vast golfing landscape, to say nothing of the Firth of Forth itself. Power is no prerequisite on this 479-yarder, but precision is. Again, the fairway is not wide. Eight pot

bunkers along the way and four at the green combine with the rough to give this hole punch. What ought to be an automatic par turns out to require 3 sound strokes, and we end up conceding, however grudgingly, the appropriateness of the 3rd's selection to *The 500 World's Greatest Golf Holes.*

For some of us, the 5th merited this honor but, inexplicably, did not receive it. A 436-yarder, it bends smartly left around deep pits in the elbow of the dogleg, then climbs to a large green carved out of the hillside. To reach the green in regulation calls for two first-rate swings. And to get down in two putts is almost as difficult a feat, so steeply sloping from back to front is this putting surface. Which may be a good time to add that Gullane's greens are among the finest in Scotland.

The 300-yard 6th, also uphill, brings us to the storied 7th tee, on the pinnacle of Gullane Hill. Here is the downhill hole of the world. The pulse races as we strive to take it all in. Popping up in profusion far below are innumerable flagsticks. Who can possibly keep straight the holes on the three Gullane eighteens and Luffness New from this aerie? Back-dropping them is a vast nature preserve and then the waters of Aberlady Bay. Turn some 90 degrees to the right and the elegant tracery of the Forth Road Bridge catches the eye. So do Arthur's Seat and glimpses of fair Edinburgh itself. Now turn east to command the pale green fairways of Muirfield and, beyond them, Bass Rock and Berwick Law. Finally, take a deep breath, the keen fresh sea breeze suddenly expanding your lungs, and come back to earth. The 400-yard 7th plunges all but vertically from tee to green. Shoulders open, we swing mightily, then watch in almost childlike rapture the prodigious hang time of this shot. And despite the downhill lie for our approach, which may be no more than 120 yards, we play it confidently and come away with 4, maybe 3.

The 8th, a short par 4 heading straight toward the sea, is followed by a pretty 141-yarder, paralleling the cliff edge and perhaps fifteen paces from it, our 7- or 8-iron drifting down to a spacious green ringed by eight bunkers.

The inbound half calls for stronger hitting. More than 400 yards longer than the first nine, it starts with a couple of testers, the uphill 434-yard 10th and, right beside it, the downhill 427-yard 11th, sweeping majestically toward the sea. The tees on the short par-5 12th, bending quietly right, and the 160-yard 13th, knob to knob, are both set high above the beach. Serving as unignorable reminders of the Second World War are massive gray concrete blocks, which were lodged in the thickets above the beach some sixty-five years ago to thwart the German tanks that never came.

The 409-yard 14th, straight and almost indiscernibly rising, is serious stuff, and so is the 15th, which reminds us of Babe Didrickson

Zaharias's dominance of the 1947 British Ladies' here. The first American ever to win this championship, Babe was not only larger than life, she was also longer by a country mile than any woman who had ever struck a golf ball. The 15th measured 535 yards for the championship. The first 350 yards are level; the hole then climbs steeply to a hillside green. In one of her matches, Babe, assisted by a moderate breeze, followed a crushing drive with a bullet 4-iron shot that rolled to a stop at the back of the green. A few locals, very elderly now, recall with awe that display of unbridled—and unladylike—power. It was also on this occasion that Babe's costume was declared unfit. When she appeared for one of her matches sporting red-and-white-checked shorts, officials politely requested that she change her attire. Babe graciously complied.

After 14 holes on the sea side of Gullane Hill, we turn our back on the water and tee it up on the 17th to head for home, gazing out now from this spectacular height over golden beige fields, if it be an August evening,

awaiting the harvest. And at last we even the score for that punishing climb we endured on the 2nd. The 17th goes straight downhill, with the wind, our drive quite possibly a clout of 310 yards. The 80-yard pitch that's left just may result in birdie, something that is not out of the question on the rolling 340-yard final hole as well. Talk about finishing with a flourish—the irresistible Gullane No. 1 gives us every chance to do just that.

OTHER GULLANE COURSES

The **No. 2 Course** measures 6,244 yards against a par of 71. It has several quite forgettable holes and not enough holes like the terrific 13th, which edges right as it climbs to a two-tier plateau green. As for **Gullane No. 3**, it is much too short—5,166 yards, par 66—but it is not without charm and spirit. A number of hillside and dell green sites are particularly attractive. And the 169-yard 15th is the most steeply plunging one-shotter in my experience: sheer fun!

Above: Gullane No. 1, 8th.
Opposite: 13th.

NEARBY COURSES

Luffness New, laid out along the lower flanks of Gullane Hill, had Old Tom Morris as its originator, in 1894, and Willie Park Jr. and Tom Simpson as its remodelers. The fairways are ribbons of green framed by waving wheat-colored rough; the bunkers feature nearly vertical revetted faces; and the greens—Bobby Locke, who knew something about putting, believed there were none better anywhere—are firm, fast, and reliably true. Though total yardage is only 6,122 (par 69), there are five par 4s comfortably over 420 yards. This easy-walking course, which often looks out over Aberlady Bay, turns out to be more testing than we might have expected.

Three miles away, on a low headland between Aberlady Bay and Gosford Bay, lies **Kilspindie**, laid out by Willie Park Jr. in 1898. Only 5,500 yards long, par 69, it is not a challenge unless a brisk breeze is blowing. But it is a delightful place for the game, with the sea in view on seventeen holes and in play, to catch the push or slice, on four of them. Two holes are memorable, both along the strand: the 513-yard 2nd, a "par 6" into a westerly, and the 162-yard 8th, where the shot must often be started out over the beach if there is to be any chance of holding the green.

Abutting Kilspindie is newcomer **Craigielaw**, laid out by Donald Steel's associate Tom McKenzie. It measures 6,601 yards from the medal tees, 6,043 yards from the regular markers (par 71), and it reveals gorgeous views of Aberlady Bay and Gosford Bay. The green complexes border on the tumultuous, with the result that we find ourselves, hole after hole, pitching and chipping and putting out of hollows and over knobs to teasingly spotted cups. On a man-made course that is not a true links, the fun—and occasional frustration—of true links golf is with us here at every turn.

Just five minutes from Craigielaw, along the coast road toward Edinburgh, lies **Longniddry**, designed by Harry Colt in 1921. It is a hybrid, an appealing mix of links and parkland golf, the broad fairways often framed by tall umbrella pines. Only 6,260 yards from all the way back and with a par of just 68, Longniddry has no par 5s. What it does have is eight two-shotters over 400 yards. Once aboard, it can be very difficult to get off the dreaded bogey train.

Archie Baird plays regularly for Gullane in the winter club match against Longniddry. A couple of years back, when Longniddry was the venue, tee markers were rather too far forward to suit the visitors. Called upon, as he often is, for after-dinner remarks, Archie congratulated the hosts on the excellence of the wine and the cooking and on their victory in the competition. Then he added, "But perhaps the next time the match is here a way might be found to set up the course so that we do not play *Short*niddry."

At Gullane No. 1 there is a one-room museum next to the pro shop, and I urge you to visit it. Archie Baird is its founder, owner, curator, and conductor of what turns out to be a forty-minute tour of his Heritage of Golf Museum. The exhibition contains the fruits of his half century of collecting golf memorabilia. Through a skillfully arranged—and utterly absorbing—selection of old paintings, prints, postcards, and photographs, of old balls (including priceless featheries) and clubs and bags and costumes, of antique medals of silver and antique buttons of brass, and of so much more, Archie presents the evolution of golf from its origin some 550 years ago down till today. Listening to him and examining his acquisitions close up is a once-in-a-lifetime experience. Visits are by appointment only. A telephone call to the maestro (0875–870–277) is all that is needed to open this treasure chest.

A word of caution: If you should elect to embark on this marvelous guided tour courtesy of Scotland's quintessential golf purist, be prepared to come away conceding that golf was *not* born in Scotland.

LODGING AND DINING

In recent years the **Golf Inn**, on Gullane's Main Street, has earned a good following. The guest rooms, some small, are cheerful and up-to-date. No views, but the cooking is top-notch, with a menu full of appetizing dishes.

Aberlady is all of five minutes from Gullane. On the main street is the hospitable **Old Aberlady Inn**. Rooms are modest and modestly priced, the atmosphere might be called "olde worlde," and both bar (crackling log fire) and beer garden are well patronized by the locals.

Two Gullane restaurants of note:
- The **Old Clubhouse** (the original golf club-house) is a large and lively spot, very bistro in feeling, with a strong sense of times long past (high beam ceiling, dark paneling, old fireplaces) and good food at what is some-times called "popular" prices.
- **La Potiniere** is small and smart. The choices are quite limited, but the cooking is imaginative.

Archie Baird's Heritage of Golf Museum.

MUIRFIELD

On September 1, 1971, I played Muirfield for the first time. With me were my two sons, seventeen-year-old Jim and sixteen-year-old John. At the east end of Gullane, the one driveway leading left off the main street had only a tiny gray-blue sign with the letters H.C.E.G. peeping up out of the grass. Ignoring it as of no consequence, I drove on, perhaps half a mile farther. Since we knew where the course lay, having looked down on it from atop Gullane Hill the day before, this inability to get to it was maddening. There was no point in continuing toward Dirleton, so I turned around and headed back. This time the minuscule sign communicated: H.C.E.G. stands for Honourable Company of Edinburgh Golfers.

Down the driveway to Muirfield we sped—it was now 9:22 and our tee time was 9:30—and zipped into the extensive parking garage. Shoes and clubs in hand, the three of us now sprinted along the tarmac to the clubhouse. An official-looking man in a navy blazer, ruddy-cheeked, solidly built, in his early fifties, came out of the clubhouse and intercepted us. His face wore no welcoming smile.

"James Finegan?" he asked peremptorily.

"Yes," I said. "Yes, sir."

"And these, I presume, are your sons. No time for introductions."

He did not volunteer to shake hands. "Do you see that two-ball?" Three pairs of eyes followed his finger as he pointed beyond a nearby green and a short distance down the fairway leading to it. "They started on the tenth and are now finishing their first nine right there, on the eighteenth. They will then proceed to the first tee"—he pointed some thirty yards to our left—"and if you have not driven off before they get there, it is entirely possible that you will not play golf at Muirfield today. I suggest you put on your golf shoes at once. That door leads to the changing room. You can pay your green fee when you finish—that is, if you start." The legendary curmudgeon Captain P.W.T. Hanmer (H. M. Royal Navy, retired,) pointed the way with that imperious finger toward a clubhouse door, and we fled on the prescribed line.

Not ninety seconds later we were back, breathless, discombobulated, but nonetheless determined to beat the looming twosome to the 1st tee, fishing our gloves and balls and tees from our golf bags as we scurried and stumbled toward the markers. A powerful, shrieking wind—55 miles per hour may not be storm force, but it is ruinous where the golf swing is concerned—was raking the links. And the level, straightaway 1st hole, measuring 425 yards, played dead into it. I caught my drive flush and advanced it about 110 yards, precisely half the distance of my normal tee shot in those days. We all laughed. The boys outhit me, both off somewhere in Muirfield's infamous tall rough. Heads down and leaning fiercely forward, wind whistling past our ears, we set out toward the distant flag.

My ball had gained the fairway by no more than a pace. I pulled out my brassie (2-wood). At 130 pounds and standing a fraction under six feet, I was no match for a fifty-five-mile-an-hour wind. Now, having anchored myself as solidly as possible, I had no choice but to swing. As I drew the club back, a particularly violent guest rocked me. Throwing the club from the top in a desperate effort to bring it back to the ball, I slammed the wood into the firm turf about eight inches behind the ball and, to my horror, felt the club bounce up and fly cleanly over the ball as I followed through.

"I missed it!" I screamed into the wind. "I whiffed it! I never touched it!"

The boys, out ahead of me in the rough on the right, turned as my voice reached them. The wind made it impossible for them to understand me. I pointed to the ball and shouted again, mimicking my swing. Now they understood, and the wind carried their laughter back to me in a rush.

I tried again. This time the ball, thinly struck, stayed low, burrowing its way a bit farther than my drive had traveled. I finished the hole with a 7. John also had a 7 and Jim nipped us with a heroic double-bogey 6.

Nothing would be gained by describing this round in detail. It was an unremitting struggle, and, for the most part, details were lost in the conflict. I remember realizing, as we walked from the 2nd green to the 3rd tee, that the faint clicking sound reminiscent of hail tapping on a window pane was actually grains of sand ricocheting off the slats of a sand fence. Without that barrier, we would have been stung repeatedly by particles blown off the dune behind the 3rd tee. I also recall Jim's choosing a pitching wedge on

Opposite: Muirfield, 4th.

the tee of the 187-yard 4th and then begging the ball to stop as it ran 35 feet past the cup. And I recall making an easy 4 on the 516-yard 5th by chipping *back* from just over the green, where my *second* shot had finished—this by the same player whose drive on the 1st had eaten up all of 110 yards. Still, that birdie 4 was twice as many strokes as Johnny Miller needed here in 1972 (the hole measured 560 yards for the Open), when he followed a 280-yard drive by holing a 280-yard 3-wood for an albatross (double eagle).

The final tallies were ludicrous: 110 for John, 101 for Jim, 96 for me (48 each way). There was nothing to do now but pay the green fee: £1.50 (just under $3), change our shoes, and retreat.

A year after this harrowing round, the Open Championship was held at Muirfield for the eleventh time. Lee Trevino, victor at Royal Birkdale in 1971, carried off the claret jug for the second straight year. This win was astonishing. Three times in the last 21 holes, he holed out from somewhere off the green. Scrambling for the lead late in the third round, he pulled his 6-iron on the par-3 16th into a bunker, the ball coming to rest on a down-slope and too close to the back of the pit to permit a full swing. Off balance as he chopped awkwardly to make contact, he almost fell down as the ball, skulled, flew across the green, bounced once, and disappeared into the cup for a 2. His opinion was that a 5 seemed likely as the ball left the clubface. Twenty minutes later, after his 5-iron shot on the 18th rolled over the green into thick rough, he pitched in from thirty feet for a 4 and a 66 that gave him a 1-stroke lead over Tony Jacklin.

When Trevino and Jacklin, paired in the final round, came to the 71st hole, they were tied at the top. Jacklin hit a couple of very good woods on this 528-yarder, followed by an indifferent chip from just in front of the green that came up about 18 feet short of the hole. Trevino pulled his drive into a bunker, then made three more bad swings—there is no other way to say it—which left him lying 4 in a troublesome spot halfway down the low, grassy mound that rings the 17th green. Hurriedly—in truth, it appeared to this TV viewer, carelessly, even halfheartedly—he jabbed at the ball, and it raced some fifty feet across the green and neatly into the cup as though no other conclusion to the shot were imaginable. Later Trevino would say candidly that he had believed he had no chance with the shot: "I thought I might have given up. I felt like I had."

Jacklin then did what you and I might have done in the circumstances: he three-putted, this despite the eighteen-foot stretch he had to negotiate being flat, presenting no problem of pace or borrow. The first putt exploded to three feet past the cup, and the jittery comebacker never looked

like going in. Shattered, Jacklin had to accept a 6, falling a stroke behind Trevino. Then, needing a birdie on the home hole to tie (the Texan would par it) and still shaken by the cruel turnabout on the 71st, he could do no better than bogey. The man who had captured the Open Championship in 1969 at Royal Lytham and the U.S. Open in 1970 at Hazeltine, and here had walked onto the green of the penultimate hole with every expectation of winning his third major, would never again contend in either the British or U.S. Open.

John and I returned to Muirfield in September of 1973. This time the day was pretty and our golf was sound. He posted an 82, I a 76. But neither score was quite so gratifying to me as the brief exchange after the round with Captain Hanmer. I noted that grandstands had been erected at the 18th green.

"Yes, yes," he said. "The preparations for the Ryder Cup are well in hand." He paused, then added, "Were you thinking of playing the afternoon round?"

"I was," I said, "but John thinks he's had enough for today."

"Perhaps you might want to play from the Ryder Cup tees," said the secretary, "to see firsthand what they'll be up against. It's a lot more length than you're used to here, much the same as the Open, a little over sixty-nine hundred yards, but I think you'd find it interesting."

I said I'd be delighted to try and that I was much in his debt for the kindness.

There was no sign of Captain Hanmer that afternoon when I teed off, blithely shouldered my light canvas bag, and, however overmatched, headed down the 1st in high spirits, my 215-yard tee shot making certain that I could not reach the green on this 447-yarder in regulation.

By Scottish standards, Muirfield, twenty miles east of Edinburgh and built in 1891, is not an old course. It is actually about the same age as the first American courses, such as Shinnecock Hills, Newport, Philadelphia Country Club's original eighteen, and Chicago Golf Club. The Honourable Company of Edinburgh Golfers was founded in 1744. The club minutes have been kept ever since and constitute the oldest continuous record of any golf club. Shortly after its founding, the Honourable Company drew up the first "Rules of Golf."

Following long stays at Leith (only five holes) and Musselburgh, the club headed farther east, finding its way to Muirfield. None other than Old Tom Morris gets credit for the basic design of the new course, a highly unusual scheme for the time, and one that in its general outline

was maintained even when the course was drastically reconstituted some thirty years later: The first nine moves in a clockwise arc outside the counterclockwise pattern of the second nine. The golfer's struggle with the winds off the Firth is thus a constantly shifting one.

The 1892 Open was a milestone. It was the first to be played at Muirfield, itself only a year old, and the first at 72 holes (instead of 36). Prize money, formerly £20, soared to £110. But the winner didn't get a farthing, because he was an amateur: Harold Hilton, a twenty-three-year-old Englishman who went on to claim the claret jug again five years later and won the Amateur Championship in 1900, 1901, and 1911, and the U.S. Amateur in 1911.

In the years to come, the Opens at Muirfield would be won by many of the greatest players in the game: Lee Trevino, Jack Nicklaus, Harry Vardon, James Braid twice, Walter Hagen, Henry Cotton, Gary Player (in 1959, the first of his three British Opens—despite a double bogey on the final hole!), Tom Watson, Nick Faldo (1987 and 1992, the 1987 victory by dint of 18 pars in the final round), and Ernie Els.

ON THE COURSE

The course sits splendidly above the Firth of Forth and at rather a remove from it. Still, the nobility, remoteness, and tranquillity of its location are enormously appealing. Herbert Warren Wind characterizes Muirfield as "a linksland course with a touch of meadowlands about it." And in *The Golf Courses of the British Isles,* Bernard Darwin comes at it with the sensibility of a poet: "There is a fine view of the sea and a delightful sea wood, with the trees all bent and twisted by the wind; then, too, it is a solitary and peaceful spot, and a great haunt of the curlews, whom one may see hovering over a championship crowd and crying eerily amid a religious silence."

Though Old Tom Morris was the initial architect of the links, the course today is more appropriately attributed to Harry Colt (Royal Portrush, Wentworth's West and East Courses, Sunningdale New, Swinley Forest, not to mention counseling with George Crump on the routing of Pine Valley). In 1925 Colt, one of the towering figures in the history of golf course architecture, extensively revised eleven holes here and created seven new ones. The result of his efforts was indisputable greatness, although it is, almost curiously, of a quite orderly sort. For in the pantheon of great courses—and Muirfield is unfailingly ranked in the world's top ten, on occasion as high as third—Muirfield is neither thrilling (Pebble Beach is) nor spectacular (Ballybunion Old is) nor breathtaking (Royal County Down is) nor dramatic (Pine Valley is). There are no hills, no trees, no water hazards, no unnerving forced carries over gorse- or heather-studded ravines. "Death or glory" shots are absent. Nonetheless, there is a rightness about the holes that adds up to excellence, so much so that we never find ourselves longing for attributes that are not present.

At the root of this excellence is what Ben Crenshaw calls "its beautiful honesty as a test of golf." Each hole states its requirements with unfailing frankness: no surprises, no tricks. Except for the drive on 11, there are no blind shots. Except on the 9th, there is no out-of-bounds. As targets, the greens are clearly etched and staunchly sand-defended. As putting surfaces, they are readable and manageable: They have character but are never excessively contoured. On terrain that very gently undulates, there is essentially nothing in the way of hillocks and hummocks to send the ball skittering crazily—confoundingly—off line. Muirfield is less mysterious, less "foreign" in feeling than other British seaside courses. Here we get exactly what the shot is worth—the good shot is properly rewarded, the poor shot is properly punished—and it all takes place within full view. Small wonder that whenever the world's best golfers are polled, Muirfield emerges as the favorite course on the Open rota.

Wherein, then, lies the challenge? The answer is simple: You have to hit the ball long and straight while, more often than not, battling a stiff breeze. From the regular markers, the course measures nearly 6,700 yards against a par of 70. That's a lot of golf. Then there is the bunkering: 165 meticulously crafted and stringently penal sod-wall sandpits (an average of more than nine per hole), every bit as intimidating when they patrol the fairways as when they defend the greens. Finally, there is the rough, deep, throttling, often mattresslike to walk on and to hack out of, that puts intense pressure on the swing by duping the player into believing the fairways to be narrower than they actually are. Muirfield is one of the game's most rigorous tests of driving.

Among the half dozen or so truly great holes are three long par 4s, all of them unyielding except to full-blooded strokes of genuine precision. The 443-yard 6th, swinging left, presents a nest of gathering bunkers (*all* Muirfield bunkers strike us as voracious) in the crook of the dogleg and a deceptive dip—dead ground—in front of the green to complicate club selection. The 8th, also 443 yards, bends right: Set in the elbow of the dogleg this time are six bunkers, three of them actually in the right side of the fairway itself, three in the adjacent rough, all lurking to snare the push or slice. Equally superlative is the 18th. It is 415 yards long for daily play (448 for the Open or the Ryder Cup), it is level, and it edges almost imperceptibly left. It is blockaded across the front and bracketed by sand. A nerveless second shot is demanded here, the type of shot summoned by Nicklaus in 1966, Trevino in 1972, and Faldo in 1987, when anything other than a pure stroke might well have cost the title. This hole was chosen for *The 500 World's Greatest Golf Holes*.

Still, on a course noted for its two-shotters, we don't want to ignore the par 3s and the par 5s. Two of them, the 9th (a two-shotter at 465 yards for member play, a three-shotter at 505 yards for the Open and the Ryder Cup), and the one-shotter 13th have been singled out in the *500 World's Greatest* volume as among the hundred best. The level 9th, more often than not played into the breeze, may show par 4 on the card when you tackle it, but you will not be upset to walk away with a 5 on a hole that demands strict control from start to finish. The fairway, which moves a shade right in the tee-shot landing area, is pinched there to about 20 yards by two bunkers on the left and tenacious rough on the right. Running the entire length of the hole on the left and becoming increasingly intrusive as we draw closer to the green is a stone boundary wall not quite five feet high. A pulled or hooked second shot—into a stiff headwind, even a third shot—can easily sail over the wall. A long second with even a suggestion of cut is likely to be wolfed down by any of four pits. And in the middle of the fairway, 65 yards short of the green and exactly where many a soundly struck second shot will come to rest, awaits Simpson's Bunker, Tom Simpson's sole contribution to Muirfield, and what an indelible memento it is! Played as a par 5, the hole yields its share of birdies and, in the Open, eagles as well from time to time. For instance, in the 1972 championship's final round, Jacklin and Trevino, head to head, drove into the right rough but reached the green comfortably with long irons and holed for eagles. On the other hand, in 1959 Peter Thomson, seeking his fifth Open (he would gain it in 1965) and squarely in the hunt, squandered his chances by hooking his 3-wood second shot over the wall in the last round.

The 13th, 160 yards, plays uphill to a long, narrow green perfectly sited in a cleft between two dunes—and zealously guarded by five deep pits eating into the putting surface, three on the right, two on the left. This green slopes maliciously down from back to front. It was here in 2002 that Ernie Els played one of the most brilliant shots of his career, somehow lifting the ball almost vertically from the very base of the mas-

sive forward wall of the larger left-hand pit and watching calmly—but doubtless relievedly—as it touched down perhaps a dozen feet from the hole and trickled to within 18 inches for a certain par.

For the record, that afternoon in 1973 I shot 80 from the Ryder Cup tees. The Match, contested three weeks later, saw the visitors field what must have looked to be an impregnable team, headed by Nicklaus, Trevino, Palmer, Casper, and Weiskopf. At the end of the first day the British/Irish side led 5½ to 2½. The U.S. squad reversed this score on the second day, and on the final day whipped the home team to retain the cup. The Honourable Company has also hosted the Walker Cup (twice), the Curtis Cup (twice), and the Amateur Championship (seven times).

As I walked up the 18th that day, I spotted Captain Hanmer standing in front of the clubhouse, scanning the links with his binoculars as he might have scanned the sea from the bridge of a warship during his years of service in the royal navy. Now, however, he was focusing on a dilatory foursome approaching the 12th green as the explanation for the holdup on the second nine. He intercepted me as I left the home green to point out that I had neglected to pay the green fee for my second round and that he would accept it now. The tariff was £2. (Today it is £125.) Visitors unaccompanied by a member are permitted to play only on Tuesdays and Thursdays. Muirfield must strike some sort of balance between the need to protect the rights of members and the obligation, acknowledged by The Honourable Company, to permit the faithful to come and worship at

the shrine. Somehow, and not without a touch of asperity from time to time, the secretaries have managed to walk this tightrope with considerable success and without compromising the principles of how a great golf club should be run. Still, a couple of them, Captain Hanmer and Colonel Brian Evans-Lombe, could fairly be labeled dictatorial.

Evans-Lombe, a retired cavalry officer, "reigned" from 1947 to 1964. Among the stories illustrative of his style is the one that finds him, on a Sunday morning, noting an unfamiliar figure sitting alone in the smoking room. When he inquired of the chap whose guest he might be, Evans-Lombe was sharply informed that he was speaking to a member of twenty years' standing. "In that event," the secretary replied, "you should come more often; then I would recognize you."

Evans-Lombe was not merely astringent. He could also be witty, as in this light verse he composed for a meeting of the Monks of St. Giles, a group of amateur versifiers:

Club Members to me, I think you'll agree,
Are as to a shepherd, his sheep;
I chase them off here and pen them in there,
And I count them as I go to sleep.

I have to listen as their eyes glisten
And they tell me of marvelous putts.
All I've seen them sink is a great deal of drink;
It's gradually driving me nuts.

They tell me with force what to do with the course
And how drinks are cheaper in pubs.
I'd like to suggest, if I ever was pressed,
What they could do with their clubs.

And when at last the ultimate blast
Of the dear old trumpet calls,
They'll all expect me on the first fiery tee
With a box of asbestos balls.

Captain Hanmer ("Paddy," I'm told, to his friends) was Muirfield's secretary from 1968 till 1983. I played the course five or six times during that period but actually had only a couple of brief, pleasant exchanges with him (after the first one, that is). In 1993 I ran into him at the house of a mutual friend in Gullane. Privately, he told me that he had regretted being forced out at Muirfield after fifteen years' service ("I suppose there were those who believed I had become too powerful"), particularly since he had aimed to hold the position three more years and eclipse the seventeen-year tenure of Evans-Lombe, the record for an Honourable Company secretary. He went on to say that he never really considered his activities at Muirfield a job but rather a nice pastime, something to occupy him that he enjoyed and could do well. "My compensation was less than the girls' in the dining room," he said. "I made it clear to the committee when I took the post that I did not require more."

Often portrayed as an ogre who took keen pleasure in turning away visiting golfers, he claimed, on the contrary, that he strove to make Muirfield more accessible to them, especially Americans. He took credit for the special arrangement now in effect with Greywalls (to be covered shortly) and made unaccompanied visitors feel at home by encouraging local members to join the visitors in the evening for a drink. He seemed surprised that I, a golf writer, was not aware of what he had done.

I recall that he told an Augusta National story with considerable relish: "One of our members," he said, "was not only turned away at the gates of Augusta National but was even refused permission to use the guard's telephone so that he might try to reach Hord Hardin, a friend of his, and have Mr. Hardin tell the guard to let him in.

"A year later," Captain Hanmer continued, "four Augusta members arrived at my office requesting the privilege of playing. They had not contacted me in advance to reserve a tee time. I carefully detailed the sorry experience of the Honourable Company member at their club and concluded by regretting that they would not be permitted to play Muirfield. I suggested that they try Gullane Number Three. They laughed. They thought I must be joking. When I made it clear that I was in dead earnest, they uneasily shuffled out of my office and headed toward their car. I let them get almost out of sight and then called out, inviting them to return. I said that they could indeed play here now that they understood what their club had put a Muirfield man through."

I never saw Captain Hanmer again, not at Muirfield nor at Pine Valley, where he had become an overseas member in 1983. He died in 2000.

Opposite: Muirfield, 13th.

H.C.E.G.

- Play the great **Muirfield**, the favorite Scottish course of many knowledgeable Americans.

- Down the storied five-course lunch with wine in the **club dining room** amid the spirited camaraderie of its members.

- Make a day of it here by **playing the links again**, after lunch, this time in a swift-paced foursomes (alternate stroke) match.

- Dine in **Gullane at La Potiniere**, where the cooking is creative.

- Spend the night just off the 10th tee at clubby **Greywalls**, the favorite Scottish inn of many knowledgeable Americans.

airborne for all of 40 yards, vanished into the right rough. Said the perpetrator with an easy smile, "If you don't mind, I'll play a mulligan."

Replied Archie, "You, sir, may play whatever you wish—I'm playing golf."

On those occasions when visitors are authorized to play two rounds in a day, the second round will, by edict of the secretary, almost always be foursomes (two balls, alternate stroke). Such a game takes about two and a half hours, a circumstance that pleases the secretary—and his constituents—no end. Slow play, which some Scots incline to view as America's principal contribution to the game, is not tolerated at Muirfield.

Off the northeastern boundary of the club's property, near the 6th, 7th, and 8th holes, loom the gnarled trees of Archerfield Wood, where, in 1882, Robert Louis Stevenson set his suspenseful novella *The Pavilion on the Links.* "On summer days," Stevenson wrote, "the outlook was bright and even gladsome, but at sundown in September, with a high wind, and a heavy surf rolling in close along the links, the place told of nothing but dead mariners and sea disasters." That was 125 years ago. Today it tells of nothing but new golf courses, two of them, on a six-hundred-acre site nestled along the strand between the corner of Muirfield and the 9th hole at North Berwick.

For this sand-based tract, it is actually a return to golf. Years ago there were two courses here, Archerfield and Fidra. Some claim that the first Archerfield holes—just six—were laid out in the sixteenth century. Not till the late 1800s would there be eighteen. Fidra was not created until the 1930s; the villagers of Dirleton fashioned the nine, with each hole built and maintained by a different family. Both the eighteen and the nine fell victim to the Second World War, when they were plowed up in order to grow vegetables.

The man behind this ambitious undertaking today is Kevin Doyle, a local businessman/entrepreneur, who also has plans for housing and a hotel here. Turning his back on the marquee names in golf course architecture, he entrusted the design of the two links eighteens to a little-known architect, David Williams, and a little-known professional golfer, D. J. Russell. As for the clubhouse, that honor falls to Archerfield House itself, an impressive pile that once housed Winston Churchill and Franklin D. Roosevelt as they planned the Normandy invasion but much more recently has functioned as a hay shed. Restoring it was almost as ambitious a task as building the two courses. Fidra opened in 2004, Dirleton, as the second course is now called, in 2006. And if The Honourable Company is keeping an eye on its new neighbors, it is surely not with bated breath.

In recent years my games at Muirfield have been with Archie Baird. About six or seven years ago, he and I had set a date for a round there well in advance, expecting that just the two of us would play. But when I arrived shortly before nine o'clock, he took me aside to say that there would be a three-ball. The other player was also a visiting American. Archie had not met him before this morning, but had felt compelled to have him join us when one of his Muirfield clubmates, a friend of this American, had asked Archie to let him come along, adding that the fellow, an avid golfer who had never played Muirfield, would have no other opportunity to do so till the next time he came to Scotland, which might not be for several years. I sensed that Archie had only grudgingly acquiesced. On the 1st tee he insisted that his two guests precede him, naming me to go first. I hit off. Now it was the unknown quantity's turn. He took a couple of practice swings (just one such preliminary would normally be enough to set Archie's teeth on edge), teed his ball up, stepped carefully back to sight down the intended line, set his stance and his grip, and swung. The half-topped shot,

Regrettably, the clubhouse is off limits to women, though the links is not. This mock-Tudor structure is the very image of what most golfers hope it to be: aging wooden lockers, handsome paneling, antique silver, oil paintings of revered golfing or club figures, an abundance of golf books, and grand views over the links. Upstairs are a half-dozen guest rooms, for members.

Frank Hannigan, former senior executive director of the USGA, once wrote: "Muirfield has everything desirable in golf—a fascinating mixture of holes, history, wind, stunning scenery and a great lunch." How enthusiastically, following the morning round, we tuck into that great lunch, in a spacious, bright, high-ceilinged dining room that will accommodate sixty to seventy golfers and a corresponding decibel level. We sit at long club tables—this promotes camaraderie and we are thus likely to talk with a member or two seated opposite or beside us. I might mention that the law is well represented in The Honourable Company—solicitors, barristers, judges—which may help to account for the lively talk, the ribbing, and the ripostes.

The choices on the luncheon menu are almost as daunting as the two-shotters on the great links. To start, trout in oatmeal and almonds or gazpacho or cullen skink, an especially hearty native cream soup featuring smoked haddock and potatoes; then sirloin of beef or loin of lamb or perhaps fillet of pork *en croûte*; five or six vegetables, often among them a delicious cauliflower au gratin; a selection of sweets that may include assorted meringues, chocolate cream pie, and a superb rhubarb crumble; and, finally, a variety of cheeses. The house wine, a chardonnay or a claret or both, will help sustain us through this trencherman's trove, and coffee at the conclusion will help restore our equilibrium, an especially useful development in the event that the secretary has approved our request for an afternoon foursome.

Is it, you may ask, a meal that measures up to the fabled luncheon at the National Golf Links of America,

which opens with cold half lobsters accompanied by a club-secret mayonnaise and works its way through three more courses, including shepherd's pie? Perhaps, perhaps. It is awfully good, this Muirfield meal.

GREYWALLS

Muirfield's next-door neighbor—they share the same driveway, off the main street—is Greywalls, backdropping the 10th tee. This twenty-two-room country-house hotel looks out in the rear over the links to the sea and in the front over the gardens to the distant Lammermuir Hills. It was in 1901 that Edward Lutyens, England's foremost residential architect in the early twentieth century, designed the graceful crescent-shape house of honeyed sandstone, and there is a sense of gentle embrace as, within the garden walls, we move down the pebbled drive to it. The equally redoubtable Gertrude Jekyll, often the architect's collaborator, fashioned the ravishing gardens, with their roses often in riotous bloom, their lavender borders and holly hedges, their long perspectives and secret nooks.

The house was built as a holiday home for a serious golfer who wanted to be within a mashie-niblick of the 1st tee. At one point over the years it was occupied by a woman who happened to catch King Edward VII's fancy. A charming story, possibly apocryphal, stems from one of the royal visits. In a bridge game one evening, the king took the lady, who was his partner, to task for her play. She replied, "To tell you the truth, sir, I am so tired that I can't tell the difference between a king and a knave!"

It was in 1948 that the private house became a hotel. How wonderfully it still echoes the Edwardian Age—the gardens, the open fires, the dark paneling, the snug bar. Photos of Nicklaus and Watson mix amiably with antiques and books and, one suspects, half the framed prints in Scotland. Neatly indicative of the overall ambience is, in the library, an old phonograph complete with a selection of early dance-band records. Clublike in feeling, Greywalls has both warmth and style.

Bedrooms, attractively appointed in traditional fashion (chintzes and faux antiques) can be very small, a drawback of a couple of those with links views. (Consider requesting Room 16, and avoid rooms over the kitchen.)

The cuisine is of a high standard, with cooking to match the excellence of the ingredients. Three dishes that might well be offered on a given evening: fish mousseline with a sauce of saffron and golden caviar to start, followed by breast of duck with a confit of the leg, and, for dessert, warm chocolate pithivier with espresso coffee sauce.

One final point about Greywalls: It can sometimes do for you what no letter, e-mail, fax, phone conversation with the secretary, or impassioned plea by an Honourable Company member of long standing can do: get you on Muirfield. Tee times for visitor play (Tuesday and Thursday only) are generally reserved a year in advance. But for the person who cannot commit that far ahead—and has very capacious pockets—Greywalls just may save the day. On certain Friday afternoons and Monday mornings, hotel guests have access to a limited number of Muirfield starting times.

COURSES

Alyth Golf Club
Alyth, Perthshire PH11 8JJ
Tel: 44-1828-632-411
www.alythgolfclub.co.uk

Anstruther Golf Club
Anstruther, Fife
Tel: 44-1333-310-956
www.anstruthergolf.co.uk

Arbroath Golf Links
Arbroath, Angus DD11 2PE
Tel: 44-1241-875-837
www.scottishgolfcourses.com
/heartland/arbroath.html

Auchterarder Golf Club
Auchterarder, Perthshire PH3 1DZ
Tel: 44-1292-313-471
www.aucherfieldgolf.co.uk

**Barassie Links, Kilmarnock
Golf Club**
Barassie, Troon, Ayrshire KA10 6SY
Tel: 44-1292-313-920
www.kbgc.co.uk

Belleisle Golf Club
c/o S. Ayrshire Council, Burns House
Burns SQ, Ayrshire KA7 1UT
Tel: 44-1292-441-258

Blairgowrie Golf Club
Rosemount, Blairgowrie PH10 6LG
Tel: 44-1250-872-622
www.theblairgowriegolfclub.co.uk

Boat of Garten Golf and Tennis Club
Boat of Garten, Inverness-Shire
PH24 3BQ
Tel: 44-1479-831-282
www.boatgolf.com

Braid Hills–Braids No. 1
Edinburgh EH10 6JY
Tel: 44-1-31-447-6666
www.greenfeesavers.co.uk
/southeast/braidhillsone.html

Brora Golf Club
Brora, Sutherland KW9 6QS
Tel: 44-1408-621-417
www.broragolf.co.uk

Bruntsfield Links Golfing Society
Davidson's Mains, Edinburgh
EH4 6JH
Tel: 44-1-31-336-2006
www.sol.co.uk/b/bruntsfieldlinks

Carnoustie Golf Links
Carnoustie, Angus DD7 7JE
Tel: 44-1241-853-789
www.carnoustiegolflinks.com

Charleton Golf Course
Colinsburgh, Fife KY9 1HG
Tel: 44-1333-340-505
www.charleton.co.uk

Craigielaw Golf Club
Aberlady, East Lothian EH32 0PY
Tel: 44-1875-870-800
www.craigielawgolfclub.com

**Crail Golfing Society–Balcomie
and Craighead Links**
Fifeness, Crail KY10 3XN
Tel: 44-1333-450-686
www.crailgolfingsociety.co.uk

Cruden Bay Golf Club
Cruden Bay, Peterhead AB42 0NN
Tel: 44-1779-812-414
www.crudenbaygolfclub.co.uk

**Dalmahoy Hotel,
Golf & Country Club**
Kirknewton, Lothian EH27 8EB
Tel: 44-1-31-333-1845
http://marriott.co.uk/Channels/global
Sites/propertypage/UK/edigs

Downfield Golf Club
Dundee, Angus DD2 3QP
Tel: 44-1382-825-595
www.downfieldgolfclub.co.uk

Duddingston Golf Club
Duddingston Road West, Edinburgh
E15 3QD
Tel: 44-1-31-652-6057
www.golftoday.co.uk/clubhouse/course
dir/scotland/Midlothian/duddingston.html

Duke's Course, The
Craigtown, St. Andrews, Fife
KY16 89S
Tel: 44-1334-474-371
www.oldcoursehotel.co.uk

Dunaverty Golf Club
Southend, Argyll PA28 6RW
Tel: 44-1586-830-677
www.dunavertygolfclub.com

Dunbar Golf Club
East Links, Dunbar, East Lothian
EH42 1LT
Tel: 44-1368-862-317
www.dunbar-golfclub.co.uk

Edzell Golf Club
Edzell, Angus DD9 7TF
Tel: 44-1356-647-283
www.edzellgolfclub.net

Elgin Golf Club
Hardhillock, Morayshire IV30 8SX
Tel: 44-1343-542-884
www.elgingolfclub.com

Elie, The Golf House Club
Elie, Fife KY9 1AS
Tel: 44-1333-330-301
www.golfhouseclub.org

Forfar Golf Club
Forfar, Angus DD8 2RL
Tel: 44-1307-465-683
www.forfargolfclub.com

**Fortrose and Rosemarkie
Golf Club**
Fortrose, Ross-Shire IV10 8SE
Tel: 44-1381-620-529
www.fortrosegolfclub.co.uk

Glasgow Golf Club–Glasgow Gailes
Glasgow Golf Club, Killermont,
Bearsden G61 2TW
Tel: 44-141-942-2011
www.glasgowgailes-golf.com

Opposite: Loch Lomond
Course, 5th.

HOTELS

Ardell House
Machrihanish, Argyll PA28 6PT
Tel: 44-1586-810-235

Auchendean Lodge
Dulnain Bridge, Inverness-Shire
PH26 3LU
Tel: 44-1479-851-347
www.auchendean.com

Auchterarder House Hotel
Auchterarder, Perthshire PH3 1DZ
Tel: 44-1764-663-646

Balcomie Links Hotel
Crail, Fifeness, Fife KY10 3TN
Tel: 44-1333-450-237
www.balcomie.co.uk

Balmoral Hotel
1 Princes St., Edinburgh EH2 2EQ
Tel: 44-1-31-556-2414
www.thebalmoralhotel.com

Blenheim House Hotel
North Berwick, East Lothian
EH39 4AF
Tel: 44-1620-892-385
www.blenheimhousehotel.co.uk

Boat Hotel
Boat of Garten, Inverness-Shire
PH24 3BH
Tel: 44-1479-831-258
www.boathotel.co.uk

Boath House
Auldearn, Nairn, Nairnshire IV12 5TE
Tel: 44-1667-454-896
www.boath-house.com

Burghfield House Hotel
Dornoch, Sutherland IV25 3HN
Tel: 44-1862-811-006
E-mail: burghfield@uhi.ac.uk

Caledonian Hilton
Princes Street, Edinburgh EH1 2AB
Tel: 44-1-31-222-8888
www.hilton.com/caledonian

Cameron House Hotel
Alexandria, Dunbartonshire GH3 8QZ
Tel: 44-1389-755-565
www.devereonline.co.uk/our-locations/
cameron-house.html

Carlogie House Hotel
Carnoustie, Angus DD7 6LD
Tel: 44-1241-853-185
www.scotlands-golf-courses.com/a/
carlogie

Carnoustie Golf Hotel
Carnoustie, Angus DD7 7JE
Tel: 44-1241-411-999
www.oxfordhotelsandinns.com/
ourhotels/carnoustie

Cartland Bridge Hotel
Lanark, Lanarkshire ML11 9UF
Tel: 44-1555-664-426
www.cartlandbridge.co.uk

Channings
South Learmonth Gardens, Edinburgh
EH4 1EZ
Tel: 44-1-31-315-2226
www.channings.co.uk

Craigsanquhar House
Cupar, Fife KY15 4PZ
Tel: 44-1334-653-426
www.craigsanquhar.com

Crusoe Hotel
Lower Largo, Fife KY8 6BT
Tel: 44-1333-320-759
www.crusoehotel.co.uk

Culloden House
Culloden, Inverness-Shire IV2 7BZ
Tel: 44-1463-790-461
www.cullodenhouse.co.uk

Culzean Castle Apartments
Culzean Castle, Maybole, Ayrshire
KA19 8LE
Tel: 44-1655-884-455
www.culzeanexperience.org/
accomodation.asp

**Dalmahoy Hotel,
Golf & Country Club**
Kirknewton, Lothian EH27 8EB
Tel: 44-1-31-333-1845
http://marriott.co.uk/Channels/global
Sites/propertypage/UK/edigs

Delnashaugh Hotel
Ballindalloch, Banffshire AB37 9AS
Tel: 44-1807-500-255
www.delnashaughhotel.co.uk

Dornoch Castle Hotel
Dornoch, Sutherland IV25 3SD
Tel: 44-1862-810-216
www.dornochcastlehotel.com

Fairmont St. Andrews
St. Andrews, Fife KY16 8PN
Tel: 44-1334-837-000
www.fairmont.com/standrews

Five Gables House
Arbroath, Angus DD11 2PE
Tel: 44-1241-871-632
www.arbroathbandb.com

Glebe House
North Berwick, East Lothian EH39 4PL
Tel: 44-1620-892-608
www.glebehouse-nb.co.uk

Gleneagles Hotel
Auchterarder, Perthshire PH3 1NF
Tel: 44-1764-662-231
www.gleneagles.com

Golf Inn
Gullane, East Lothian EH31 2AB
Tel: 44-1620-843-259
www.golfinn.co.uk

Golf View Hotel
Nairn, Nairnshire IV12 4HD
Tel: 44-1667-452-301
www.crerarhotels.com/ourhotels/golf_
view_hotel/

Golf View Private Hotel
Prestwick, Ayrshire KA9 1QG
Tel: 44-1292-671-234
www.golfviewhotel.com

Opposite: St. Andrews Bay,
17th. Above: 10th.

PHOTO CREDITS

All golf course photographs are by Laurence C. Lambrecht, except for page 49. All photographs in "Off the Course" sections are by Tim Thompson, except for those listed below:

P. 28—top, courtesy of Myres Castle
P. 33—right, courtesy of St. Andrews Bay Hotel
P. 49—courtesy of the Golf House Club, Elie
P. 98—right, both courtesy of Gleneagles Hotel
P. 119—lower right, courtesy of Udny Arms
P. 123—bottom right, courtesy of Boat Hotel
P. 130—center, P. Tomkins/Visit Scotland/Scottish Viewpoint
P. 131—middle row, center and right, courtesy of Boath House
P. 135—both courtesy of Carnegie Club
P. 145—top left, courtesy of Royal Marine Hotel
P. 157—top right, courtesy of Rossdhu House
P. 170—center, top, courtesy of the Landmark Trust
P. 207—bottom row, center, Allan Devlin/Scottish Viewpoint
P. 220—bottom left, courtesy of the Landmark Trust
P. 253—courtesy of Greywalls Hotel
P. 272—courtesy of John Finegan

ABOUT THE AUTHOR

JAMES W. FINEGAN, after four decades of crisscrossing the British Isles, is America's leading expert on the golf courses of Scotland. He has authored five revered books on golf, including *Where Golf Is Great: The Finest Courses of Scotland and Ireland*; *Blasted Heaths and Blessed Greens*; and *Emerald Fairways and Foam-Flecked Seas*. Jim has also contributed to all the major golf magazines. For many years a 2-handicap, he lives in Villanova, Pennsylvania.